Learn Microsoft® Visio® 2002

by Ralph Grabowski

For users of:
Microsoft Visio Standard 2002
Microsoft Visio Professional 2002

Wordware Publishing, Inc.

Library of Congress Cataloging-in-Publication Data

Grabowski, Ralph
   Learn Microsoft Visio 2002 / by Ralph Grabowski.
     p. cm.
   Includes index.
   ISBN 1-55622-818-X (pbk.)
   1. Computer graphics. 2. Microsoft Visio. I. Title.
   T385 .G69264 2001
   650'.0285'66869--dc21   2001026779
                                   CIP

ISBN 1-55622-818-X
10 9 8 7 6 5 4 3 2 1
0106

All inquiries for volume purchases of this book should be addressed to the address above. Telephone
inquiries may be made by calling:

(972) 423-0090

Vaughan
T385
.G69264
2001
c. 1

Contents

Contents

Acknowledgments

No author is an island. In that regard, I would like to thank Jim Hill, the publisher of Wordware, for his enthusiasm and support. My wife, Heather, and our three children accepted Dad working evenings and weekends in exchange for taking time off during other people's "working hours."

And, as I well know, no author can ever edit his own writing. I am grateful for Judy Lemke's critical eye, which scanned my manuscript for technical accuracy. Without her help, this would be a poorer book.

Soli Deo Gloria.

Ralph Grabowski
Abbotsford BC, Canada

Wordware Publishing, Inc. would like to thank the Microsoft Visio staff for their continued support of our books on this unique product. We look forward to continuing our working relationship.

Introduction

Getting Started

Microsoft Visio is software for creating diagrams. Unlike other technical drawing programs, such as computer-aided drawing software, Visio is easy to use. To make a drawing, you don't need to know how to draw! You drag shapes from stencils onto the page — it's that simple. When you prefer to draw freehand, Visio includes a number of tools for drawing lines, circles, boxes, and curves.

The shapes are called *SmartShapes* because they know where to connect with each other. They resize appropriately and contain other "smarts." For example, the lines that connect shapes, such as in flowcharts, are smart because they stretch when you move any connected shape.

With SmartShapes and dynamic connectors, Visio creates intelligent drawings. Typical drawings include organization charts, process flow charts, directional maps, and network diagrams.

Which Visio is for You?

Microsoft Visio 2002 is available in two flavors: Standard and Professional. Which product is best for you?

▶ Visio Standard 2002 is for general business diagramming needs. Use this software for creating organization charts, basic network diagrams, Gantt charts, cross-functional flowcharts, and process flowcharts.

▶ Visio Professional 2002 is for designing and documenting information systems and business processes. It is also for creating 2D technical drawings, such as space plans, HVAC (heating, ventilating, air conditioning) designs, fluid power schematics, and factory floor layouts, and for working with AutoCAD and MicroStation drawings.

About This Book

Learn Microsoft Visio 2002 covers Visio Standard 2002 and Visio Professional 2002. This book discusses features common to both programs.

This book is designed to be modular. Instead of chapters, this book has modules. Every module is independent of the other modules.

Think of this book as a cookbook: You don't need to start at the beginning and work your way though to the end. If you already know how to open and save files, and how to use the Clipboard, you can easily skip those modules. Once you have mastered the subjects covered in this book, consider *Learn Microsoft Visio 2002 for the Advanced User*, also by author Ralph Grabowski. The advanced book teaches you how to customize Visio for the way you work. You learn how to create templates and custom styles. You go "behind the curtain" and learn how the ShapeSheet operates, and find out why it is fundamental to all that goes on in Visio. You also learn how to create diagrams automatically, and how to hook up Visio with database files.

Starting Visio

To start Visio 2002, either (1) select **Start | Programs | Microsoft Visio**; or (2) double-click the shortcut icon on the Desktop. (To exit Visio at any time, press **Alt+F4** or select **File | Exit**.)

A Guided Tour

When Visio first starts, it displays the Choose Drawing Type window. This acts like a control panel, where you can:

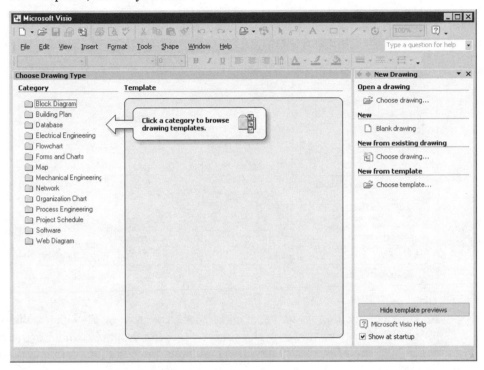

▶ Start with a specific solution, such as a flowchart or floor plan.

▶ Start a new, blank drawing.

▶ Open an existing drawing.

▶ Use an existing drawing as the basis for a new drawing.

Under the Category heading, Visio has many *solutions*. (The following illustration shows Visio Professional, which has more categories than Visio Standard.) A solution consists of a single drawing page, usually scaled and oriented appropriately for the drawing type. It also includes a set of commonly used stencils. You'll see one such solution shortly.

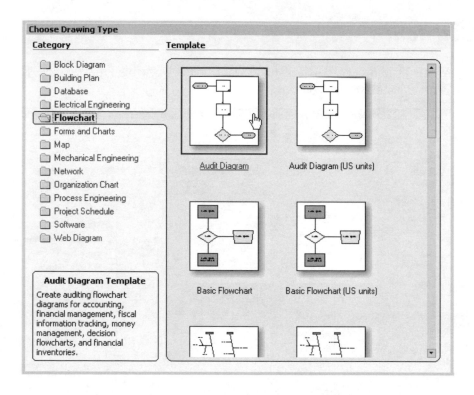

As you click a category name, such as Block Diagram or Flowchart, Visio displays previews of drawing types in the center pane. For example, under Flowchart, you can select one of several templates, including the Audit Diagram and the Basic Flowchart. Notice that they are available in metric and U.S. (imperial) units.

Pause your cursor over one of the drawing previews to see a tooltip describing the drawing type. The *tooltip* is a yellow square of text that appears in the lower-left corner. The tooltip describes the drawing type.

Select a solution, such as Audit Diagram. Once you select a drawing type, the Visio screen comes to life.

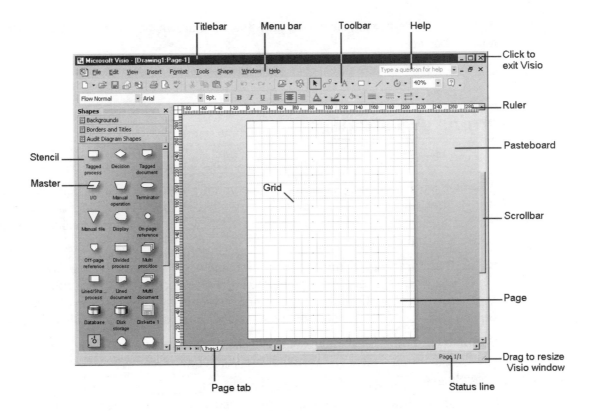

Titlebar Menu bar Toolbar Help

Click to exit Visio

Ruler

Pasteboard

Stencil

Master

Grid

Scrollbar

Page

Drag to resize Visio window

Page tab Status line

Along the top of the window are the toolbar and the menu bar. The menu bar contains most — but not all — Visio commands.

Below the menu bar are *toolbars*. By default, two toolbars are displayed: Standard and Formatting. To add and remove toolbars, right-click on the toolbar and select (or deselect) the name from the shortcut menu.

At the left is a *stencil* with *masters*. You can open more than one stencil at a time; three stencils are open in the illustration (two are shown just by their title bars). Each stencil in the illustration includes one or two dozen masters. To use a master, simply drag it from the stencil to the page.

The largest part of the Visio window is the drawing area, which displays a page. While most of the time you will probably work with a standard 8½ x 11-inch page, Visio accommodates a wide variety of page sizes — all the way up to 36 x 48". You can have up to 200 pages in a drawing, although only one page is displayed at a time.

The page tabs make it easy to switch between pages, as well as add, remove, and reorder pages.

Surrounding the page is the *pasteboard*. You can store shapes there; the pasteboard does not print.

Scroll bars let you move the page around the window. The *rulers* measure distances.

Diagramming Assistants

Visio uses many visual hints to help you draw quickly and accurately:

Grid: On a blank drawing page, all you see initially are the grid lines. The grid helps you position objects; you can choose to have shapes *snap* to the grid for accurate horizontal and vertical positioning. You may change the grid spacing, including independent x- and y-spacing.

Ruler: The ruler reports the size of the drawing in scaled units. By holding down the Ctrl key, you can drag the 0-point (from the intersection of the two rulers) to a new zero point. Like the grid, the ruler helps you position objects; you can have shapes snap to the ruler increments for accurate horizontal and vertical positioning.

Connection point: Small blue x shapes appear whenever you select a shape that you dragged from a stencil. These indicate the points where you can connect one shape to another.

Selection handle: Perhaps the most important visual clue is the selection handle. Its shape and color change, alerting you to its properties. The most common selection handle is a small, green square. This indicates the points where you can change the size and rotation of the object. Click and hold the square, drag (to change the size or the angle), then let go of the mouse button. In brief, selection handles can take on the following colors and shapes:

- Green square: selection handle.
- Red square: glued connection.
- Padlock: a locked shape.
- Round: a rotation handle for rotating the object.
- Diamond: a vertex point on objects such as arcs.

The red color indicates the object is *glued* to another object. When you move a shape that is glued to another shape, the shapes stay connected.

Drawing with Visio is Better and Faster

You can create a drawing with Visio in exactly the same manner as with other drawing and CAD software: draw lines, circles, and other shapes, and then edit them. In addition, Visio offers a much more powerful — and faster — method of drawing rarely found in other software. Follow these easy steps:

Step 1:   Start a new drawing.
Step 2:   Open the appropriate template.
Step 3:   Drag shapes into the drawing.
Step 4:   Connect shapes as required.
Step 5:   Save and print the drawing.

Using the predrawn shapes saves you the time it takes to draw objects from scratch. If the shape isn't exactly what you need, it can be easily edited.

Connections between shapes work like magic. Small blue x markers tell you where the connections are located on each shape. When two shapes connect, the connector endpoints turn red. When you move one of the shapes, the connector stays glued to it — until you decide to disconnect them. Visio includes many tools for accurate, automatic positioning and shape manipulation.

When you have drawings that were created in other software programs, you can import them into a Visio drawing. When you have data that resides in database files, you can link the data with Visio drawings, and then access the database from within Visio. Visio can export its drawings in many vector (CAD) and raster (paint) formats; Visio can also export its drawing as a Web page.

Visio is a powerful program for working with graphics and data. This book will show you how easy it is to harness that power.

A Brief History of Visio

ShapeWare Corp., as Visio Corp. was first called, was founded in 1990 by two of the founders of Aldus Corp. (of PageMaker fame, later merged with Adobe of PostScript fame). When Visio v1.0 was introduced in 1992, the software quickly became popular because it did not present a blank page to the new user. Instead, it invited the user to drag shapes and drop them into the page.

In 1993, ShapeWare began shipping optional stencils and shapes to Visio called "Visio Shapes." When it was renamed the Visio Solutions Library in 1996, the library included add-ons developed by ShapeWare and third-party vendors. One example is the Visio Business Modeler, which lets you analyze business models found in the SAP R/3 Reference Model.

After shipping Visio v1, v2, v3, and v4, ShapeWare began creating specific releases of Visio. Visio Technical was introduced in 1994 as companion software to CAD products (the first version of Technical was called "version 4.1"). In 1995, ShapeWare Corp. changed its name to Visio Corp. and went public on the NASDAQ stock exchange under the symbol "VSIO."

Visio Professional was released in 1996 for IT professionals (the first version of Professional was called "version 4.5"). In 1997, Visio delivered Visio Map for GIS users, with mapping technology licensed from ESRI, one of the largest GIS software companies.

In 1998, Visio began shipping IntelliCAD (aka "Phoenix"), an AutoCAD-compatible CAD system Visio obtained by purchasing Boomerang Technology, a former division of Softdesk, which had merged with Autodesk a year earlier. At about the same time, Visio help establish the OpenDWG Alliance (www.opendwg.org) to unravel the mysteries of the AutoCAD DWG file format. Just 18 months later, Visio handed IntelliCAD over to the IntelliCAD Technical Consortium (www.intellicad.org) to market the software as "open source software."

Also in 1998, Visio released Visio Enterprise as an advanced version of Visio Professional that replaced Visio Network. Later in the year, Visio Standard and Technical were updated with the Visio Plus editions. Visio opened up its eVisio Web site, where the software and its components could be purchased over the Internet, then couriered to you on CD-ROM.

In 1999, Visio began shipping its more powerful Visio 2000 in four editions: Standard, Technical, Professional, and Enterprise. And, in a surprise move, Microsoft purchased Visio Corp. for $1.3 billion; the purchase was finalized in early 2000.

In 2001, Microsoft reduced the Visio stable to two editions: Standard and Professional. The features of the old Technical Edition were included with Visio 2002 Professional Edition, while the networking functionality of Enterprise Edition was repackaged as an add-on to Professional called "Visio Enterprise Network Tools." Microsoft Visio Network Center, a subscription-based Web site, provides access to new network equipment shapes and documentation.

For more information about Visio, check the Web site at www.microsoft.com/office/visio.

About the Author

Ralph Grabowski is the author of over 50 books about the Internet, computer-aided design, and technical drawing, including the *Learn AutoCAD LT* series for Wordware Publishing. Ralph is the former senior editor of *CADalyst* magazine, and was a contributing editor to *Cadence* magazine. He helped launch *Technical Design Solutions* magazine for Visio Technical and IntelliCAD users, and was the editor of the *Drawing-Design* Webzine for Actrix, iGrafx, Imagineer Technical, and Visio users.

Ralph is currently the editor of *upFront.eZine*, the weekly CAD news e-newsletter distributed free by e-mail. (To subscribe, send the message "subscribe upfront" to editor@upfrontezine.com.) He is also the editor of *AutoCAD User* magazine and the *CRCeZine* e-newsletter. He can be reached via e-mail at ralphg@xyzpress.com and his Web site at www.upfrontezine.com.

Starting a New Drawing

File | New

In this chapter you'll learn about:

✓ **Starting with a new drawing**

✓ **Beginning with a solution**

✓ **Creating a new drawing with a wizard**

Uses

You reach for a piece of blank paper. That's the first step you take when you start a new drawing. In Visio, it is no different: you start with a new drawing *page*.

A new drawing is like a blank sheet of paper. Visio 2002 lets you start a new drawing in several ways:

▶ Start with a blank drawing.

▶ Start with a solution (aka template).

▶ Start a new drawing with a wizard.

In this module, you learn about all three of these methods of starting a new drawing.

Tip: To again see the Create New Drawing window, from Visio's menu bar, select **File | New | Choose Drawing Type**.

After you start Visio 2002, it displays a window with two lists of drawing types, and a preview area in the center. The **Category** list on the left of the Choose Drawing Type window sorts solutions into many categories, such as block diagrams, flowcharts, and networks.

The center area displays previews of templates listed in the categories.

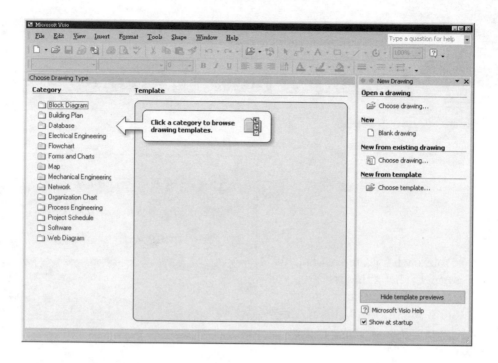

The **New Drawing** list on the right is perhaps misnamed, since it allows you to open "old" (existing) drawings, as well as a blank new drawing, or a new drawing based on existing drawings and templates:

▶ **Open a drawing**: Click **Choose drawing** to open an existing drawing. This can be one of the sample drawings that comes with Visio, or a drawing that you or someone else created previously. Visio displays the Open dialog box.

▶ **New**: Click **Blank drawing** and Visio opens a new, blank drawing with no stencils.

▶ **New from existing drawing**: Click **Choose drawing**, which allows you to use an existing drawing as a template for a new drawing. Visio displays the From Existing Drawing dialog box with the My Documents folder open.

▶ **New from template**: Click **Choose template** to select a template drawing. Visio displays the Browse Templates dialog box with the Visio\Solutions folder open.

Tip: When you pause the cursor over a template or drawing name, a tooltip shows the full pathname (drive and folders) of the drawing.

Start with a New Drawing

Visio provides two ways to start with a new drawing.

Here is the first method: When you start Visio, it displays the Choose Drawing Type window. Under **New**, click **Blank Drawing**. Visio opens a blank drawing: an 8½" x 11" sheet of paper in portrait orientation, a scale of 1:1, and no stencil or shapes loaded. Starting with a blank drawing is best when you want to create a new drawing from scratch, with no assistance from Visio stencils or wizards.

A new, blank drawing opened by Visio.

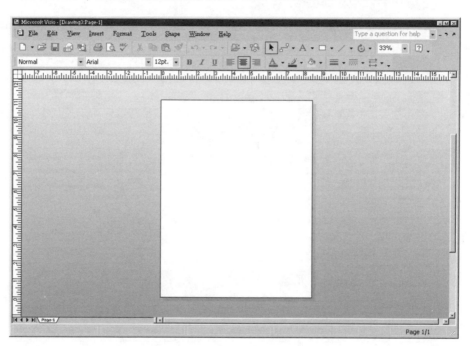

Here is the second method: After starting Visio, you can open another blank drawing page. When you press **Ctrl+N** (or select **File | New | New Drawing** from the menu bar), Visio opens a new drawing with the same settings as the current drawing.

Begin with a Solution

A *solution* is a customized drawing environment for a specific discipline or vertical market, such as flowcharts, electronics, or facilities management. When you open a solution, Visio opens related stencils; configures the drawing page with a suitable size, scale, and orientation; and in some cases may add an item to the menu bar. (Solutions are based on Visio's *.VST template files, *.VSS stencil files, and additional menu items.) Opening a template is the same as opening a solution.

3

The two editions of Visio 2002 — Standard and Professional — come with a different collection of solutions files. (If you are familiar with older versions of Visio, then you may be interested to learn that Visio 2002 Professional combines the Technical, Professional, and Enterprise editions of Visio 2000.) As with creating a new drawing, Visio provides a couple of ways to access solutions.

Here is the first method: When you start Visio, it displays the Choose Drawing Type window. Under **Category**, select a category name. The categories listed vary according to the edition you are using.

The Choose Drawing Type dialog box displayed by Visio 2002 Professional Edition.

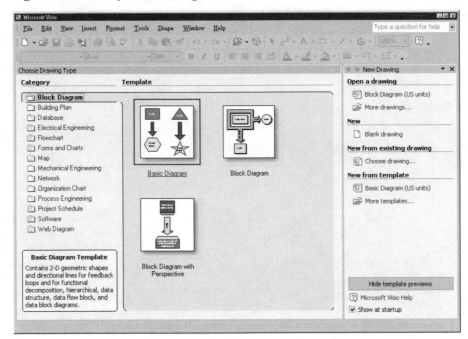

🔑 **Tip:** Pause the cursor over the template preview image. Notice that Visio displays a tooltip describing the solution.

Here is the second method: Within Visio, you access the solutions by selecting **File | New** from the menu bar. The menu lists the solution categories. As an alternative, you can click the small arrow next to the **New** icon on the toolbar to display the list of categories.

Selecting a solution from within Visio 2000.

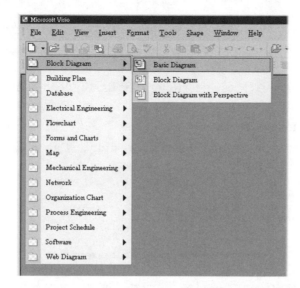

No matter which method you use, Visio opens a blank, new drawing with appropriate stencil(s) and page setup. Depending on the solution, Visio may also open a toolbar, additional menu items, and/or a wizard.

The Process Engineering solution provided with Visio 2002 Professional.

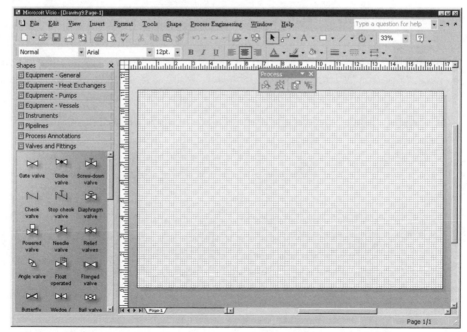

You are not stuck with the solutions that Visio provides. Feel free to modify any solution to suit your needs; just remember to save it as a template drawing (*.VST) with a different name or store it in another folder (see Module 2 "Saving Files").

The properties you can save in a template drawing include:

▶ Layers, scale, and page settings (see Module 4 "Setting Up Pages and Layers").

▶ Snap and glue settings (see Module 6 "Rulers, Grids, Guidelines, and Page Breaks").

▶ Color palette (see Module 13 "Formatting Shapes").

▶ Shape styles and text styles (see Module 15 "Creating and Applying Styles").

▶ Print setup (see Module 20 "Printing Drawings").

▶ Window size and position.

You can save a template so that it opens stencils.

Tip: By creating your own templates, you create a consistent look for all your drawings. Templates are an excellent way to affirm corporate standards. For example, to ensure that the corporate logo and copyright statement appear in every drawing, create a layer with that information, and then save the drawing as a template.

Start a New Drawing with a Wizard

The Visio package includes *wizards* that guide you through the steps of setting up a preliminary drawing. Along the way, you are prompted to fill in information and select options. Wizards are available for creating flowcharts, office layouts, organizational charts, project timelines, and other specialized drawings.

There are, however, two disadvantages to using a wizard: (1) you may find it becomes tedious answering the wizard's many questions and then waiting for the wizard to complete its work; and (2) you sometimes end up doing more work editing the drawing created by the wizard than you would have by starting the drawing from scratch.

You find wizards in the Tools menu. From the menu bar, select **Tools | Macros**, then look at options such as Flowchart, Organization Chart, and Visio Extras. You learn more about wizards in later modules in this book.

Selecting a wizard from the Tools menu.

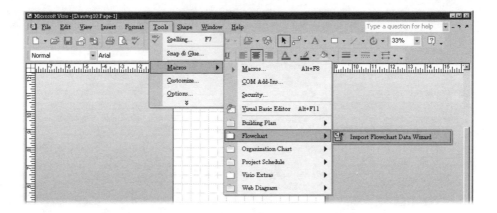

Procedures

When you start Visio, it automatically displays the Choose Drawing Type window. From this window, you select a solution or a drawing file. Alternatively, you can start a new drawing anytime you are in Visio with the New command. The shortcut key is:

Function	Key	Menu	Toolbar Icon
New	Ctrl+N	File | New	

Starting a New Drawing

Use the following procedure to start a new drawing:

1. Select **New** from the **File** menu.

2. Select a solution category, such as **Block Diagram**.

3. Select a solution, such as **Basic Diagram**.

4. Notice that Visio opens a blank, scaled drawing with the appropriate stencils.

Selecting a solution from the New menu.

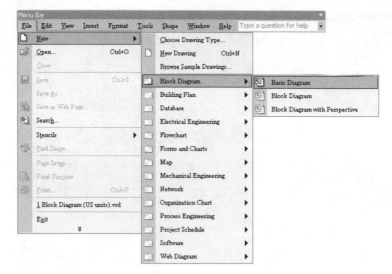

Starting a Blank, New Drawing

Use the following procedure to start a new drawing without a template:

1. Select **File | New | New Drawing** from the menu bar.

2. Notice that Visio opens a blank drawing and no stencil.

Starting a New Drawing with a Wizard

Use the following procedure to start a new drawing with a wizard:

1. Select **File | New** from the menu bar.

2. Select a category from the menu, such as **Organization Chart**. (The list of categories and wizards varies, depending on whether you installed the Standard or Professional edition.)

3. Select a wizard name from the list. For example, under Organization Chart, choose **Organization Chart Wizard**.

4. Notice that Visio opens a scaled, blank drawing with the appropriate stencils, and starts the wizard.

5. Follow the instructions provided by the wizard's dialog boxes.

*The
Organization
Chart Wizard.*

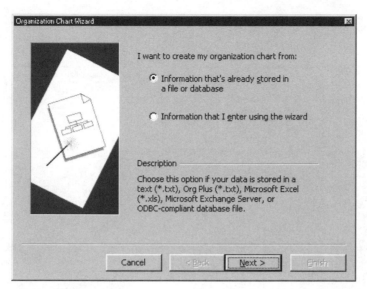

Hands-On Activity

In this activity, you open a new drawing.

1. Start Visio to begin the activity. Notice that Visio displays the Choose Drawing Type window.

2. In the Category list, click **Forms and Charts**.

3. In the Template area, click the **Charts and Graphs** preview image.

*Selecting
Charts and
Graphs from
the window.*

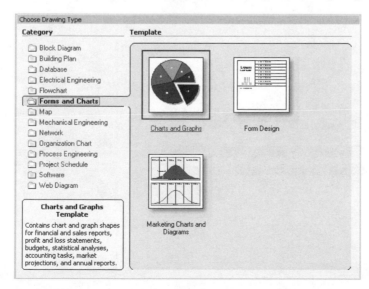

Stencils with shapes at left, and the new drawing at right.

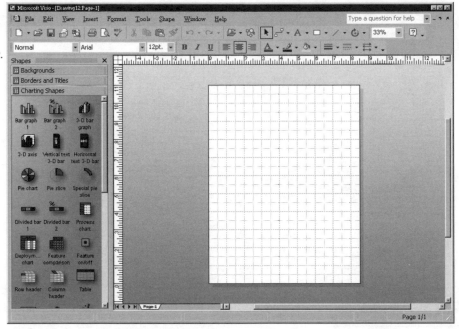

Notice that Visio opens a new drawing that looks like a sheet of graph paper. On the left side are several stencils, with the Charting Shapes stencil visible.

4. To get a feel for how Visio works, drag the **Bar graph 1** shape from the stencil to the drawing page. Notice the Custom Properties dialog box, which prompts you for the number of bars in the bar chart. (You learn more about *custom properties* in Module 34 "Custom Properties.")

Specifying properties.

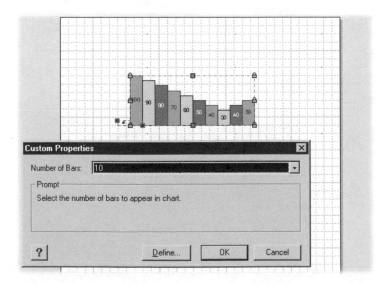

5. Accept the default of 10 bars by clicking **OK**.

6. Enlarge the view of the bar chart to make it easier to see. Right-click the bar chart shape. Choose **View | 100%**. Visio zooms in on the shape.

Clicking on the right mouse button displays the shortcut menu.

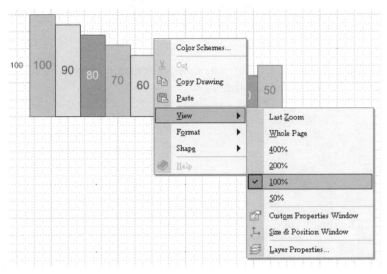

7. Let's add a label to the bar chart. Double-click the chart. Notice that you can type a label for the bar chart, below the bars. Enter **My Bar Chart**.

Adding a label to the bar chart.

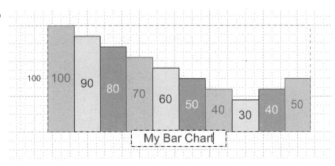

8. Let's see Visio's dynamic nature in action. From the toolbar, select the **Text** tool by clicking the button with the icon that looks like a capital letter **A**.

Selecting the Text tool.

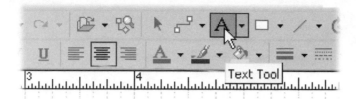

9. Click the second bar and enter a negative number, such as **–90**. Notice that bar drops down below the zero line.

Changing the value of a bar changes its height.

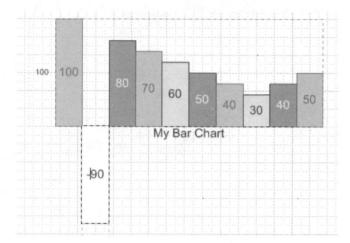

This completes the hands-on activity for opening a new drawing. Do not exit Visio or the drawing because you need both for the next module.

Module 2 Saving Files

File | Save, Save As, Properties

In this chapter you'll learn about:
✓ **Using the Save and Save As commands**
✓ **Exploring the File Properties** *dialog box*
✓ **Saving a drawing as a template**

Uses

The **Save** command on the **File** menu saves the *current* drawing. Recall that Visio, like many other Windows programs, can have more than one drawing open at a time. Selecting a command from a menu applies to the topmost (or current) drawing. Here is how to tell which drawing is current: When the drawing windows are maximized, the current drawing is the one you can see. When the drawing windows are not maximized, the current drawing is the one with the highlighted title bar.

Saving the drawing to the computer's disk drive lets you work with the drawing again later. If you have more than one Visio drawing open, you must save each one individually.

When a drawing is new and unnamed, Visio displays the generic name "Drawing1" on the title bar. The first time you save the drawing, Visio asks you to provide a name for the file. You can enter a filename up to 255 characters long. You may want to limit filenames to eight characters if the drawing will be used by an older version of Visio running on a Windows v3.1 system.

After the first time you save the file by name, Save no longer prompts you for the name. Instead, it silently and quickly saves the drawing to disk; the only indication is the hourglass cursor.

When you attempt to exit Visio without saving the drawing, Visio asks, "Save changes to Drawing1?" This gives you a final chance to save the drawing. Click **Yes**.

This dialog box saves you from accidentally closing a drawing without saving it.

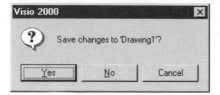

Tip: You are wise to periodically save (every 10 minutes or so) while you are working on a drawing. That way, you don't lose your work if the power goes out or your computer freezes. A large, 1MB Visio drawing takes only four seconds to save on a slow Pentium. That's a short time to wait for a large investment in your valuable work. Visio 2002 adds an automatic recovery feature, which is turned off by default. To turn it on, from the menu bar select **Tools | Options**, and then click the **Save** tab. Click the check box next to **Save AutoRecover info every *x* minutes**. Click **OK**.

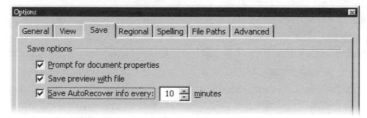

Turning on Save AutoRecover info.

Save As

When you want to save the file by a different name, use the **File | Save As** command, which displays the Save As dialog box. The Save As command also lets you save the drawing in a different file format, such as AutoCAD, Adobe Illustrator, Corel Draw, and earlier versions of Visio.

File Properties

The first time you save a drawing, Visio displays the Properties dialog box:

The Properties dialog box.

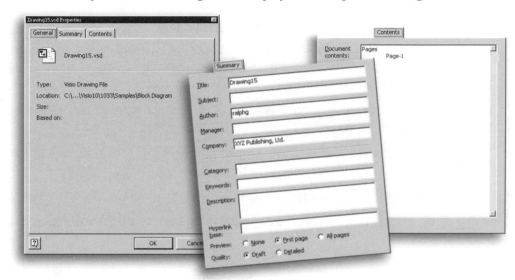

This dialog box has three tabs, which display information about the drawing and allow you to enter information about the drawing.

General This tab displays details about the file that come from the operating system; you cannot edit this data.

▶ **Type** describes the class of Visio file, such as "Visio Drawing File."

▶ **Location** lists the path to the folder (subdirectory) where the file is located; if the path is too long, an ellipsis (...) truncates the full path name.

▶ **Size** indicates the size of the file in bytes and KB (kilobyte = 1,024 bytes).

▶ **Based on** tells you the name of the template file on which this drawing is based. This field is blank when no template was used.

Summary This tab records information that describes the drawing file. In most cases, you can type up to 63 characters in each field. You can change the information at any time via **File | Properties**; use the **Field** command to automatically modify the information.

▶ **Title** is a descriptive title of the drawing.

▶ **Subject** describes the contents of the drawing.

▶ **Author** identifies the author.

▶ **Manager** is the name of your boss.

▶ **Company** is your firm or client.

▷ **Category** is a brief description of the drawing, such as map or floor plan.

▷ **Keywords** identifies topics related to the file: project name, version number, etc.

▷ **Description** allows up to 191 characters.

▷ **Hyperlink base** specifies the base URL (uniform resource locator) to be used with the filename. URL is the universal file naming system used by the Internet to identify the location of any file.

(Preview is no longer available for Visio files; however, it is still available for other types of files, such as TIFF.)

Contents This tab displays a list of the pages and *master* shapes in the file. A master shape is the "source" shape in the stencil.

(The Output Format tab, found in Visio 2000, was removed from Visio 2002.)

To change the file properties at any time, select **File | Properties** from the menu bar.

File Dialog Boxes

All file dialog boxes in Visio allow you to manage files on your computer, as well as other computers connected to yours via a network and locations on the Internet via FTP (file transfer protocol). To select another folder or another drive, click the **Save in** list box.

The Save As dialog box.

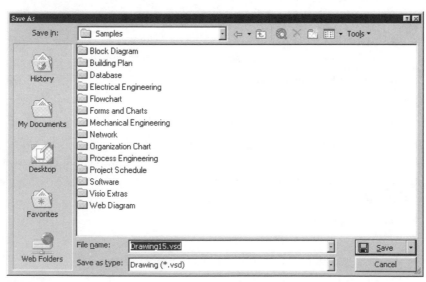

Notice that next to the **Save in** list box are several icons:

The file dialog box's toolbar.

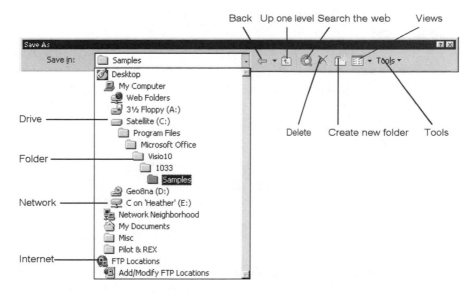

Back (light blue arrow) returns you to the previous folder, just like the back button on a Web browser.

Up One Level button moves up one level in the folder structure.

Search the Web opens the default Web browser and goes to the search.msn.com Web site.

Delete erases the selected file or folder.

Create New Folder creates a new folder. Windows gives the new folder the default name of "New Folder" and allows you to change the name to something more meaningful. Like a filename, a folder name can be up to 255 characters long.

Views displays the files and folders in a variety of formats:

▶ **Large icons** displays the files and folders as larger icons, which may be easier to see.

▶ **Small icons** displays the files and folders as smaller icons, which lets you see a larger number of icons.

▶ **List** displays just the file and folder names (the default view). Windows attempts to display as many names as it can.

▶ **Details** adds the size, type, and last-modified date. I find this the most useful view.

▶ **Preview** uses half of the dialog box to display a preview of the file; in some cases, a preview image may not be available.

▶ **Thumbnails** displays multiple preview images at once.

Click the **Details** button to display the name, size, and date for every file. Windows displays the details in three columns but does not ensure that all text is visible. The Details listing allows you to sort the files in several ways: by filename, size of file, and date last modified. To sort, click the column header:

▶ Click **Name** to sort the filenames in alphabetical order, from A to Z. Click a second time to reverse the sort, listing filenames from Z to A.

▶ Click **Size** to sort the files in order of size, smallest to largest. Click a second time to reverse the sort, from largest to smallest.

▶ Click **Modified** to sort the files in order of the date and time stamp, from newest to oldest. The time stamp indicates when the file was last modified. Click a second time to reverse the sort, from oldest to newest.

Note: By default, Windows does not display file extensions. To have Windows and Visio display file extensions, start Windows Explorer. From the menu bar, select **View | Options**. When the View dialog box appears, click the radio button next to **Hide file extensions for known file types**. Ensure no check mark appears next to this option. Click **OK** to close the dialog box.

In the Save As dialog box, right-click a filename to display the shortcut menu. This menu lets you perform additional file management functions (your computer system may have additional functions displayed by the shortcut menu).

Right-click a filename to display the shortcut menu.

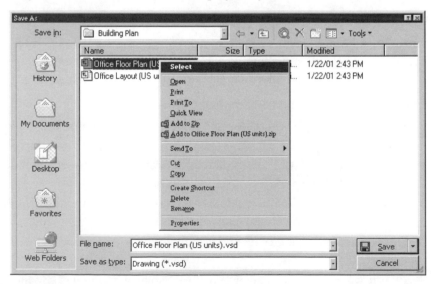

Select: Selects the highlighted filename for the **File name** text box and saves the drawing.

Open: Opens the selected filename in Visio; same as using the **Open** command. The Save As dialog box remains open.

Print To: Launches a second copy of Visio with the selected file, and prints the drawing with the default printer. When printing is complete, the second copy of Visio closes itself. This command fails if the selected drawing is already open in another copy of Visio.

Quick View: Launches the Visio Drawing Viewer.

Send To: Sends the drawing to another drive or software application, such as fax and e-mail.

Cut: Copies the file to the Windows Clipboard so it can be pasted into another application. What happens in the other application varies: a word processor pastes the Visio drawing; an e-mail program places the file as an attachment. You may need to cancel the Save As dialog box in Visio for the other program to complete its paste operation. Note that the Cut option does not actually cut (erase) the file.

Copy: Works the same as the Cut option.

Create Shortcut: Creates a shortcut to the selected file in the same folder. You can then drag the shortcut to the desktop.

Delete: Sends the file to the Recycle Bin. Windows asks if you are sure.

Rename: Allows you to change the name of the file.

Properties: Displays the Properties dialog box with the properties of the file.

The **Save** area of the Save As dialog box gives you two options for saving the drawing with extra attributes. These come into effect the next time you load the drawing:

Workspace: Saves the drawing, along with the position of windows. This ensures the drawing comes up looking exactly the same way the next time you load it.

Read Only: Saves the drawing with the read-only bit set. This means that the next time you load the drawing, you cannot save it. This prevents you (or another user) from making changes to the drawing.

The **Save As Type** list box lets you save the drawing in a large number of different file formats. This is also known as *exporting* the drawing. (See Module 29 "Exporting Drawings.") Visio 2002 can export drawings in a variety of formats, which varies according to the edition you are using.

Procedures

Before presenting the general procedure for saving the drawing, it is helpful to know about the shortcut keys. The first two save the drawing, while the last two trigger an option to save the drawing when it has changed:

Function	Keys	Menu	Toolbar Icon
Save As	Alt+FA	File | Save As	...
Save	Ctrl+S	File | Save	💾
Properties	Alt+FI	File | Properties	...
Close	Ctrl+F4	File | Close	☒
Exit	Alt+F4	File | Exit	☒

Saving a Drawing for the First Time

Use the following procedure to save a drawing the first time.

1. Choose **File | Save** from the menu bar.
2. In the **File name** field, type a name for the drawing.
3. Click the **Save** button.
4. When the Properties dialog box appears, fill in as much as you care to, or are required to by the corporate policy and procedures manual.
5. Click **OK** to close the Properties dialog box. Notice that Visio saves the drawing.

Saving a Drawing the Next Time

Use the following procedure to save a drawing.

1. Use **File | Save** (or press **Ctrl+S** or click the diskette button on the toolbar).
2. Notice that Visio saves the drawing to disk.

Saving a Drawing as a Template

Use the following procedure to save the drawing as a template.

1. Use **File | Save As**.

2. In the **File name** field, type a name for the drawing.

3. Click the down-arrow next to the **Save as type** list box. The list box drops down.

Saving a drawing as a template file.

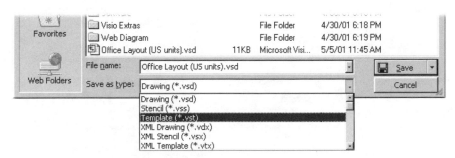

4. Select **Template (*.vst)** from the list.

5. Click **Save**. Visio displays the Properties dialog box.

6. Click **OK**. Visio renames the drawing "Drawing1.Vst." The "t" at the end of Vst is a reminder that the file is now a template drawing.

Hands-On Activity

In this activity, you use the Save As function to save the current drawing. Ensure Visio is running and the drawing you created in Module 1 is displayed.

1. Press **Ctrl+S** to save the drawing.

2. Note that Visio displays the Save As dialog box. The default filename, "Drawing1," is highlighted since this is the first time the drawing is being saved.

Using the Save As dialog box to give the drawing its name.

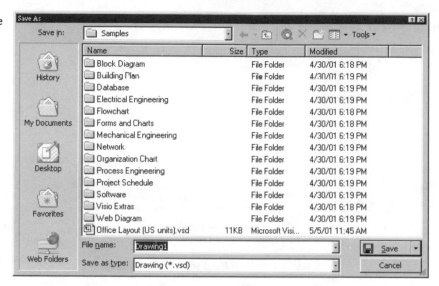

3. Type the filename **module-02**.

4. Click **Save**.

5. Notice that Visio displays the Summary tab of the Properties dialog box. Fill in the information requested by this dialog box:

Filling out the Properties dialog box.

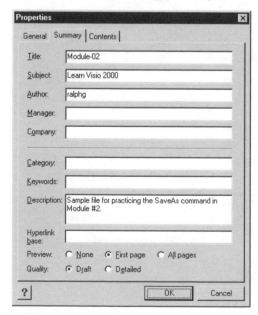

▶ Title: **Module-02**

▶ Subject: **Learn Visio 2002**

▶ Author: *your name*

▶ Description: **Sample file for practicing the SaveAs command in Module #2.**

Leave the other fields blank.

6. Click **OK**. Visio saves the drawing to disk and changes the name of the drawing to "Module-02.vsd" on the title bar.

7. Press **Alt+F4** to exit Visio. Click **Yes** in the Save Changes dialog box.

This completes the hands-on activity for saving the drawing.

Opening Existing Drawings

File | Open

Uses

In this chapter you'll learn about:

✓ *Importing non-Visio files*

✓ *Opening a Visio drawing*

You can open a drawing in
Visio by three methods:

Open an existing file when Visio starts. You can select a drawing from the **New Drawing** pane. This window lists the drawings opened most recently; under **Open a drawing**, click **More drawings** to look for other files. Visio 2002 uses a Web-like interface, which means that selected options are underlined, and you click just once to open (as opposed to double-clicking in the standard Windows interface).

*Opening
existing
drawings with
the New
Drawing pane.*

Open a file from within Visio. The **Open** selection of the File menu opens an existing Visio template, drawing, stencil, or workspace:

▶ A *template* file (with the .VST extension) is a drawing file that contains custom settings; new drawings are based on a template file.

▶ A *stencil* file (extension .VSS) contains shapes that you dragged onto the drawing page.

▶ A *workspace* file (extension .VSW) records the size and placement of Visio drawing and stencil windows.

You have the option of opening files in three modes. **Original** means that Visio opens the drawing file and you can make changes to it. **Copy** means Visio makes a copy from the original file; when you save the drawing, Visio prompts you for a different filename. **Read-only** means Visio opens the file, but you can't modify it.

Open a file from Windows Explorer. You can double-click a Visio file (files with the .VSD, .VST, .VSS, and the older .VSW extensions) in Explorer; Windows automatically starts Visio and loads the drawing.

You can open more than one drawing at a time in Visio. Simply use **File | Open** for each drawing you want to open. As an alternative, you can select more than one drawing at a time in the Open dialog box: Hold down the **Ctrl** key to select more than one file.

Open multiple files by holding down the Ctrl key.

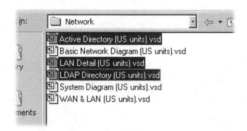

Tip: The Visio Open dialog box displays the contents of the folder you specify in the Drawings field of the File Paths tab. You can find this in the Options dialog box (**Tools | Options**, on the File Paths tab). You can specify the file path for each of the fields listed in this dialog box. To specify more than one path, separate each with a semicolon.

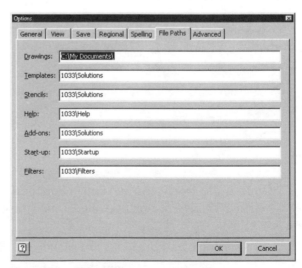

The Options dialog box.

Importing Non-Visio Files

You are not limited to opening files created by Visio; Visio can *import* drawings created by other programs such as ABC FlowCharter, AutoCAD, CorelDraw, Micrographx, and MicroStation, as well as raster images created by paint programs.

Vector Formats	Extension
ABC FlowCharter	AF2 or AF3
Adobe Illustrator	AI
AutoCAD and IntelliCAD drawings	DWG
Other CAD software	DXF
Computer Graphics Metafile	CGM
Compressed Enhanced Metafile	EMZ
CorelDraw drawing	CDR
CorelFLOW chart	CFL
Corel Clipart	CMX
Encapsulated PostScript	EPS
Enhanced Metafile	EMF
Initial Graphics Exchange Specification	IGS
MicroGraphx Designer v3.1 drawing	DRW
MicroGraphx Designer v6 drawing	DSF
MicroStation drawing	DGN
PostScript	PS
Windows Metafile	WMF
Raster Formats	**Extension**
Graphics Interchange Format	GIF
JPEG	JPG
Macintosh PICT	PCT
Portable Network Graphics	PNG
Tagged Image File Format	TIFF
Windows Bitmap	BMP or DIB
Z-Soft PC Paintbrush	PCX
Tagged Text Formats	**Extension**
ASCII text	TXT
Comma-separated value text	CSV

Caution: When Visio imports a vector file created by another program, it must translate the data. In some cases, the translation is not perfect. Some objects may be erased, while other objects may look different in Visio than in the originating application.

Procedures

Before presenting the general procedures for Open, it is helpful to know about the shortcut keys. These are:

Function	Keys	Menu	Toolbar Icon
Open	Ctrl+O	File | Open	

Opening a Visio Drawing

Use the following procedure to open a Visio drawing:

1. Start Visio. Notice the Choose Drawing Type window.

2. In the New Drawing pane, under **Open a drawing**, select **More drawings**. Notice the Open dialog box displays names of Visio drawings.

3. If necessary, use the **Look in** drop-down list to go to the drive and folder where the drawing is located.

4. Double-click the drawing name. Notice that Visio opens the drawing and associated stencils.

Importing a Non-Visio File

Use the following procedure to import a non-Visio file:

1. Start Visio. Notice the Choose Drawing Type window.

2. In the New Drawing pane, under **Open a drawing**, select **More drawings**. Notice the Open dialog box displays names of Visio drawings.

3. If necessary, use the **Look in** drop-down list to go to the drive and folder where the drawing is located.

4. Double-click the drawing name. Notice that Visio opens the drawing and associated stencils.

5. Click the down arrow in the Files of type box.

6. Select the extension of the file to import.

7. Double-click the filename.

8. Visio opens the file in a drawing.

Hands-On Activity

In this activity, you use the Open function. Begin by starting Visio.

1. From the **File** menu, click **Open**.
2. Notice the module-02 filename you saved in Module 2.

The Open dialog box.

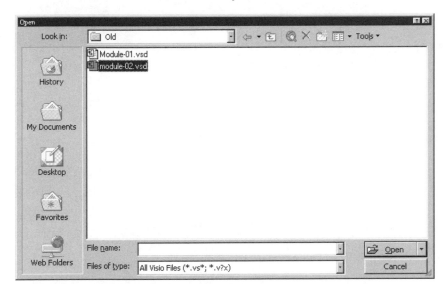

3. Double-click the filename.
4. Visio opens the file in a drawing.
5. Press **Alt+F4** to exit Visio.

This completes the hands-on activity for opening a drawing.

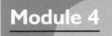

Module 4 | Setting Up Pages and Layers

File | Page Setup
Insert | Page
View | Layer Properties

Uses

> **In this chapter you'll learn about:**
> ✓ **Drawing pages**
> ✓ **Inserting pages**
> ✓ **Background pages**
> ✓ **Drawing scale**
> ✓ **Layers**

A Visio drawing can contain one or more pages. This makes Visio like a combination word processor and drawing software: You can easily create multi-page documents with mixed text and graphics. Unlike a word processor, though, text and graphics don't "flow" from one page to the next; each page is independent. A Visio drawing can have up to 200 pages.

You view only one page at a time, except for *background* pages and when Visio is in print preview mode. (Actually, that's not quite true: You could use the **Window | Tile** command to display all pages.)

Each drawing page can have a set of *layers*, which are a way to separate objects logically and are common with CAD (computer-aided design) software, such as AutoCAD. For example, selecting all shapes on a page does not select shapes on a locked layer. In Visio, a shape can be assigned to two or more layers.

Drawing Pages

Each new Visio drawing contains a single page. To create more pages, right-click the page tab at the bottom of the drawing; Visio calls this "inserting" a page. The shortcut menu inserts, deletes, renames, and reorders pages.

> **Tip:** There is a case where Visio creates pages on its own. When you drag a shape from the Backgrounds stencil (found in Visio Extras), Visio automatically creates a new page called "Background" and places the shape on that page.

Right-click a page tab to create additional pages.

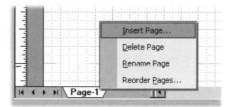

Pages not in the right order? Visio lets you drag pages around by their tabs. (The Background page cannot be moved.) The small arrow shows you where the page ends up.

Drag a page tab to reorder the pages.

Inserting a Page

To add a page to the drawing, right-click any page tab and select **Insert Page**. Visio displays the Page Setup dialog box with the Page Properties tab showing.

The Page Setup dialog box's Page Properties tab.

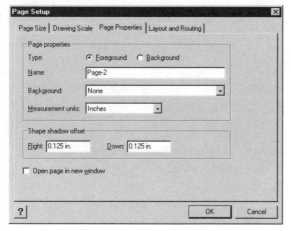

This dialog box can be intimidating, with its many tabs and options. Let's concentrate on just the Page Properties tab:

Type: Specifies whether the page is a foreground or a background page.

Name: Describes the page with a name up to 31 characters long.

Background: Lists the names of the background pages in the drawing, if any.

Measurement units: Specifies the units of measure for the page, if you want it different from the units set for the drawing (see Drawing Scale tab).

Shape shadow offset: Specifies the offset distance for "shadows" applied to shapes; a negative distance makes the shadow offset to the top or left of the shape.

Open page in new window: When on, the page is opened in a new window; when off, the page is displayed in the current window.

Tip: You can use pages to give a slide show, as a substitute for PowerPoint. First, create your multi-page drawing. Then, from the menu bar, select **View | Full Screen**; the drawing is displayed all by itself on your computer's screen (background pages are not displayed). To move through the pages, press **N** or the → key; press **P** or the ← key for the previous page. You can right-click to display a shortcut menu, too. Press **Esc** to return to "normal" view.

Background Pages

As mentioned earlier, you see only one page at a time, with one exception. The *background* page shows through to a foreground page (most pages in a Visio drawing are foreground pages). You can use a background page to display a common graphic element, like a background texture, the corporate logo, or a title block on many pages. Even though you can see the shapes on the background page, you cannot edit them until you switch to the background page. (If you are a CAD software user, you can think of the background page as a layer or xref common to all pages. If you use PageMaker for desktop publishing, a background page is similar to a master page.)

The world map graphic is on the background page.

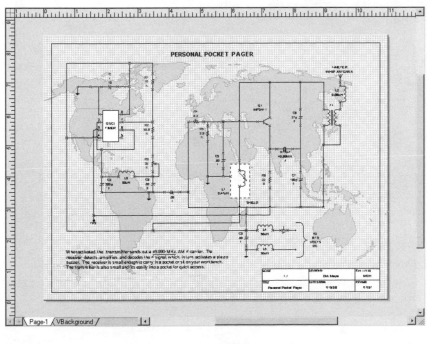

In many cases, you must assign the background page to each foreground page individually. If you want all the pages in your drawing to use the same background, set up Page-1 with the correct background; any page you insert after that has the same background page associated with it.

When you create a background page, you have to tell Visio the foreground page(s) with which to associate the background page. Also, you can assign a background page to another background page. And you can convert a foreground page to background status, and vice versa. To assign a background page to a foreground page:

1.   Click the foreground page tab at the bottom of the drawing window.

2.   From the menu bar, select **File | Page Setup**.

3.   When the Page Setup dialog box appears, click the **Page Properties** tab.

4.   From the **Background** list, select the name of the background page. If you want to disassociate a background page, select **None** from the list.

5.   Click **OK**.

Other Page Parameters

Unlike a word processing document, every page in a Visio drawing can have a different size, scale, and orientation. These items are handled by the Page Size tab of the Page Setup dialog box.

The Page Size tab of the Page Setup dialog box.

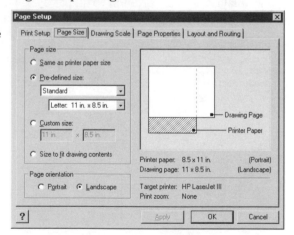

Same as printer paper size: Matches automatically the drawing page size to the printer paper (on the Print Setup tab).

Pre-defined size: Allows you to select a standard paper size. Visio includes sizes that match these standards: Standard, Metric (ISO), ANSI Engineering, and ANSI Architectural up to 34" by 44".

Custom size: Allows you to specify any size for the page. (Contrary to Visio's documentation, the size is *not* adjusted by the drawing scale.) The horizontal and vertical dimensions can be as big as 1e19" by 1e19" — which is a 1 followed by 19 zeros or ten billion, billion inches. That's an area large enough to hold 20,000 copies of our solar system — full size!

> **Tip:** You can change the size of the page interactively without needing this dialog box. Hold down the **Ctrl** key, then grab the edge of the page with the cursor. Drag the width (or height) wider or narrower.
>
> In addition, you can also rotate the page interactively. Select the **Rotation** tool, grab the corner of the page, and rotate it. Watch the status line for the angle readout. (If this doesn't work for you, go to the **General** tab by using **Tools | Options** and turn on the **Enable page rotation** option.) You would rotate the page to create an isometric drawing grid using guidelines.

Size to fit drawing contents: This handy option makes the page fit the drawing.

> **Tip:** You can have Visio center the drawing on the page automatically. From the menu bar, select **Tools | Center Drawing**.

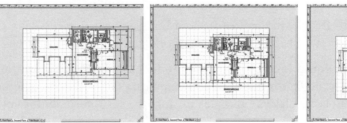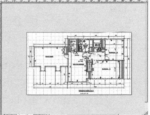

Centering the drawing (center) and fitting the page to the drawing (right).

Page orientation: Specifies the page as portrait (tall) or landscape (wide); this option is unavailable when Same as printer paper size is selected. This option affects only the drawing page; it does not change the orientation of the printer page. The preview window shows how the drawing and printer pages relate to each other. For a square-shaped page, the orientation doesn't matter.

> **Tip:** To force the drawing page to match the printer page, select **Same as printer paper size**.

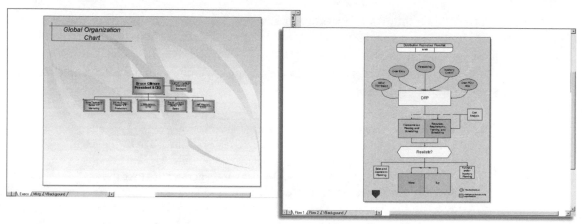

Landscape (left) and portrait orientation (right).

Drawing Scale

Scale makes a large drawing fit a small page. Or, more formally, scale is the relationship between the size of the page and the size of the objects being drawn. For example, when the scale is 1"=10', a 10-foot-wide shape is printed one inch wide. There are two ways that you can scale a drawing:

Scale to fit: If you don't care about the scale, turn on the **Size to fit drawing contents** option in the Page Size tab of the Page Setup dialog box.

Specific scale factor: If you require that the drawing be printed at a standard scale, select a scale factor from the Drawing Scale tab of the Page Setup dialog box. The following table shows examples of standard scale formats for specific disciplines:

Scale	Example
No Scale	1:1
Metric	1:100
Architectural	3/32" = 1' 0"
Civil Engineering	1" = 10' 0"
Mechanical Engineering	1/32:1
Custom Scale	1" = 12.5' or 1mm = 254m

 Warning: When you change the scale of a page, it does not affect other pages in the drawing. In particular, be aware that the scale of a page does not affect the scale of the background page; you must set the scale of the background page separately.

Specify the drawing scale in the Drawing Scale tab of the Page Setup dialog box.

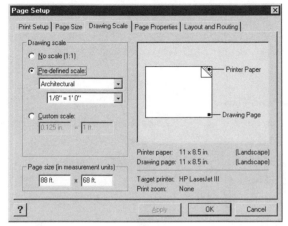

No scale (1:1): The page is not scaled.

Pre-defined scale: Allows you to select a standard scale. Visio includes scales that match these standards: Architectural, Civil Engineering, Metric, and Mechanical Engineering.

Custom scale: Allows you to enter any scale factor. The first measurement is the size of the printed page; the second is the size in the Visio drawing.

Page size: Allows you to enter any size of page in actual dimensions. For example, if you are drawing a house 25' x 50', you would enter those dimensions.

Layers

Just as a drawing can have many pages to segregate data, a page can have many layers to further segregate shapes. The difference is that all shapes on different layers can be viewed at the same time; all shapes on different pages (except background pages) cannot be viewed at the same time.

The Layer Properties dialog box.

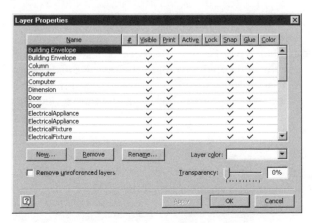

Using layers provides you a powerful tool for controlling the visibility and editability of shapes. You access the Layer Properties dialog box by selecting **View | Layer Properties** from the menu bar. A layer has the following properties:

Property	On	Off
#	Number of objects on layer	...
Visible	Objects are displayed	Objects are hidden and do not display
Print	Objects are printed	Objects are not printed
Active	Objects are added to this layer	Objects are not added to this layer
Lock	Objects cannot be edited	Objects are editable
Snap	Objects snap to other objects	Objects on other layers cannot snap to objects on this layer
Glue	Objects glue to other objects	Objects on other layers cannot glue to objects on this layer
Color	Objects display in this color	Objects display in their original color

The other controls in the dialog box have the following purpose:

New creates a new layer.

Remove deletes a layer; removing a layer also erases all objects assigned to that layer.

Rename gives the layer a different name.

Layer color assigns a color to the layer; objects take on that color as long as their color is not overridden.

Transparency makes objects on the layer see-through.

Remove unreferenced layers deletes all layers with no objects.

 Tip: A shape rests entirely on one layer; you cannot have part of a shape on one layer, and the remainder of the shape on another layer. This affects text: You *cannot* have the text of a shape on a separate layer. (If this were possible, you could turn off all the text in the draw-ing, for example.) The workaround is to create a group: Place the shape on one layer and the separate text on another layer, and then group the two together.

Visio creates layers automatically when you drag certain shapes onto the page; this occurs only when the master is pre-assigned to a layer. Unlike CAD software, a Visio object can be assigned to more than one layer at a time.

You can create new layers at any time; you can remove unused layers at a later time. The new layer is added to the current page, not all pages in the drawing. In the same way, a new page does not inherit the layers from existing pages in the drawing.

You can change the layer settings at any time independently for each layer. For example, if you want to display some text but not print it, you place the text on a layer and turn off the Print setting.

 Tip: Here's the quick way to find out which layer a shape resides on: Turn on the Format Shape toolbar. (To do this, right-click any toolbar and select **Format Shape**.) Select the shape. Observe the layer name in the Layer list box. If the shape is assigned to more than one layer, the list box reads "(Multiple layers)."

Procedures

Before presenting the general procedures for setting up the page, it is helpful to know about the shortcut keys. These are:

Function	Keys	Menu	Toolbar Icon
Size and Scale	Alt+FU	File | Page Setup	...
Layer Properties	Alt+VL	View | Layer Properties	⊜
Add a Page	Shift+F5	Insert | Page	...
Go to a Page	F5	Edit | Go To	←
			→

 Tip: The size, scale, and layer settings are not necessary for some drawings. For example, scale doesn't matter for flowcharts and graphs. Unless you need layers, it is easier to draw without worrying about layer settings.

Setting the Drawing Size and Scale

Use the following procedure to change the size and scale of a drawing.

1. Select **File | Page Setup** to display the Page Setup dialog box.
2. On the Print Setup tab, select the **Paper Orientation**.
3. Click the **Page Size** tab, and select the **Page Orientation**.
4. Click the **Drawing Scale** tab to change the scale of the drawing.
5. Select a scale factor. Notice that Visio automatically determines the drawing scale.

6. Click **OK**.

Changing the Drawing Size Interactively

Use the following procedure to make the drawing page larger or smaller:

1. Move the cursor over any edge of the drawing page.
2. Hold down the **Ctrl** key, and then drag the edge of the drawing inward (for a smaller page) or outward (for a larger page).

To change the width, grab either side of the page; to change the height, grab either the top or bottom edge; to change both width and height at the same time, grab one of the four corners.

Creating New Layers

Use the following procedure to create a new layer:

1. Select **View | Layer Properties** to display the Layer Properties dialog box.
2. Click **New** to create a new layer. Notice that Visio displays the New Layer dialog box.
3. Type a name for the layer.
4. Click **OK**. Notice that Visio adds the layer to the list of names.
5. Click **OK**.

Changing Layer Properties

Use the following procedure to change the properties of a layer in a drawing:

1. Select **View | Layer Properties** to display the Layer Properties dialog box.
2. Select a layer name.
3. Click **Visible** to change the visibility:
   - Check mark means objects assigned to the layer are displayed.
   - No check mark means the objects are not displayed.
4. Click **Print** to change the printability:
   - Check mark means objects assigned to the layer are printed.
   - No check mark means objects are not printed.
5. Click **Active** to change the layer assignments:
   - Check mark means new objects drawn are assigned to the layer.
   - No check mark means new objects are not assigned to the layer.

When more than one layer is active, new objects are assigned to all active layers. Shapes pre-assigned a layer go to that layer, not the active layer.

6. Click **Lock** to change the lock setting:
   ▶ Check mark means objects assigned to the layer cannot be selected or edited.
   ▶ No check mark means the layer is not locked.

   Locked layers cannot change their Visible, Print, Active, Snap, Glue, and Color properties.

7. Click **Snap** to change the snap setting:
   ▶ Check mark means other objects snap to objects assigned to this layer.
   ▶ No check mark means other objects do not snap to objects on this layer.

8. Click **Glue** to change the glue setting:
   ▶ Check mark means other objects glue to objects assigned to this layer.
   ▶ No check mark means other objects do not glue to objects on this layer.

9. Click **Color** to set the color; select the color from Layer Color.
   ▶ Check mark means objects assigned to the layer display in the color shown.
   ▶ No check mark means objects take their pre-assigned color.

10. Click **Visible**, **Print**, **Active**, **Lock**, **Snap**, **Glue**, or **Color** to reverse the property of all layers at once. This action has no effect on locked layers, except the Lock property. The first click changes all layers to the default setting for each property; the second click reverses the setting.

11. Click **#** to have Visio add up the number of objects assigned to each layer.

12. Click **Apply** to apply changes without leaving the dialog box; click **OK** to apply changes and close the dialog box; click **Cancel** to ignore changes and close the dialog box.

Renaming a Layer

Use the following procedure to change the name of a layer:

1. Select **View | Layer Properties** to display the Layer Properties dialog box.
2. Select a layer name.
3. Click **Rename**. Notice the Rename Layer dialog box.
4. Type a new name for the layer.
5. Click **OK.**
6. Click **OK.**

Removing a Layer

Use the following procedure to remove an unused layer:

1. Select **View | Layer Properties** to display the Layer Properties dialog box.

2. Select a layer name.

3. Click **Remove**. Notice the Layer Properties dialog box warns: "Removing this layer will delete all shapes belonging to it. Remove the layer?"

4. Click **Yes** to remove the layer.

5. To remove all unused layers (layers with no objects assigned to them), click **Removed unreferenced layers**.

Creating a New Page

Use the following procedure to create another page:

1. Right-click any page tab.

2. From the shortcut menu, select **Insert Page**. Notice the Page Setup dialog box. In most cases, the default values provided on the Page Properties tab are appropriate for a new page and you need only click **OK**.

   ▶ **Type: Foreground** (shapes are editable) or **Background** (shapes are seen but cannot be edited).

   ▶ **Name:** Type a name up to 31 characters; Page-2 is the default name.

   ▶ **Background**: Assign a background page to this new page.

   ▶ **Measurement units**: Select units for the rulers (you may have a different measurement system for each page).

   ▶ **Shapeshadow offset**: Applies equally to all shapes on this page that have the shadow option turned on (to cast the shadow up or to the left, use negative values).

   ▶ **Open page in new window**: When on, the page displays in an independent window; when left unchecked, switching to another page replaces the current page.

3. Click **OK**. Notice that Visio displays a new, blank page and states the page number on the title bar.

Hands-On Activity

In this activity, you use the size, scale, and layer functions to set up a new drawing. Begin by starting Visio.

1. In the New Drawing pane, under **New**, click **Blank Drawing** to create a new empty document. Notice that Visio displays an upright 8½" x 11" page. If the grid is turned on, you also see grid lines. The grid lines that are one inch apart are somewhat heavier. This is important, since we will observe the grid lines to notice changes in scale.

2. If necessary, turn on the grid. From the menu bar, select **View | Grid**.

Visio displays an upright 8½" x 11" drawing page.

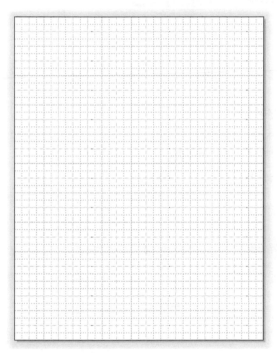

3. Select **File | Page Setup**.

4. In the Page Setup dialog box, select the **Print Setup** tab:

   Select **Landscape.** Click **Apply.** Notice that underneath the dialog box, Visio changes the page from vertical to horizontal orientation.

Visio rotates the page to make it landscape.

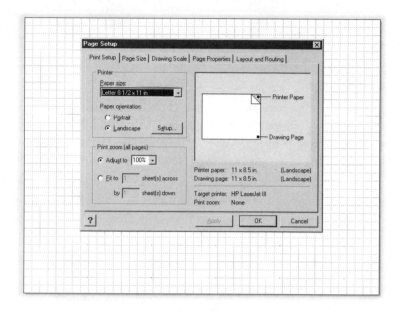

5. Click the **Drawing Scale** tab:

    Select **Pre-defined scale.**

    Select **Architectural** in the Drawing Scale area of the dialog box.

    Select Scale of **1/2" = 1'0".**

    Click **Apply.** Notice how Visio adjusts the drawing size to 22ft 0in x 17ft 0in.

The sheet is larger.

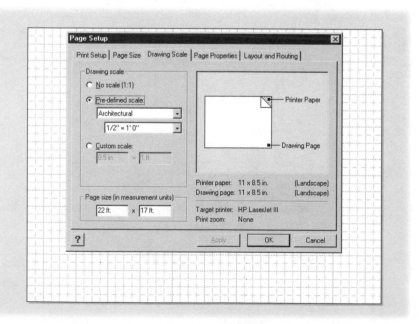

6. Click **OK** to close the dialog box. Notice that the rulers now show the distance as feet, such as 4'6".

The ruler shows scale distances.

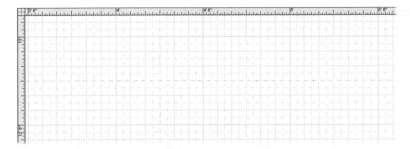

7. Select **View | Layer Properties**. Notice the Layer Properties dialog box has no layer names since this is a new drawing.

Empty Layer Properties dialog box.

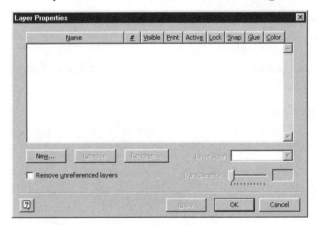

8. Click **New** to create a new layer. Notice the New Layer dialog box.

9. Type **Non-printing text** in the Layer Name box.

Name that layer.

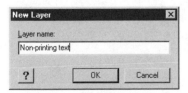

10. Click **OK**. Notice that the Layer Properties dialog box lists layer "Non-printing text."

11. Click **Layer color** at the bottom of the dialog box and select color #7, cyan (light blue). You may need to scroll though the list of colors to find 7.

12. Uncheck **Print** to turn off printing of this layer. We are making this a non-printing layer.

13. Check **Active** to make this layer the active layer. When the next objects are placed, they will be on this layer.

The newly created layer is active and cyan but won't print.

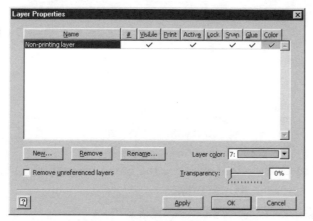

14. Click **OK** to close the dialog box.

15. Select the **Text** tool (looks like the letter A next to the Pointer tool) to place text on the newly created layer.

16. Click near the upper-left corner of the page.

17. Type **Drawing for.** The text is placed on layer Non-printing Text and appears in cyan (light blue) color.

18. Notice that Visio enlarges the page and places a boundary box (the dashed lines) around the text.

19. Press **Enter.**

20. Type **Module 4.**

Placing text in the drawing.

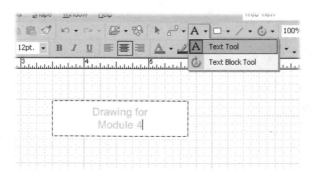

21. Click anywhere else on the page. Notice that Visio returns the page to its original size.

22. Select the **Pointer** tool (looks like an arrow).

23. Click the text. Notice the handles or grips (green squares).

24. Right-click the text. Notice the shortcut menu.

25. Select **View | Layer Properties**.

26. Click **OK** to close the dialog box.

27. Use **File | Save As** and save this drawing as **Module-4.Vsd**.

Do *not* exit Visio or the drawing because you need both for the next module. This completes the hands-on activity for setting up the drawing's size, scale, and layers.

Module 5 Views, Zooms, and Pans

View

In this chapter you'll learn about:

✓ **The Pan & Zoom window**

✓ **Zooming in on a detail**

✓ **Returning to previous zoom level**

Uses

The zoom selections of the View menu enlarge and reduce your view of the page. The term *zoom* comes from the camera zoom lens, which brings objects in a scene closer.

The scroll bars along the edge of the Visio window pan the page. *Pan* means to move the view of the page around without changing the zoom level.

Visio enlarges and reduces the view by a percentage of the actual size. Actual size is *100%*. Smaller than actual size is less than 100 percent. For example, 50% is half-size: objects on the page are half their full-drawn size and you see twice as much of the page. The minimum zoom level is 1%, which makes the page 100 times smaller than actual size. This is useful for seeing a very large drawing on the computer's relatively small screen.

Larger than actual size is more than 100 percent. For example, 400% is four times larger: objects in the page are four times their full-drawn size and you see one-quarter of the page. The maximum zoom is 3098%, which makes the page 31 times larger than actual size.

The **View** menu contains commands that adjust the zoom according to the page area:

▶ **Zoom | Last Zoom** returns to the previous zoom level.

▶ **Zoom | Page Width** means the page is zoomed so that its width fits the Visio window.

▶ **Zoom | Whole Page** means the entire page is zoomed to fit the window.

▶ **Full Screen** removes the toolbars and other user interface displays, showing the entire drawing. You can draw and edit in full-screen mode using function and control keys. Press **Esc** to return to Visio's normal screen.

By using the mouse buttons with the **Ctrl** and **Shift** keys, Visio performs quick zooms and pans. When you hold down the Ctrl and Shift keys, Visio displays a magnifying glass cursor to remind you it is now in zoom mode. By holding down together the Ctrl and Shift keys, you change the view as follows:

View Action	Ctrl + Shift keys plus Mouse Action
Zoom in	Click left mouse button; each click doubles the zoom percentage.
Zoom out	Click right mouse button; each click halves the zoom percentage.
Zoom window	Drag left mouse button; windowed area becomes new view.
Pan	Drag right mouse button; view pans until button is released.

As you hold the Ctrl and Shift keys and drag with the right mouse button, the view pans around the page, and the cursor changes to the hand cursor.

An alternative to zooming in is the *windowed* zoom. Hold down the Ctrl and Shift keys, and then draw a rectangle with the right mouse button; that rectangle becomes your new view.

The Pan & Zoom Window

The Pan & Zoom window provides an overview of the entire drawing. A heavy red border indicates the current zoomed-in view. (This window is known in CAD software as the "bird's-eye view" or the "aerial view.")

The Pan & Zoom window.

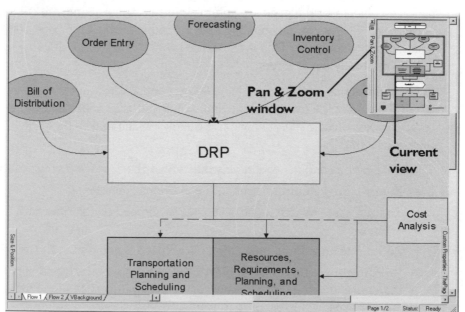

50

To see the Pan & Zoom window, from the menu bar select **View | Pan & Zoom Window**:

▶ To zoom into the drawing, click and drag the cursor. Notice the heavy red rectangle that outlines the zoomed-in view.

▶ To pan the view, grab inside the red rectangle and move it around.

▶ To change the zoom level, grab a corner or an edge of the red rectangle and stretch it. As an alternative, you can once again click and drag a new rectangle.

Procedures

Before presenting the general procedures for setting zoom levels, it is helpful to know about the shortcut keys. These are:

Function	Keys	Menu	Toolbar Icon
Actual Size	Ctrl+I	View | Actual Size	...
Last Zoom	Alt+VZL	View | Zoom | Last Zoom	...
Page Width	Alt+VZP	View | Zoom | Page Width	...
Pan	Ctrl+Shift+Right Drag	...	...
Pan & Zoom window	Alt+VP	View | Pan & Zoom Window	...
Whole Page	Ctrl+W	View | Whole Page	...
Zoom	F6	View | Zoom	150%
Zoom In	Ctrl+Shift+Left Drag	...	...
Zoom In	Ctrl+Shift+Left-click	...	🔍
Zoom Out	Ctrl+Shift+Right-click	...	🔍

Zooming in on a Detail

Use the following procedure to enlarge a detail in the page:

1. Click an object to zoom in on.

2. Select **View | Zoom | 400%**.

3. Alternatively, press function key **F6**, and select **400%**.

4. Alternatively, right-click the object and select **View | 400%**.

5. Alternatively, select **400%** zoom from the toolbar.

Returning to Previous Zoom Level

Use the following procedure to return to the previous zoom level:

1. Select **View | Zoom | Last Zoom**.

2. Alternatively, right-click and select **View | Last Zoom**.

3. Alternatively, select **Last** zoom from the toolbar.

Hands-On Activity

In this activity, you use the zoom functions. Ensure Visio is running and the Module-4.Vsd drawing is displayed.

1. Click the text to select it.

2. Notice that Visio surrounds the selected text with a dashed green line and green handles (or grips). That's how Visio gives you feedback. Notice also that Visio tells you the width, height, and rotation angle of the selected object on the status bar.

3. Hold down the **Ctrl** and **Shift** keys. Notice that Visio changes the cursor to a magnifying glass with a + sign in it.

4. Move the cursor to the upper left of the text.

5. Press the left mouse button.

6. With the **Ctrl** and **Shift** keys and the mouse button all held down, move the cursor down and right.

7. Notice how Visio draws a rectangle, which stretches as you move the mouse.

The zoom preview rectangle.

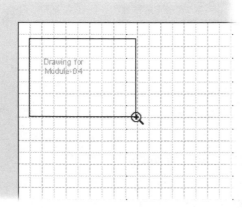

8. Let go of the mouse button. Notice how Visio zooms in and enlarges the text.

The selected object after zooming.

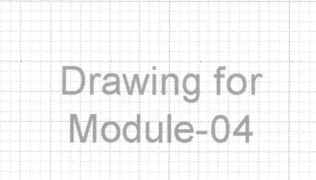

9. Glance at the **Zoom** list box. It should be higher than 100%.

10. Hold down the **Ctrl** and **Shift** keys, and press and hold down the right mouse button.

11. Move the mouse. Notice how the cursor changes from the magnifying glass to an open hand. Notice, too, how the entire drawing moves as you move the mouse.

12. Hold down the **Ctrl** and **Shift** keys and press the right mouse button repeatedly. As you do, notice how the text becomes smaller as Visio zooms out.

13. In the Zoom list box, select **Page** to see the entire page again. As an alternative, you can press **Ctrl+W**.

14. Press **Alt+F4** to exit Visio. Click **No** in the Save Changes dialog box.

This completes the hands-on activity for zooming in and out of the page.

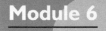

Rulers, Grids, Guidelines, and Page Breaks

View | Rulers, Grid, Guides
Tools | Ruler & Grid
Snap & Glue

> **In this chapter you'll learn about:**
> ✓ **Horizontal and vertical rulers**
> ✓ **Grid lines**
> ✓ **Guidelines and guide points**
> ✓ **Snap distance**
> ✓ **Shape extensions**
> ✓ **Dynamic grid**

Uses

The **Ruler, Grid, Guides**, and **Page Breaks** selections of the View menu toggle the display of the rulers, grid lines, guidelines, and page breaks. The term *toggle* comes from the light switch that turns the lights on and off. You may change the ruler, grid, snap, and page breaks settings at any time without affecting shapes already placed in the drawing.

Horizontal and Vertical Rulers

The *ruler* runs along the top and left edges of the drawing window. The ruler's measurement system matches that of the units selected for the drawing scale (see Module 4 "Setting Up Pages and Layers"). You select the number of tick marks to display between Fine, Normal, and Coarse.

You can move the ruler's origin (zero point) to anywhere in the page by holding down the Ctrl key and dragging the ruler. The horizontal ruler's zero point is normally at the upper-left corner of the page; the vertical ruler's zero point is normally at the lower-left corner of the page. Double-click the rulers to reset them.

*Rulers, grid,
guidelines,
guide point,
and page
breaks.*

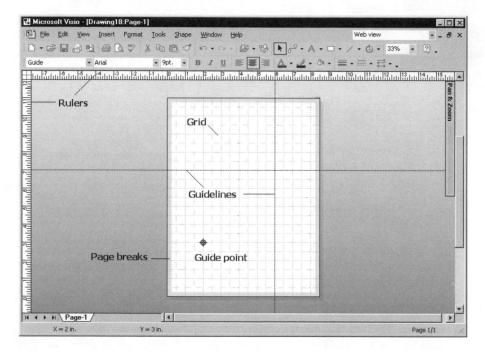

The Grid Lines

The *grid* consists of the horizontal and vertical lines on the page. It helps you line up objects as you draw. The grid has four settings: Normal, Fine, Coarse, and Fixed. You specify how far apart the grid lines are. You can also move the origin of the grid to align with an object on the page.

Grid lines do not print, nor are they copied to the Clipboard.

 Note: The ruler and grid settings of Fine, Normal, and Coarse are relative terms. In *normal* spacing, the ruler and grid spacing change as you zoom in or out; *fine* displays twice as many grid lines as normal spacing, while *coarse* displays half as many grid lines.

The Fixed setting establishes the grid at a constant distance. When you zoom in and out, the spacing between grid lines doesn't change. This is more similar to the type of grid IntelliCAD users are familiar with.

Guidelines and Guide Points

The *guideline* is like a customizable grid line. You create a guideline by dragging the guideline from the ruler (horizontal or vertical) over onto the page. Guidelines help you align shapes; shapes can be "glued" to the guideline (see Module 11 "Connecting Shapes"). Pause the cursor over the ruler to view a tooltip regarding guidelines. CAD users may be familiar with guidelines by the name of "construction line" or xline.

A *guide point* is a small cross marking a point. You create it by dragging from the intersection of the two rulers. Pause the cursor over the rules' intersection to view a tooltip regarding guide points.

To remove a guideline or guide point, select it and press the **Del** key.

 Tip: A page can have as many guidelines and guide points as you need, although too many begin to obscure the drawing. Guidelines and guide points do not print. As well, they do not show up when you copy and paste the drawing from Visio into another application.

Snap Distance

Snap is the ability of Visio to cause objects to snap to objects or other elements such as guidelines or ruler subdivisions. Snap makes it easier to create an accurate drawing because you can use this feature to quickly align your shapes. Think of snap as making shapes magnetic, so that they attract each other. With the Snap & Glue dialog box's General tab (which you find via the menu by selecting **Tools | Snap & Glue**), you can specify that Visio snap a shape to:

The General tab of the Snap & Glue dialog box.

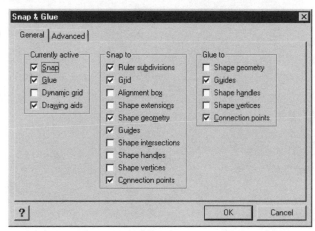

▶ **Ruler subdivisions**: Snaps to tick marks on the ruler.

▶ **Grid**: Snaps to the grid lines.

▶ **Alignment box**: Snaps to the shape's alignment box (the green, dashed rectangle that surrounds every shape).

▶ **Shape extensions**: Snaps to a shape's extension; this option works only with the Line, Arc, Freeform, Pencil, Ellipse, Rectangle, and Connection Point tools.

▶ **Shape geometry**: Snaps to the visible edges of the shape.

▶ **Guides**: Snaps to guidelines and guide points.

▶ **Shape intersections**: Snaps to intersection of two shapes; to the intersection of a shape extension and a shape; and to the intersection of a shape edge and a grid line.

▶ **Shape handles**: Snaps to shape selection handle.

▶ **Shape vertices**: Snaps to a shape's vertex.

▶ **Connection points**: Glues to a shape's connection point.

You can adjust the snap's strength. For example, you set the snap "strength" to 5. When the cursor is within five pixels of a grid line, the snap takes place. Other default values are within three pixels of a ruler tick mark, and ten pixels of a guideline or a guide point. (Snap is not the same as *glue*, which is the ability of shapes to stay together when moved or resized.) To change the strength of the snap, select the **Advanced** tab of the Snap & Glue dialog box.

The Advanced tab of the Snap & Glue dialog box.

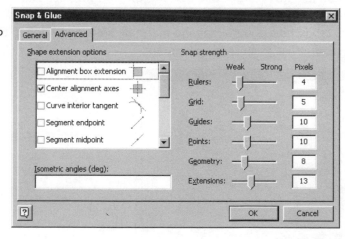

Shape Extensions

Also in the Advanced tab of the Snap & Glue dialog box are *shape extensions* options. Shape extensions display a dashed line that extends from some portion of a shape's geometry. For example, Curve Interior Tangent causes a dashed line to appear when the cursor is over an arc or curve. The dashed line is called an *extension line*, and shows you the tangency to the curve's midpoint. In some cases, the extension is an arc or ellipse.

The gray dashed lines are called extension lines.

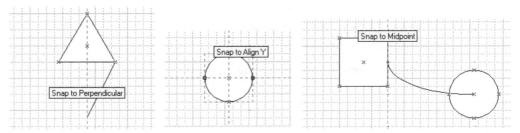

This option works only with the Line, Arc, Freeform, Pencil, Ellipse, Rectangle, and Connection Point tools. Visio 2002 includes a long list of shape extensions:

Shape extensions marked with the check mark are turned on, by default.

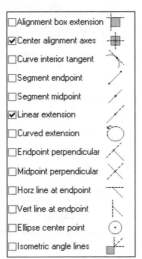

Alignment Box Extension displays the extension line from the shape's alignment box.

Center Alignment Axes displays the extension line from the center of the shape's alignment box.

Curve Interior Tangent displays the extension line from the curve's tangent at the midpoint of the arc segment.

Segment Endpoint displays the extension line from the endpoint of a line segment or arc; the line segment includes the lines that make up a polygon.

Segment Midpoint displays the extension line from the midpoint of a line segment or arc.

Linear Extension displays the extension line from the nearest endpoint of the line.

Curved Extension displays the extension ellipse of an arc segment or freeform shape.

Endpoint Perpendicular displays the extension line perpendicular to the nearest endpoint of a line or an arc.

Midpoint Perpendicular displays the extension line perpendicular to the line or arc's midpoint.

Horz Line At Endpoint displays the extension line horizontal to a line or an arc's endpoint; the line is considered "horizontal" when horizontal to the screen, not the page.

Vert Line At Endpoint displays the extension line vertical to a line or an arc's endpoint; the line is considered "vertical" when vertical to the screen, not the page.

Ellipse Center Point highlights the center of an ellipse or a circle.

Isometric Angle Lines displays the extension line from the vertex at the angle specified in the **Isometric Angles (Deg.)** field.

Isometric Angles (Deg.) allows you to specify up to ten angles (in degrees), each separated by a comma. For example, angles in 15-degree increments are commonly used: 15, 30, 45, 60, 75, and 90.

Dynamic Grid

In addition to the many drawing aids discussed above, Visio 2002 can display a *dynamic grid*. Although Visio calls it a "grid," it looks the same as a shape extension — a dashed gray line. It is called dynamic because it is not static, as is the drawing grid.

When turned on, the dynamic grid shows you the center of adjacent shapes. This makes it very easy to line up shapes. For example, you can easily center a potted plant on a table. Dynamic grid is turned off by default, so you need to turn it on in the Snap & Glue dialog box before you can employ this useful tool.

The vertical and horizontal dashed lines are called the dynamic grid.

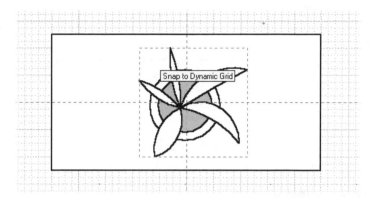

Page Breaks

Page breaks is a non-standard term for displaying the margin around the edge of the page. The *margin* is the unprintable area along the edges of the page; the printer needs this thin strip (usually 0.3" or less) to feed the paper through the printer.

Procedures

Before presenting the general procedures for ruler, grid, snap, and page breaks settings, it is helpful to know about the shortcut keys. "Toggle" means to turn on and off. These are:

Function	Keys	Menu	Toolbar Icon
Snap toggle	Shift+F9	...	[icon]
Ruler toggle	Alt+VR	View | Rulers	...
Guides toggle	Alt+VU	View | Guides	[icon]
Grid toggle	Alt+VG	View | Grid	[icon]
Ruler & Grid dialog box	Alt+TR	Tools | Ruler & Grid	...
Snap & Glue dialog box	Alt+F9	Tools | Snap & Glue	...

Setting the Snap

Use the following procedure to set the snap:

1. Select **Tools | Snap & Glue**. Notice the Snap & Glue dialog box.
2. Select the items you want Visio to snap to in the **Snap To** section.
3. Click the **Advanced** tab.

4. Move the slider bars in the **Snap Strength** section:

   ▶ **Weak:** The cursor is as close as 1 pixel from the point.

   ▶ **Strong:** The cursor is as far away as 30 pixels from the point.

5. Click **OK**.

Setting the Ruler and Grid

Use the following procedure to set the ruler and grid:

1. Select **Tools | Ruler & Grid**. Notice the Ruler & Grid dialog box.

The Ruler & Grid dialog box.

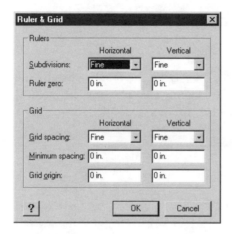

2. Select settings for the ruler from the **Rulers** section:

   ▶ **Subdivisions:** Select from Fine, Normal, or Coarse.

   ▶ **Ruler Zero:** Specify a horizontal and vertical scale distance from the default point.

3. Select settings for the grid from the **Grid** section:

   ▶ **Grid Spacing:** Select from Fine, Normal, Coarse, or Fixed. Fine spacing displays twice as many grid lines as the normal setting; Coarse displays half as many grid lines as normal spacing.

   ▶ **Minimum Spacing:** For Fine, Normal, and Coarse, specify the minimum distance between grid lines. For Fixed, specifies the distance between grid lines. Visio always displays the fixed grid lines, no matter the zoom level.

   ▶ **Grid Origin:** Specify a horizontal and vertical grid distance from the default origin.

4. Click **OK**.

Toggling the Snap

Use the following procedure to turn off and on the snap:

1. Press function key **Shift+F9**.

2. Alternatively, press the **Snap** button on the toolbar.

Toggling the Glue

Use the following procedure to turn off and on the glue:

1. Press function key **F9**.

2. Alternatively, press the **Glue** button on the toolbar.

Creating a Guideline

Use the following procedure to create one or more guidelines:

1. Move the cursor to the horizontal or vertical ruler. Notice that you can create guidelines at any time.

2. Click the mouse button, and then drag into the drawing. Notice the blue line moving with the cursor; this is the guideline.

3. Release the mouse button once the guideline is in position. Notice that the guideline turns green, indicating it is selected.

Tip: You can drag as many guidelines into the drawing as you require:

▶ Dragging from the horizontal ruler results in a horizontal guideline.

▶ Dragging from the vertical ruler results in a vertical guideline.

Guidelines respect the setting of snap, grid, ruler, connection points, etc. To position the guideline accurately, make use of the positioning aids. Note that an unselected guideline is colored blue.

Repositioning a Guideline

Use the following procedure to reposition a guideline:

1. To reposition a guideline, select the **Pointer** tool icon.

2. Select the guideline. Notice that its color changes from blue to green.

3. Drag the guideline to a new position.

4. To move more than one guideline at a time, hold down the **Shift** key while selecting guidelines. The first guideline you select turns green; the additional guidelines you select turn cyan (light blue).

Removing a Guideline

Use the following procedure to remove one or more guidelines:

1. To remove a guideline, select the **Pointer** tool icon.
2. Select the guideline. Notice that it turns green.
3. Press the **Delete** key. Visio deletes the guideline.
4. To delete more than one guideline at a time, hold down the **Shift** key while selecting guidelines, then press the **Delete** key. To erase all guidelines and guide points, select from the menu bar **Edit | Select by Type**. In the Select by Type dialog box, click **None**, then check **Guides**. Click **OK**, then press **Delete**.

Creating and Removing Guide Points

Use the following procedure to create and remove guide points:

1. Move the cursor to the intersection of the rulers (upper-left corner of Visio's drawing area).
2. Click and drag the guide point into the drawing. Notice the two blue lines moving with the cursor.
3. Let go of the mouse button when the guide point is in position. The guide point looks like a small green + sign.
4. To delete the guide point, select it and press the **Delete** key.

Toggling the Display of Guidelines and Points

Use the following procedure to turn off and on the display of guidelines and points:

1. Select **View | Guides**. The check mark indicates guide display is on; no check mark means the guides are not displayed.
2. Alternatively, press the **Guides** button on the Snap & Glue toolbar.
3. Alternatively, create a new layer and place guides on that layer. Toggle the visibility of the guidelines and points by turning the visibility of that layer off and on.

Toggling the Grid Display

Use the following procedure to turn off and on the display of grid lines:

1. Select **View | Grid**. The check mark indicates grid display is on; no check mark means the grid is not displayed.

2. Alternatively, press the **Grid** button on the toolbar.

Relocating the Ruler Origin

Use the following procedure to move the zero setting of the ruler:

1. Move the cursor over the vertical or horizontal ruler.

2. Hold down the **Ctrl** key.

3. Hold down the left mouse button.

4. Drag into the drawing. Notice that a black line moves with the mouse into the drawing.

5. Let go of the **Ctrl** key and mouse button. Notice that the zero point on the ruler has moved.

6. To reset the ruler's zero point back to its default position, double-click the *other* ruler.

To change both rulers at the same time, Ctrl + drag from their intersection at the upper-left corner. To reset both rulers at the same time, double-click the intersection point.

Hands-On Activity

In this activity, you use the ruler and grid functions. Ensure Visio is running and start a new drawing.

1. Select **Tools | Ruler & Grid**. Notice the Ruler & Grid dialog box. All settings are either Fine or 0.

2. Select **Fine** for the Horizontal and Vertical ruler Subdivisions.

3. Select **Coarse** for the Horizontal and Vertical Grid Spacing.

4. Click **OK**. Notice the coarse ruler tick mark spacing and the fine grid line spacing.

Coarse grid spacing and fine ruler spacing.

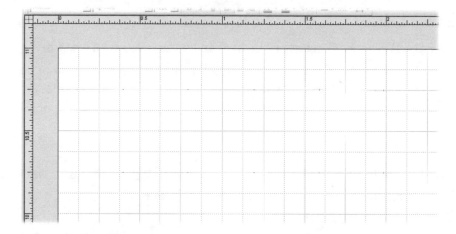

5. To place a vertical guideline, move the cursor to the vertical ruler (located at the left edge of the Visio drawing area). Notice that the cursor becomes a horizontal double-ended arrow.

6. Hold down the left mouse button.

7. Drag the mouse into the drawing. Notice the blue vertical line moving with the mouse.

8. Let go of the mouse button. Notice that the guideline changes from blue to green.

9. Exit Visio by pressing **Alt+F4**. Click **No** in the Save Changes dialog box.

This completes the hands-on activity for setting the ruler and grid.

Opening Existing Stencils

File | Stencils

Uses

In this chapter you'll learn about:

✓ **The Find Shape tool**

✓ **Opening a stencil file**

✓ **Adjusting the Stencil window**

The **Stencils** selection of the **File** menu lets you open one or more stencil files. You use stencils to place shapes in the page. The term *stencil* comes from the green plastic stencils used by drafters to quickly draw commonly used shapes.

This plastic stencil was used to create flowcharts.

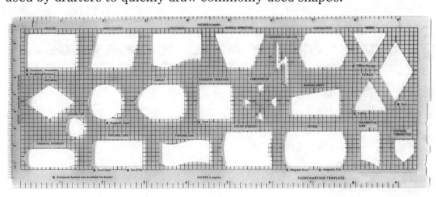

In Visio, stencils contain predrawn objects, called *shapes*. Visio shapes have more intelligence than the shapes cut out of the green plastic. The shapes know their logical connection point and are automatically assigned a layer name. Unlike the plastic stencil shapes, Visio shapes are easy to resize and modify, and are in full color.

Visio comes with many stencil files, which are files with extension .VSS (found in the \Solutions folder). Each stencil file typically includes 10 to 45 shapes. Additional specialized stencil files are available from Microsoft and third-party developers. To help you find stencil files, whether on your computer or your firm's network or the Internet, Visio includes the Find Shape feature.

Samples of Visio stencils.

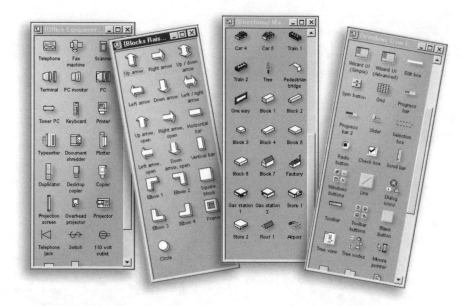

You use a shape in two steps: (1) open the stencil file; and (2) drag the shape from the stencil to the page. In this module, you learn the first step, opening the stencil file.

Dragging a shape from the stencil to the drawing.

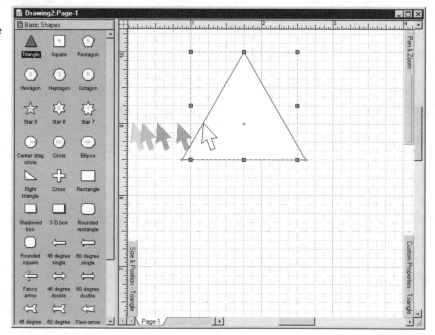

Note: The shape in the stencil is called the *master shape* because Visio makes a copy of the master when you appear to drag the shape into the drawing.

Finding Shapes

Since Visio includes thousands of shapes, it can be difficult looking for a specific shape: which stencil is it stored in? To solve this problem, Visio provides two ways to search for a shape. One solution is to categorize the shapes. Click the small arrow next to the **Open Stencil** button on the toolbar; Visio displays a list of stencil categories (which correspond to folders in the \Solutions folder). The exact contents of the list varies, depending on which edition of Visio you are operating.

The toolbar lists stencils by categories. Clicking on the Open Stencil button displays a list of stencils by categories.

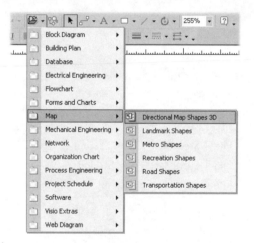

The second solution is the Find Shape tool (known as the Shape Explorer in Visio 2000). This tool searches for shapes on your computer and the Internet.

The Find Shape tool searches for shapes.

Type a word or phrase that describes the shape in the Search For box. For example, when I enter "map," the Find Shape tool returns 87 shapes in several stencils.

▶ **All of these words**: Find Shape searches for an exact match to the words you type. This is equivalent to using quotation marks, such as "Blocks with Perspective." When you type a single word, the Find Shape tool searches for items that contain only that word. For example, typing "block" returns "Block Diagram" but not "Blocks Raised."

▶ **Any of these words**: Find Shape searches for items that have any of the words in the search phrase, such as "blocks," "with," and "perspective." This could include "Block Diagram," "Blocks Raised," and "Blocks with Perspective."

Once you have found the shape you are looking for, drag the shape into the drawing.

Procedures

Before presenting the general procedures for opening a stencil file, it is helpful to know about the shortcut keys. These are:

Function	Shortcut	Menu	Toolbar Icon
Open stencil file	Alt+FTO	File | Stencils | Open Stencil	
Open blank stencil	Alt+FTN	File | Stencils | New Stencil	...
Find Shape	Alt+FF	File | Find Shape	

Opening a Stencil File

Use the following procedure to open a stencil file:

1. Select **File | Stencils | Block Diagram | Basic Shapes**. Notice how Visio groups the stencil files by categories.

2. You can have more than one stencil open at a time. Repeat the above procedure and select another stencil name.

*Opening a
stencil via the
File menu.*

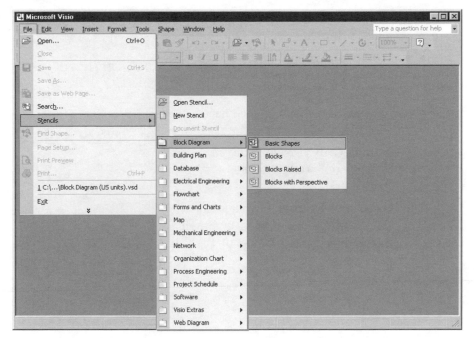

Adjusting the Stencil Window

Use the following procedure to change a stencil window:

1. Open a new drawing.

2. Select **File | Stencils | Block Diagram | Basic Shapes**.

3. Click the icon on the stencil's title bar (as shown in the following illustration). Notice the options:

   ▶ **Close:** Closes (removes) the stencil.

   ▶ **Edit:** Makes the stencil editing command available (right-click a shape to view a shortcut menu with editing options).

   ▶ **Save:** Saves changes made to the stencil in Edit mode.

   ▶ **Save As:** Saves the stencil to another filename.

   ▶ **Properties:** Displays the Properties dialog box for the stencil (available in Edit mode only).

   ▶ **Find Shape:** Displays the Find Shape window.

   ▶ **Drawing Explorer Window:** Displays the Drawing Explorer window of the stencil window (see Module 31 "Drawing Explorer").

▶ **Float Window**: Makes the window undock (float).

▶ **Icons and Names**: Displays the shapes with icons and names (the default, as illustrated).

▶ **Icons Only**: Displays the shapes with icons only.

▶ **Names Only**: Displays the shapes by name only (takes up less space).

▶ **Icons and Details**: Displays the shapes with icons, names, and their tooltip descriptions (takes up the most space).

The stencil's menu is located in its title bar.

The stencil displays shapes in a number of different ways.

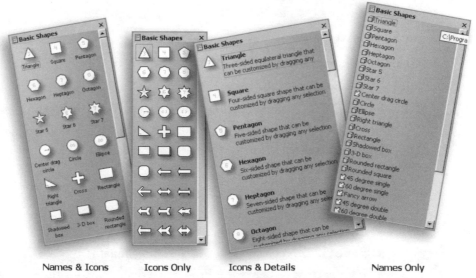

Names & Icons   Icons Only   Icons & Details   Names Only

4. Drag the slider bar to see more shapes in the lower part of the stencil.

5. Right-click on a shape in the stencil. Notice the options; most are grayed out, unless **Edit** it turned on (as noted earlier):

Each shape has its own shortcut menu.

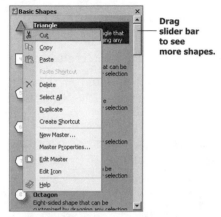

Drag slider bar to see more shapes.

▶ **Cut:** Cuts (removes) the shape from the stencil and copies it to the Clipboard.

▶ **Copy:** Copies the shape to the Windows Clipboard in picture (WMF) format.

▶ **Paste:** Pastes a shape from the Clipboard into the stencil; this option is available only when the Clipboard contains a shape.

▶ **Paste Shortcut:** Pastes a shortcut to a shape on another stencil.

▶ **Delete:** Erases the shape from the stencil.

▶ **Select All:** Selects all shapes in the stencil.

▶ **Duplicate:** Makes a copy of the stencil.

▶ **Create Shortcut:** Creates a shortcut to a shape on another stencil.

▶ **New Master:** Creates a new, blank shape.

▶ **Master Properties:** Displays the Master Properties dialog box.

▶ **Edit Master:** Opens the master in a window so that the master can be graphically edited.

▶ **Edit Icon:** Opens the master's icon in an icon editor.

▶ **Help:** Displays help that answers the following questions: "Where is this shape located?", "How do I use this shape?", "How do I use Visio shapes?", and "How do I find other shapes?".

Modifying masters and creating new stencils is beyond the scope of this book. See *Learn Microsoft Visio 2002 for the Advanced User*, also from Wordware Publishing.

Hands-On Activity

In this activity, you open two stencil files. Ensure Visio is running.

1. Select **File | New | Building Plan | Floor Plan** from the menu bar. Notice that Visio sizes the page window to accommodate the Walls, Shell and Structure and other stencils.

Visio sizes the stencil and page to fit the window.

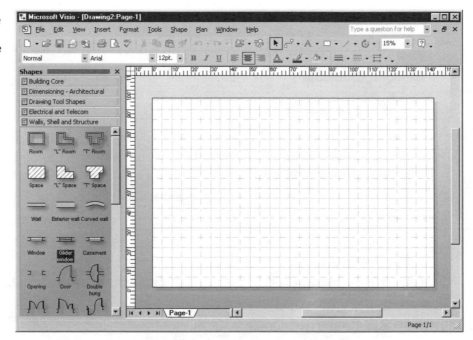

2. Drag the stencil's scroll bar to look at the 35 shapes in the stencil.

3. Open a second stencil by selecting **File | Stencils | Forms and Charts | Marketing Diagrams**. Notice how the newly opened stencil covers up the first stencil. (In case you don't see it, the title bar of the Office Layout stencil may be at the top or bottom of the stencil window.)

The title bar of stencils can be at the top or bottom of the stencil window.

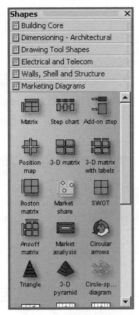

4. To bring the first stencil back into view, click the **Walls, Shell and Structure** title bar. Notice how it reappears, covering over the Marketing Diagrams stencil.

5. To see both stencils at the same time, drag the **Marketing Diagrams** stencil by its title bar. Drag the stencil to the right side of the drawing area.

Two stencils visible at the same time.

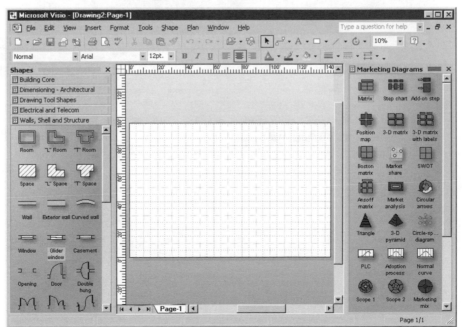

6. To make more room for the drawing area, you have three options:

   ▶ Drag the side of the stencil to make it narrower.

   ▶ Right-click on either stencil's title bar. Select **Icons Only** or **Names Only** from the floating menu. Notice that the window size of both stencils change.

   ▶ Right-click the title bar and select **Float Window**. Notice that the stencil becomes an independent window and can be placed anywhere on your screen, even outside of Visio.

Floating the stencils.

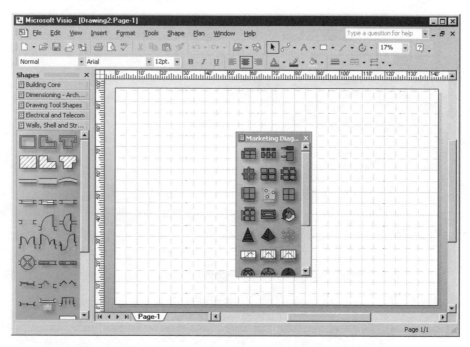

⊷ Tip: To move a floating stencil, drag it by the title bar. To prevent a stencil from docking, hold down the **Ctrl** key as you move the stencil. To resize a stencil, drag it by one of its four corners.

---

7. Exit Visio with **Alt+F4**. Click **No** in the Save Changes dialog box.

This completes the hands-on activity for opening and positioning a stencil file.

Dragging Masters into the Drawing

Uses

In this chapter you'll learn about:

✓ **Dragging shapes into a drawing**

To use a shape, you drag it from the stencil to the drawing. There are no menu selections, toolbar icons, or shortcut keys for placing shapes in the drawing.

Note: Visio terminology can be confusing sometimes. While in the stencil, the "shape" is called a *master*. When you drag the master into the drawing, Visio makes a copy of the master. Visio places an *instance* of the master in the drawing. The instanced master is called a *shape*.

Procedures

Use the following procedure to drag a shape from the stencil to the page. Ensure Visio has at least one stencil file open and a drawing page displayed.

1. Move the cursor over a master in the stencil.

2. Drag the master to the page. To *drag*, you hold down the left mouse button, move the master onto the page, and then let go of the mouse button.

 Tip: You can drag the master from the stencil to the page many times. A Visio stencil does not "run out" of shapes. You can delete a shape by dragging it back onto the stencil.

Dragging the master into the drawing.

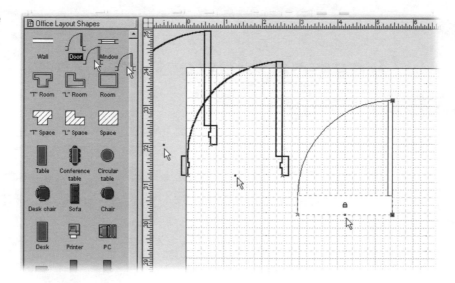

Hands-On Activity

In this activity, you start to create an office drawing by dragging shapes onto the page. Ensure Visio is running. Open a new drawing via **File | New | Building Plan | Floor Plan**. Visio should be displaying the **Walls, Shell and Structure** stencil.

1. Move the cursor over the **Room** master shape in the stencil. Notice that after a second or two, Visio displays a tooltip that helps you use the shape.

Each shape contains a tooltip that displays helpful information.

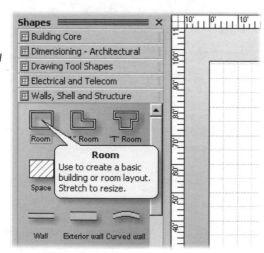

2. Drag the **Room** master to the drawing. Notice that Visio adds walls to the room after a few seconds. (You may need to zoom into the room shape to see it more clearly.)

3. Right-click the shape to display the shortcut menu. The options found on the menu vary, depending on the shape. The following options are common to all shapes:

   ▶ **Cut** removes the shape from the drawing and places it in the Windows Clipboard.

   ▶ **Copy** copies the shape to the Clipboard. It is available to Visio and other Windows applications in different formats: Visio drawing, Visio drawing data, Picture (WMF), Enhanced Picture (EMF), and ANSI text of the shape name. See Module 12 "Cutting, Copying, and Pasting."

Right-click a shape to view its shortcut menu.

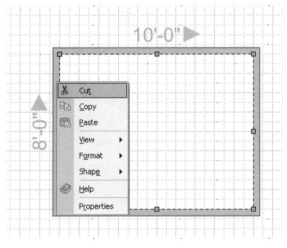

   ▶ **Paste** pastes whatever is currently in the Clipboard into the center of the drawing.

   ▶ **View** lets you change the zoom level and toggle the display of drawing aids, such as grids and rulers.

   ▶ **Format** lets you change the formatting of the lines and text that make up the shape. (See Modules 13 and 14 "Formatting Shapes" and "Formatting Text.")

   ▶ **Shape** lets you change the position of the shape, such as flipping it. (See Module 9 "Sizing and Positioning.")

   ▶ **Help** displays the same help box we saw earlier.

▶ **Properties** displays the Custom Properties dialog box. For this room shape, it allows you to change the width and length. (The data can be extracted to a database to help you create an inventory listing.) Other shapes have other custom properties. See Module 34 "Custom Properties."

4. Exit Visio with **Alt+F4**. Click **No** in the Save Changes dialog box.

This completes the hands-on activity for placing a shape in the drawing.

Sizing and Positioning

Shape | Rotate or Flip
Shape | Order | Bring to Front, Send to Back
Tools | Center Drawing
View | Size & Position Window

Uses

Much of the time, you probably will use the shape's handles (the green squares) to size and position the shape. With shape handles, you change the size of a shape. You can perform the following actions with the handles on a 2D shape:

In this chapter you'll learn about:
✓ *The Size & Position window*
✓ *Resizing the shape*
✓ *Changing the height of the shape*
✓ *Rotating the shape*
✓ *Flipping the shape*
✓ *Bring to Front and Send to Back*
✓ *Centering the drawing*

▶ Corner handles: Size the shape proportionally.

▶ Side handles: Size the shape horizontally.

▶ Bottom or top handles: Size the shape vertically.

You can perform the following actions with the handles on a 1D shape:

▶ Begin and end handles: Change the length of the shape.

▶ Center handle: Widen the shape relative to its base.

When you see small gray padlocks instead of green squares, it means the shape is locked. (The small blue x markers are connection points.)

Every shape has sizing handles, whether movable (left) or locked against resizing (right).

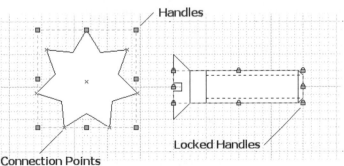

Handles

Connection Points

Locked Handles

Each time you use one of the **Rotate** selections of the **Rotate or Flip** option (found in the Shape menu), it rotates the shape at right angles (90 degrees). **Rotate Left** rotates the shape counterclockwise by 90 degrees; **Rotate Right** rotates the shape 90 degrees clockwise. In addition, Visio has the **Rotation** tool that lets you rotate the shape any angle.

The **Flip** selections of the **Shape | Rotate or Flip** menu transpose the shape. **Flip Horizontal** transposes the left and right halves, while **Flip Vertical** reverses the top and bottom halves.

The **Order** selections of the Shape menu change the overlap of shapes. **Bring to Front** brings a shape visually in front of an overlapping shape; the **Send to Back** selection moves the overlapping shape behind an underlying shape. When three or more shapes overlap, the Bring Forward and Send Backward options move the selected shape by one shape at a time.

The **Center Drawing** selection of the Shape menu is a very useful tool that nicely centers the entire drawing on the page. You will find yourself using this tool after changing the size or orientation of the page.

Size & Position Window

The **Size & Position Window** selection of the View menu displays the Size & Position window. It allows you to make the changes by typing in numbers, which is more accurate than dragging handles. The data listed in the window varies according to the shape. Two examples are illustrated below:

Size and position data for a 1D shape (left) and 2D shape (right).

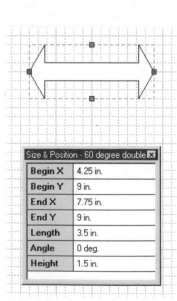

Size & Position - 60 degree double	
Begin X	4.25 in.
Begin Y	9 in.
End X	7.75 in.
End Y	9 in.
Length	3.5 in.
Angle	0 deg.
Height	1.5 in.

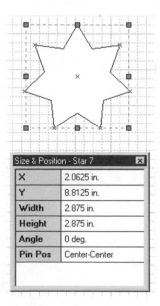

Size & Position - Star 7	
X	2.0625 in.
Y	8.8125 in.
Width	2.875 in.
Height	2.875 in.
Angle	0 deg.
Pin Pos	Center-Center

For the 1D shape, the parameters have the following meaning:

Begin X: The x-coordinate of the shape's begin point; x is measured from the ruler's 0 point.

Begin Y: The y-coordinate of the shape's begin point.

End X: The x-coordinate of the shape's end point.

End Y: The y-coordinate of the shape's end point.

Length: The length of the shape.

Angle: The angle of the shape; the angle is measured in degrees from the x-axis.

Height: The height of the shape.

You can click the data field and change the value. For example, click the field next to **Height** and change **1.5 in** to **3**; Visio changes the width of the shape to 3.0 inches. Conversely, you can size the shape via its handles, and you will see the data updating in the Size & Position window.

For the 2D shape, the parameters have the following meaning:

X: The x-coordinate of the shape's "pin" position.

Y: The y-coordinate of the shape's pin.

Width: The width of the shape's alignment box.

Height: The height of the shape's alignment box.

Angle: The angle of the shape's alignment box, relative to the pin.

Pin Pos: The location of the pin relative to the shape's alignment box.

The *pin* of the 2D shape is used by Visio to measure the distance from the page's origin (0,0). Think of sticking a pin through a memo on a bulletin board. When you click the field next to **Pin Pos**, Visio displays a list of other pin positions, such as Top-Left.

The pin position for a 2D shape.

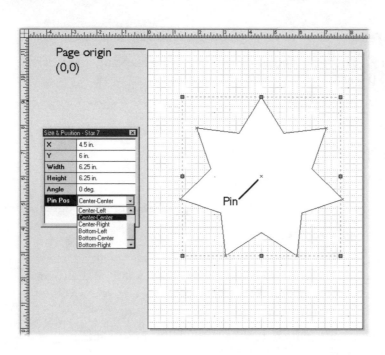

Procedures

Before presenting the general procedures for sizing and positioning it is helpful to know about the shortcut keys. These are:

Function	Keys	Menu	Toolbar Icon
Bring to front	Ctrl+OF	Shape | Order | Bring to Front	
Center drawing	Alt+TW	Tools | Center Drawing	…
Flip horizontal	Ctrl+H	Shape | Rotate or Flip | Flip Horizontal	
Flip vertical	Ctrl+J	Shape | Rotate or Flip | Flip Vertical	
Free rotation	Ctrl+0	…	
Rotate left	Ctrl+L	Shape | Rotate or Flip | Rotate Left	
Rotate right	Ctrl+R	Shape | Rotate or Flip | Rotate Right	
Send to back	Ctrl+OB	Shape | Order | Send to Back	
Size & Position window	Alt+VS	View | Size & Position Window	…

Resizing the Shape

Use the following procedure to resize the shape:

1. Select the shape.
2. Move the cursor over a corner handle. Notice that the cursor changes to a diagonal double arrow.
3. Drag the corner handle away from the shape. Notice the shape getting larger.
4. Release the mouse button. The shape is larger.

Changing the Height of the Shape

Use the following procedure to stretch the shape:

1. Select the shape.
2. Move the cursor over the bottom middle or top middle handle. Notice that the cursor changes to a double arrow.
3. Drag the handle away from the shape. Notice the thin outline of the shape stretching.
4. Release the mouse button. The shape is longer.

Rotating the Shape

Use the following procedure to rotate the shape by 90 degrees:

1. Select the shape.
2. Select **Shape | Rotate or Flip | Rotate Left**. Notice the shape has rotated counterclockwise by 90 degrees. The status line reports "Angle = 90 deg."
3. Repeat to rotate another 90 degrees.

Free Rotating the Shape

Use the following procedure to free rotate the shape:

1. Select the shape.
2. Select the **Rotation** tool button on the toolbar. Notice the shape has new handles that look like green circles:
    ▶ **Center of Rotation:** The center handle is a green circle with a small cross; the shape rotates around this handle. This handle can be moved to change how the shape is rotated.
    ▶ **Rotation Handle:** The other green circle handles are used to rotate the shape around the center of rotation.

3. Move the cursor over one of the rotation handles. The cursor changes to a pair of curved arrows. Notice the thin outline of the shape rotating as you drag the cursor. The status line reports the angle.

4. Click the **Pointer** tool button on the toolbar to exit the rotation mode.

Flipping the Shape

Use the following procedure to flip the shape:

1. Select the shape.

2. Select **Shape | Rotate or Flip | Flip Horizontal** from the menu bar. Notice the shape has mirrored about its center point. The status line reports the new angle.

The Size & Position Window

Use the following procedure to precisely change the size and rotation angle of a shape by typing numbers:

1. Select the shape.

2. Make sure the Size & Position window is visible; if it isn't, from the menu bar select **View | Size & Position Window.**

3. To change the size of the shape, enter new values in the **Width** and **Height** boxes.

4. To change the rotation, type a new angle in the **Angle** box.

5. To change the center of rotation, type new distances in the **X** and **Y** boxes.

6. Alternatively, change the center of rotation to one of nine locations by clicking on the **Pin Pos** box.

Bring to Front and Send to Back

Use the following procedure to change the visibility of overlapping shapes:

1. Select the shape.

2. Select **Shape | Order | Bring to Front** from the menu bar. Notice that the shape moves on top of overlaying shapes.

3. Select **Shape | Order | Send to Back.** Notice that the shape moves to the bottom of overlaying shapes.

Centering Drawing

Use the following procedure to center the drawing:

1. Select **Shape | Center Drawing** from the menu bar; there is no need to select the shapes. Notice that Visio centers the drawing on the page.

Hands-On Activity

In this activity, you use the size functions to resize a shape. Ensure Visio is running. Start a new drawing with the **Basic Shapes** stencil.

1. Drag the **Triangle** shape onto the drawing page. If necessary, zoom in to make the triangle look larger. Notice the eight selection handles (green squares) and one rotation handle.

The Triangle shape and its handles.

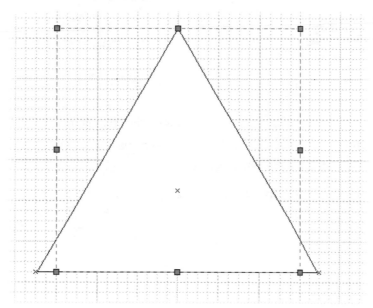

2. Ensure the Size & Position window is open. If necessary, select **View | Size & Position Window** from the menu bar.
3. Type **45** in the Angle box. Notice the triangle is rotated.

Changing the shape via the Size & Position window.

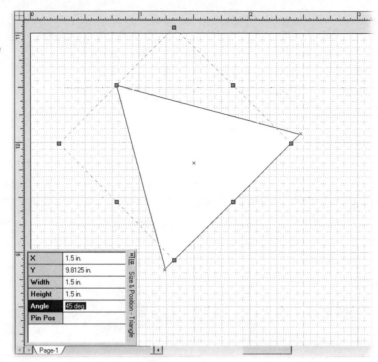

4. Type **5** for both the X and Y position. Notice the triangle moves on the page.

5. Select **Bottom-Right** for Pin Pos. Notice the triangle moves again.

6. Exit Visio with **Alt+F4**. Click **No** in the Save Changes dialog box.

This completes the hands-on activity for sizing and positioning shapes.

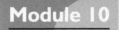

Placing Multiple Shapes

Edit | Duplicate
Shape | Operations | Offset

Uses

In this chapter you'll learn about:

✓ *Making a copy*

✓ *Duplicating more than one copy*

✓ *Making an offset copy*

Once a shape is placed in the drawing, you may want to make copies of the shape. When you change a shape, you don't want to apply those changes to every additional shape; instead, you would make copies (or *duplicates*) of the modified shape.

Sometimes you want to create shapes parallel to existing shapes. Visio allows you to *offset* lines, arcs, and similar simple objects.

Procedures

Before presenting the general procedures for placing multiple shapes, it is helpful to know about the shortcut keys. These are:

Function	Keys	Menu
Duplicate (copy)	Ctrl+drag or Ctrl+D	Edit | Duplicate
Repeat last action	F4	Edit | Repeat
Offset		Shape | Operations | Offset

Making a Copy

Use the following procedure to copy a shape within the drawing:

1. Select a shape.

2. Hold down the **Ctrl** key. Notice that a small + (plus) sign appears next to the arrow cursor. Visio is reminding you that it will make a copy of the shape, rather than move it.

3. Drag the shape, release the mouse, and then release the Ctrl key. Notice that an exact copy of the shape appears.

Making a copy of a shape.

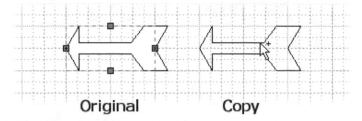

Original   Copy

⊷ **Tip:** To copy a shape in a precise horizontal and vertical direction, hold down the **Ctrl** and **Shift** keys. This constrains movement of the cursor.

Duplicating More Than One Copy

Use the following procedure to duplicate a shape several times at the same distance apart:

1. Select a shape.

2. Hold down the **Ctrl** key, drag the shape, and let go of the Ctrl key. Notice that an exact copy of the shape appears.

3. Press **F4** to repeat the action.

4. Repeat pressing **F4** until you have enough copies.

5. If you make too many copies, press **Ctrl+Z** to undo the copy action.

Making multiple copies with F4.

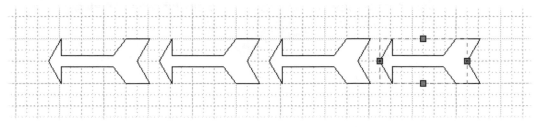

 Note: When it comes to making multiple copies, there is nothing specific about function key **F4**. It is, in fact, the shortcut for the Repeat tool (**Edit | Repeat**). This command repeats the last action you completed. You can use F4 to repeat other actions, such as applying the same formatting to more than one shape.

Making an Offset Copy

Use the following procedure to offset lines and arcs:

1. Draw a line or arc.

2. Select the line (or arc).

3. Select **Shape | Operations | Offset**. Notice the Offset dialog box.

The Offset
dialog box.

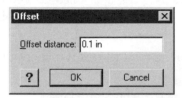

4. Enter an offset distance in the **Offset Distance** text box.

5. Click **OK**. Notice that Visio places a copy of the shape on both sides.

Offsets placed
on simple
shapes (left)
and complex
shapes (right).

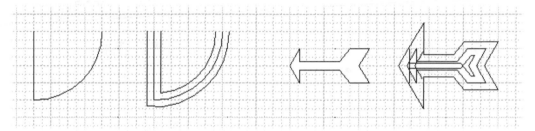

In some cases, Visio cannot accurately offset a figure, as illustrated below.

Offsets are not
always perfect.

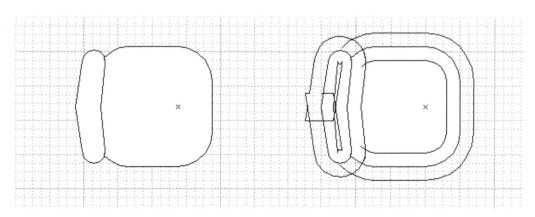

Hands-On Activity

In this activity, you use the duplicate function. Ensure Visio is running. Start a new drawing with the **Office Layout** stencil.

1. Drag the **Bookshelf** shape into the drawing.

2. Hold down the **Ctrl** key, and start dragging the shape. Then hold down the **Shift** key while you're dragging the shape. (You cannot first hold down **Shift+Ctrl**, then drag, because Visio goes into Zoom window mode.)

3. Drag a copy of the **Bookshelf** shape to the right so that it touches the first bookshelf.

4. Release the mouse, and then release the Ctrl and Shift keys.

5. Press **F4** again to place two more bookshelves.

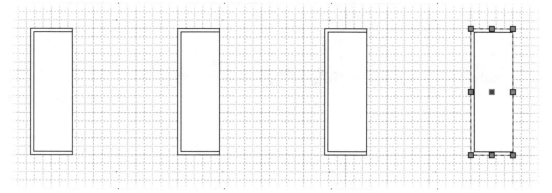

6. If necessary, use one of the **Zoom** commands to see all four bookcases.

7. Press **Alt+F4** to exit Visio. Click **No** in the Save Changes dialog box.

This completes the hands-on activity for placing multiple shapes.

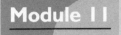

Connecting Shapes

Shape | Connect Shapes

Uses

Perhaps the most important concept in Visio is the connector. *Connectors* are the lines drawn between shapes, such as flowchart, network, and organization shapes.

In this chapter you'll learn about:

✓ **Connection points**

✓ **Glue**

✓ **Variations on connectors**

✓ **Creating connections**

Connectors connect shapes.

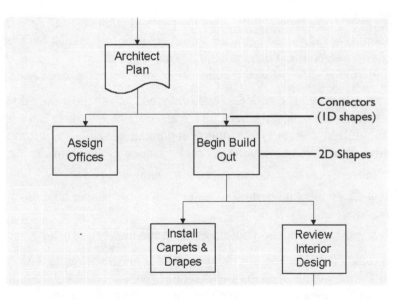

More accurately, a connector is a 1D (one-dimensional) shape that connects 2D (two-dimensional) shapes. The connector can be as simple as a line or an arc, or a more complex object that knows to stay connected, no matter how the shapes are relocated. As we see later, *any* shape can be converted to 1D and, hence, become a connector.

A connector has a start and an end. The start is where the connector was drawn first. It is important to know which end is which. It affects, for example, which end should have an arrowhead.

The start is indicated by a tiny + sign, while the end is indicated by a small x. When a successful connection is made, the end turns red.

Points on a connector, and connection points.

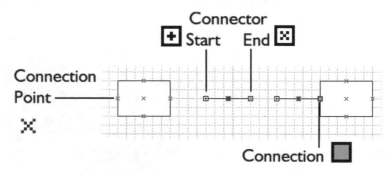

Connection Points

In most cases, the connector attaches to specified points on a shape (the exception is dynamic glue, which attaches to the "best" connection point). These points are called *connection points*. The connection point is indicated by a small blue x. When the connection is successful, the connection point becomes a red square.

Connection points can be added to and removed from shapes; they do not need to be on the shape, but can be anywhere inside and outside of it. Use the Connection Point tool to move, add, and remove connection points to a shape. (From the toolbar, select the **Connection Point** tool; you may find it hidden in the **Connection** tool flyout.)

▶ To move a connection point, drag it to the new position.

▶ To add a connection point to a shape, select the shape, hold down the **Ctrl** key, and click.

▶ To remove a connection point, select it and press the **Delete** key.

You can toggle (turn off and on) the display of connection points with **View | Connection Points**. While creating the diagram, you want connection points to be visible; when it comes time to give your presentation, you want the connection points turned off.

Connection points, like guidelines and the grid, do not print.

Glue

Connectors have a "stickiness" called *glue*. Glue is what forces the connector to stay connected to the shapes as they are moved.

Visio provides you with two types of glue: static and dynamic. *Static* glue causes the connector to stay connected to a connection point. *Dynamic* glue causes the connector to stay connected to the shape.

This means that static glue is best for connectors that you want to stay put, while dynamic glue is best when you want connectors to rearrange themselves automatically. A connector can have static glue at one end and dynamic glue at the other.

In the following illustration, a connector connects the rectangle and the triangle. At the rectangle end, the connector uses static glue; at the triangle end, the connector uses dynamic glue. As the triangle is moved, its dynamic connection jumps from connection point A (center of triangle) to B (left side), to C (top of the triangle). On the rectangle, however, the static connection stays fixed to a single connection point.

The dynamic connection jumps around the triangle, from A to B to C, while the static connection stays fixed on the rectangle.

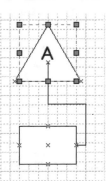
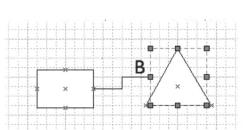
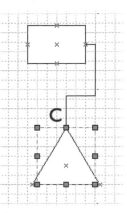

Here is how you tell whether connections are made with static or dynamic glue:

▶ **Static** connections have a red box the same size as the connector's start and end boxes.

▶ **Dynamic** connections have a larger red box.

The difference between static and dynamic glue is subtle.

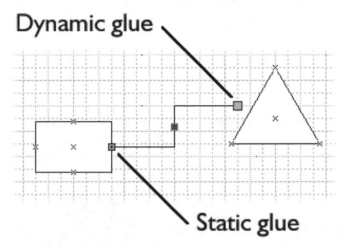

You can change the glue from static to dynamic and back:

1. From the toolbar, select the **Pointer** tool.

2. Drag the end of the connector away from its connection point.

3. Drag the end of the connector into the shape (*not* to a particular connection point). Notice that the entire shape is outlined by a thick red rectangle.

4. When you let go of the mouse button, the connector connects to the shape, not a connection point.

You can now drag the shape around and watch the connector jump from connection point to connection point.

The shape is outlined by a red rectangle when attaching a connector with dynamic glue.

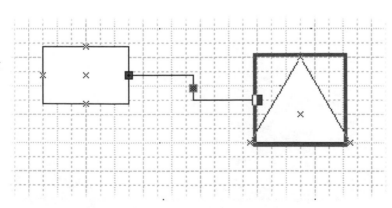

To convert dynamic glue back to static glue, follow the above procedure, but drag the end of the connector to a connection point. In this case, a heavy red square surrounds just the connection point, not the entire shape.

The connection point is outlined by a red square when attaching a connector with static glue.

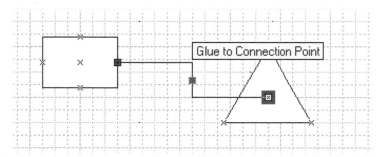

▲ **Note:** This procedure differs from earlier versions of Visio, where you held down the **Ctrl** key while dragging the end of the connector to a different connection point. Visio also refers to these connectors as "point-to-point" and "shape-to-shape."

Variations on Connectors

Visio comes with many dozens of connectors. Some are included with industry-specific stencils, such as network cabling. Others are general-purpose connectors. The **Connectors** stencil in the **Visio Extras** folder has more than 60 connectors.

Some of the connectors provided with Visio.

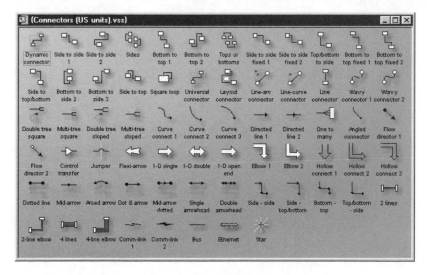

Earlier, I hinted that any shape in Visio could be a connector, provided it is a 1D shape. You turn a 2D shape into a 1D shape with the Behavior dialog box, and vice versa:

The Behavior dialog box.

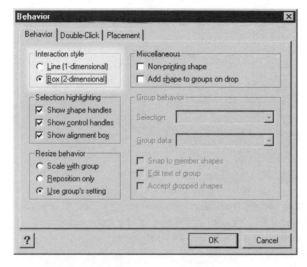

1. Select the shape.
2. From the File menu, select **Format | Behavior**.
3. In the Interaction style section, click the radio button next to either **Line (1-dimensional)** or **Box (2-dimensional)**.
4. Click **OK**.

The triangle as 2D shape (left) and 1D shape (right).

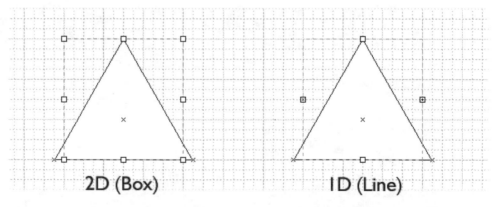

Notice that the selection handles have changed. In summary:

Feature	1D Shape	2D Shape
Handles	4	6 or 8
Top handle	Stretches relative to base	Stretches relative to base

Feature	1D Shape	2D Shape
Side handles	Stretch and rotate	Stretch only
Side handles	Connectors	Not connectors
Corner handles	None	Resize

Just like there are a couple of types of glue, there is more than one type of connector:

Connector: A 1D shape with static glue.

Dynamic connector: A 1D shape with a bend and dynamic glue.

Routable connector: A dynamic connector that routes around *placeable* shapes; these are shapes that Visio will route connectors around.

The routable connector routes around placeable shapes.

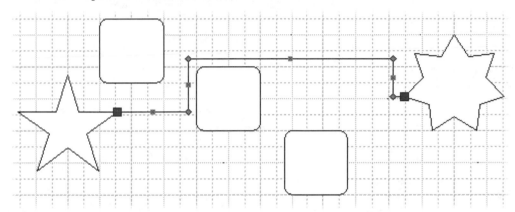

When the routable connector encounters a placeable shape between the two shapes it connects, it moves around the shape rather than crossing through it. To make a 2D shape placeable:

1. Select the shape.
2. From the menu bar, select **Format | Behavior.**
3. Select the **Placement** tab.
4. In the **Placement Behavior** section, select **Layout and Route Around.**
5. Click **OK.**

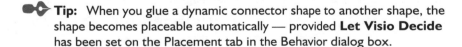
Tip: When you glue a dynamic connector shape to another shape, the shape becomes placeable automatically — provided **Let Visio Decide** has been set on the Placement tab in the Behavior dialog box.

Creating Connections

There are three ways to connect shapes:

Method 1. Select the **Connector** tool button, then drag shapes from the stencil to the page. The shapes are automatically connected.

Method 2. Drag shapes to the page. Then use the **Connector** tool to connect the shapes.

Method 3. Select **Shape | Connect Shapes** to automatically connect selected shapes.

There is a fourth method, not covered in this book. You can create a text file, a spreadsheet, or a database file that specifies the shapes and their connections. The file is imported into Visio, which creates the drawing, complete with connected shapes. See *Learn Microsoft Visio 2002 for the Advanced User.*

Procedures

Before presenting the general procedures for connecting shapes, it is helpful to know about the buttons and shortcut keys. These are:

Function	Keys	Menu	Toolbar Icon
Connector tool	Ctrl+3	...	
Connect Shapes	Ctrl+K	Shape	Connect Shapes	...
Connection Point tool	Ctrl+Shift+I	...	
Toggle display of connection points	Alt+VC	View	Connection Points	...

Connecting Shapes Automatically During Dragging

Use the following procedure to automatically connect shapes as you drag them onto the page:

1. Select the **Connector** tool. Notice that the cursor changes to a black arrow with a zigzag connector near it.

2. Drag a shape from the stencil to the page.

3. Drag another shape from the stencil to the page.

4. Notice that Visio draws a connector between the first and second shape.

5. As you drag additional shapes to the page, Visio connects them in sequential order: the shape dragged onto the drawing page connects to the currently selected shape.

Connecting All Existing Shapes Automatically

Use the following procedure to automatically connect all shapes that are already on the page:

1. Press **Ctrl+A** to select everything on the page.

2. Select **Shape | Connect Shapes**. Notice that Visio draws a connector between the shapes approximately in the order that you placed them in the drawing.

3. You may need to move some of the shapes to straighten out the connectors and make them look more pleasing. Notice how the connectors "stick" to the shapes as you move them around. This is one of the most powerful Visio features.

Tip: Visio connects shapes automatically in the order you placed the shapes. If you plan to use the automatic connection feature, think ahead about shape placement, otherwise you may end up with spaghetti-like connections.

Connecting Selected Shapes Automatically

Use the following procedure to automatically connect selected shapes already on the page:

1. Hold down the **Shift** key and select the shapes you want to connect in the order you want to connect them.

2. Select **Shape | Connect Shapes**.

3. Notice that Visio draws a connector between the shapes.

Connecting Shapes Manually

Use the following procedure to connect shapes:

1. Select the **Connector** tool.

2. Click on a shape's connection point (the small blue x).

3. Drag the connector to another shape's connection point. Notice that the connector's endpoints are red squares; this tells you the endpoint successfully connected to a connection point. If the square is green, the endpoint is not connected to a connection point.

Adding a Connection Point

Use the following procedure to add a connection point to a shape:

1. Select the **Connection Point** tool from the Standard toolbar.

2. Select the shape, and then move the cursor to the location where you want the connection point.

3. Hold down the **Ctrl** key, then click. Notice the magenta (pink) x: this is the new connection point.

Hands-On Activity

In this activity, you use the functions of the connection tools. Begin by starting Visio. Then create a new document using the **Basic Network** template.

1. Select the **Connector** tool button.

2. Drag the **Desktop PC** shape from the **Basic Network Shapes** stencil to the upper-left area of the page.

3. Drag the **Server** shape from the stencil to the upper-right area of the page. Notice that Visio draws a connector between the first and second shape.

4. Drag the **Workstation** shape to the center area of the page. Notice that Visio draws a second connector between the second and third shape.

With the Connector tool selected, Visio draws connectors between shapes automatically.

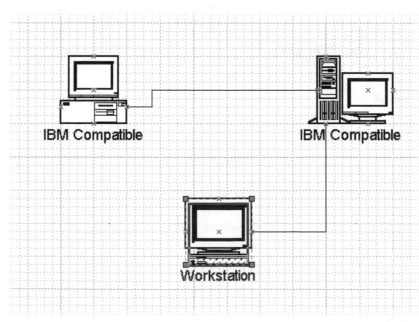

5. Select the **Pointer** tool (looks like an arrow) button on the toolbar.

6. Drag the **Power Mac G4** shape to the lower-left area of the page.

7. Drag the **iBook** shape to the upper-right area of the page. Notice that Visio no longer connects the shapes.

With the Pointer tool selected, Visio does not draw connectors between shapes.

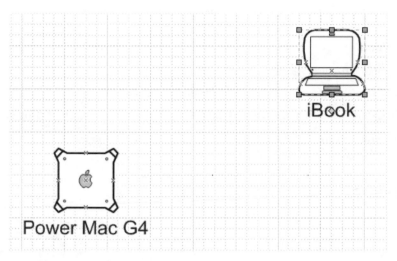

8. Press the **Connector** tool button on the toolbar.

9. Click a connection point (small blue x) of the **Power Mac G4** shape.

10. Hold down the mouse button.

11. Drag the connector to a connection point on the **iBook** shape.

12. Release the mouse button. Notice that Visio connects the two shapes and the connection points turn red.

Connecting selected shapes.

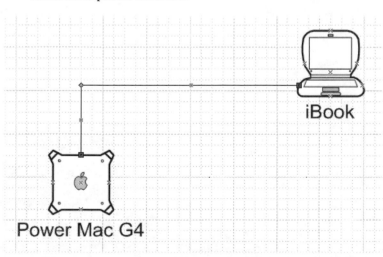

13. From the menu bar, select **Edit | Undo**. Notice that the connector disappears.

14. Press the **Pointer** tool button.

15. Select the **iBook** shape. Notice that Visio surrounds the selected shape with green squares, which acknowledge the selection.

16. Hold the **Shift** key and select the **Server** shape. Notice that Visio surrounds the selected shape with cyan (light blue) squares, which acknowledges adding to the selection.

17. Select **Shapes | Connect Shapes**.

18. Notice that Visio automatically connects the two shapes.

19. Press **Alt+F4** to exit Visio. Click **No** in the Save Changes dialog box.

This completes the hands-on activity for connecting shapes.

Module 12 *Cutting, Copying, and Pasting*

Edit | Cut, Copy, Paste, Paste Special, Paste Hyperlink

Uses

The **Cut**, **Copy**, and **Paste** selections of the Edit menu move shapes and text from one location to another. As with all software running under Windows, nearly any object can be copied and pasted between applications. For example, an Excel spreadsheet can be pasted in a Visio drawing. A Visio drawing can be pasted in a PowerPoint slide.

> **In this chapter you'll learn about:**
>
> ✓ **Cutting text and graphic objects**
>
> ✓ **Copying text and graphic objects**
>
> ✓ **Pasting text and graphic objects**
>
> ✓ **The Paste Special command**

Placing a Visio drawing into PowerPoint.

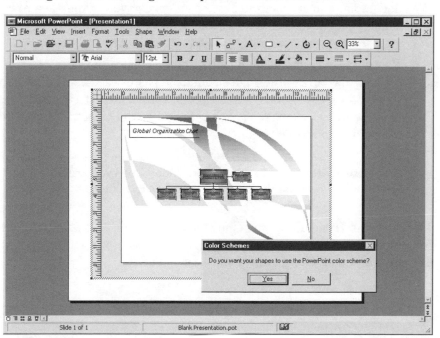

Tip: A Visio 2002 diagram automatically picks up the color scheme of a PowerPoint slide. From within PowerPoint 95, 97, or 2000, select **New Slide** from the **Common Tasks** toolbar, and then select the **Object** slide (you may need to scroll down to find this slide). Double-click the icon indicated by the slide; Visio appears in the slide.

The terms *cut* and *paste* come from a time when newspapers were put together by manually cutting strips of text and pasting them into columns to fit the page. With computers, it is more common to copy, rather than cut.

When you use the Cut and Copy commands, Windows moves the object to the Clipboard, a temporary holding area. The next time you use the Cut or Copy command, the new object replaces the previous one being stored in the Clipboard.

▶ The **Cut** command removes the object from the document; it is like deleting the object.

▶ The **Copy** command makes a copy of the object; the original object remains in place. (Do not confuse the Copy command with the **Duplicate** command: while Copy can be used for duplication, Duplicate does not send a copy to the Clipboard.)

▶ The **Paste** command copies the object from the Clipboard and places it in the document. You can use the Paste command several times in a row to paste the same object several times into one or more documents.

▶ To control the format of the object that is pasted in your document, use the **Paste Special** command, which displays a dialog box that lets you select a format. In contrast, the **Paste** command pastes the first format listed in the Paste Special dialog box. Paste Special sometimes lets you link the object back to its source. This makes it easier to update the object. There is more about linking in Module 28 "Inserting Objects."

 **Tip:** Use **Paste Special**'s **ANSI Text** option when you want Visio text formatting to override the source document's formatting.

The **Paste as Hyperlink** command works only when text is in the Clipboard. This command pastes the text as a hyperlink in the Visio document. Hyperlinks are discussed in Module 36 "Creating a Web Document."

Procedures

Before presenting the general procedures for cutting, copying, and pasting text and graphic objects, it is helpful to know about the shortcut keys. These are:

Function	Keys	Menu	Toolbar Icon
Cut	Ctrl+X	Edit | Cut	✂
Copy	Ctrl+C	Edit | Copy	📋
Paste	Ctrl+V	Edit | Paste	📋
Paste Special	Alt+ES	Edit | Paste Special	...
Paste Hyperlink	Alt+EH	Edit | Paste as Hyperlink	...

Cutting Text and Graphic Objects

Use the following procedure to cut an object from a drawing and copy it to the Clipboard:

1. Select a shape by clicking on it so that green square handles appear.
2. Select **Edit | Cut** (or press **Ctrl+X**) to remove the selected shape from the page and copy it to the Clipboard.

Copying Text and Graphic Objects

Use the following procedure to copy an object to the Clipboard:

1. Select a shape by clicking on it.
2. Select **Edit | Copy** (or press **Ctrl+C**) to copy the selected shape to the Clipboard.

Pasting Text and Graphic Objects

Use the following procedure to paste an object onto the drawing page:

1. Select **Edit | Paste** (or press **Ctrl+V**) to paste whatever is in the Clipboard onto the page.
2. If an object is in the Clipboard (from a previous cut or copy operation), it is pasted in the center of the page.
3. Drag the object into place and resize, if necessary.

Pasting an image into the Visio drawing.

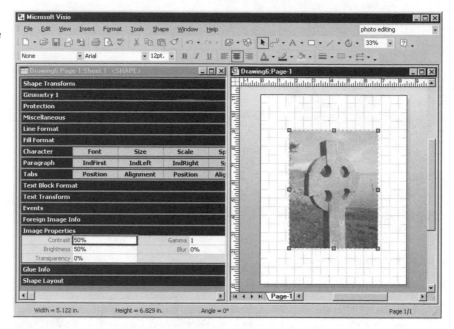

➤ **Tip:** After pasting a raster image in the drawing, you can adjust the image (the image must be pasted as a Bitmap, not a Picture). This is done with the following steps:

1. Select the raster image.

2. From the menu bar, select **Window | Show ShapeSheet**. Notice that a new window opens.

3. Scroll down the window until you reach the section titled "Image Properties." Notice the six image parameters that can be adjusted:

    Contrast increases the contrast — the difference between dark and light areas — when the value is above 50%, and decreases the contrast when below 50% (default = 50%).

    Brightness darkens the image when the value is less than 50%, and brightens the image when above 50% (default = 50%).

    Gamma makes the image brighter while leaving darks dark, when the value is above 1 (default = 1).

    Blur makes the image appear softer (default = 0%; maximum = 100%).

    Sharpen makes the image appear sharper — less blurry. The effect is created by increasing the contrast of adjacent pixels (default = 0%; maximum = 100%).

    Denoise removes "noise," which are pixels with randomly distributed color levels (default = 0%).

4. To change a value, click the value and type a new one. Notice the change to the raster image.

5. To close the ShapeSheet window, click the x (Close) button on the ShapeSheet's title bar.

Paste Special

Use the following procedure to control the paste format of an object:

1. Select **Edit | Paste Special**. Notice that Visio displays the Paste Special dialog box.

The Paste Special dialog box.

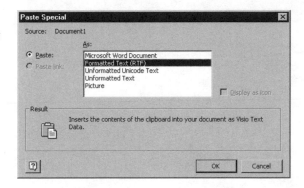

The Paste Special dialog box contains the following options:

▶ **Paste** pastes the object in the drawing.

▶ **Paste Link** pastes the object with a link back to the source application. If the source application does not allow linking, the **Paste Link** radio button is grayed out.

▶ **As** describes the formats available in the Clipboard.

▶ **Display as Icon** pastes the object as an icon. Selecting this option displays a default icon, along with the **Change Icon** button to let you select another icon.

2. Select a format from the **As** list box. When an object is available in several different formats, it may look different, depending on the format you select. When you paste a Visio object in a non-Visio format, the object loses all its intelligence, such as layers, connection points, and custom properties.

3. Click **OK**. Notice the object is pasted in the center of the page.

4. Drag the object into place and resize if necessary.

Hands-On Activity

In this activity, you use the cut, copy, and paste functions. Begin by starting Visio. Then open the **Basic Network** template file found in the Network folder.

1. Click the title bar of the **Basic Network Shapes 3D** stencil to make it visible.

2. Drag the **Personal computer** shape into the drawing. If necessary, zoom to get a better view.

Select the Personal computer shape, and copy it.

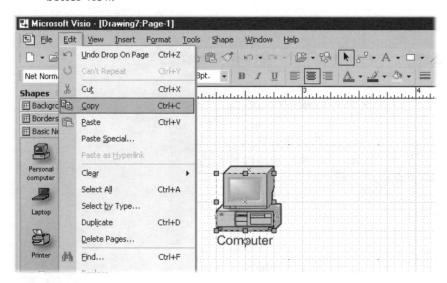

3. Ensure the shape is selected (green handle squares surround it), then press **Ctrl+C** to copy the shape to the Clipboard. Or, click the **Copy** icon from the toolbar. Or, right-click and select **Copy** from the shortcut menu.

4. Select **Insert | New Page**, and click **OK** to create a new page.

5. Press **Ctrl+V** to paste the copied shape. Notice that Visio places the shape in the center of the page. Notice, also, that the shape retains its intelligence. For example, the connection points (small blue x) are present.

6. Select **Edit | Paste Special**. Notice the Paste Special dialog box with several format options:

    ▶ **Microsoft Visio Drawing**: The drawing in Visio 2002 format.

    ▶ **Visio Drawing Data**: The drawing in a format that can be read by earlier versions of Visio.

    ▶ **Formatted Text (RTF)**: The text portion of the shape, retaining formatting.

    ▶ **Unformatted Text**: The text portion of the shape, without formatting.

    ▶ **Picture**: A vector format known as Windows Metafile or WMF, for short.

▶ **Picture (Enhanced Metafile):** A newer version of WMF.

▶ **Device Independent Bitmap:** A raster format.

*The Paste
Special dialog
box.*

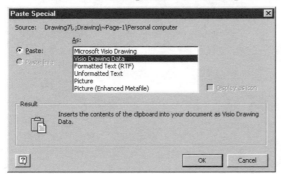

7. Select **Picture** and click **OK**. Notice that Visio places the graphic object in the center of the page. Notice, too, that the computer pasted as a Picture lacks the connection points.

8. Select **Edit | Paste Special**.

9. This time select **Unformatted Text** and click **OK**. Notice that this time Visio pastes just the word "Computer" in the center of the drawing.

*Just the
shape's text is
pasted.*

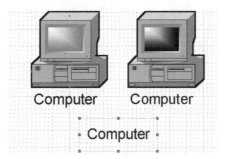

10. Press **Alt+F4** to exit Visio. Click **No** in the Save Changes dialog box.

This completes the hands-on activity for cut, copy, and paste. These functions are identical in all Windows applications. Only the available formats in the Paste Special dialog box differ.

Formatting Shapes

Format | Line, Corners, Fill, Shadow

Uses

Many Visio shapes are plain black and white. But they don't need to be! Visio lets you change the look of a shape, such as its color and the thickness of its lines. Making these changes to a shape is called *formatting* the shape.

> **In this chapter you'll learn about:**
> ✓ **Formatting lines**
> ✓ **Formatting areas**
> ✓ **Shadow casting**

Starting with a plain square, a variety of formatting is progressively applied.

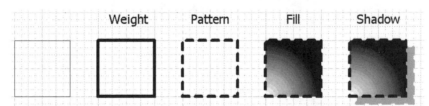

Formatting Lines

You can change the look of the lines that make up all shapes. *Line* is a generic term applying to not just lines but also circles, arcs, curves, rectangles, and ellipses. The **Format | Line** command lets you select from:

▶ **Line pattern:** Patterns of dashes and dots.

▶ **Line weight:** Varying widths of line.

▶ **Color:** Shades of gray (ranging from black to white), plus colors selected from the entire 16.7 million color Windows palette.

▶ **End caps:** Round or square ends to the line.

▶ **Line ends:** Variety of line endings, including arrowheads in seven sizes ranging from Very Small to Colossal.

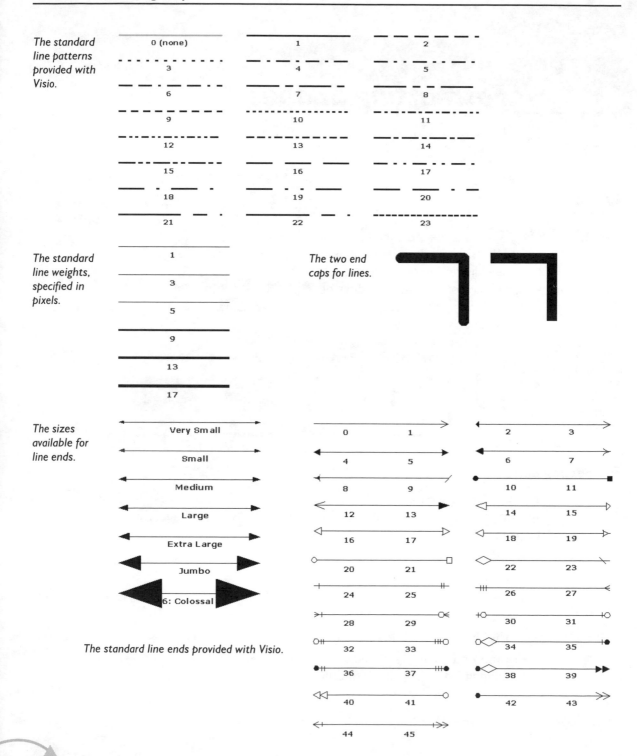

The standard line patterns provided with Visio.

The standard line weights, specified in pixels.

The two end caps for lines.

The sizes available for line ends.

The standard line ends provided with Visio.

When two lines (or arcs or curves) meet, the **Format | Corners** command lets you select from seven different radii of rounded corners, as well as the default (no rounding — a sharp corner), and a custom radius.

Rounding the corner.

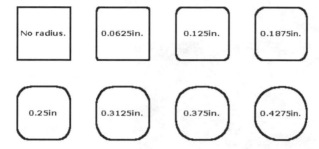

Formatting Areas

Areas are formed by lines, circles, arcs, curves, and rectangular and elliptical areas. Usually, these are empty or are filled with white color. The **Format | Fill** command lets you select from patterns of lines and dots, and colors and shades of gray, as well as gradient fills for the foreground and background. *Foreground* refers to the lines and dots that make up the pattern, while *background* refers to the underlying area.

The standard fill patterns provided with Visio.

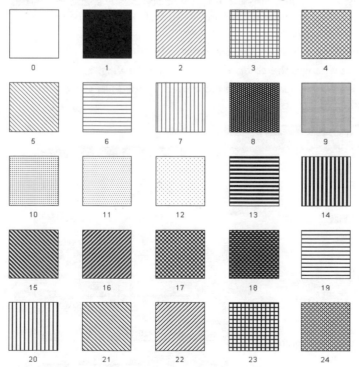

Transparency allows one shape to show through another.

*Examples of
transparency.*

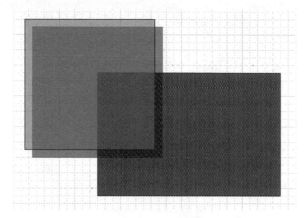

Tip: Visio 2002 includes preset color schemes, which apply colors to nearly all shapes in the entire drawing. This feature is called "single-click formatting." It does not, however, change other formatting, such as line weights, line ends, line patterns, and line caps.

Specifically, the schemes apply to underlying styles; any shape formatted with styles based on these underlying styles will change. The scheme applies color changes to:

Line color: Changes the color of all lines in the drawing.

Text color: Changes the color of all text in the drawing.

Foreground color: Changes the color used by solid fills and the foreground color of pattern fills.

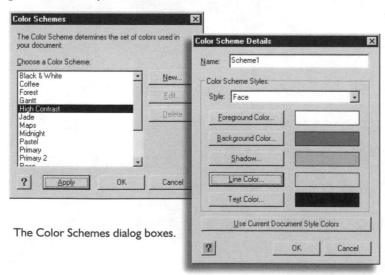

The Color Schemes dialog boxes.

Background color: Changes the background color of pattern fills.

Shadow color: Changes the color of shadows in the drawing.

From the menu bar, select **Tools | Color Schemes**. From the Color Schemes dialog box, select a named scheme. Click the **Apply** button to see the effect on your drawing. To create your own color scheme, click **New** and make your changes.

Shadow Casting

Every object — whether shape, text, or pasted object — can cast a shadow in a Visio drawing. By default, no shadow is cast; adding the shadow helps make the object stand out on the page from other objects. The **Format | Shadow** command lets you select a pattern and color for the shadow. Be careful, though, some printers print the shadow as black, no matter how you format it.

Shadow format dialog box.

> **Tip:** You can create a more interesting shadow effect by using a graduated fill pattern, such as #34, along with foreground color black and background color light gray.

The size and direction of the shadow is specified, strangely enough, in the **Page Properties** tab of the Page Setup dialog box (and not the Shadow dialog box). From the menu bar, select **File | Page Setup**. In the Page Properties tab, change the values in the **Shape shadow offset** fields. To make the shadow cast up and to the left, use negative values, such as –0.25 in. The same shadow offset values apply to all shapes on the page.

Shadow size and direction is set by the Page Setup dialog box.

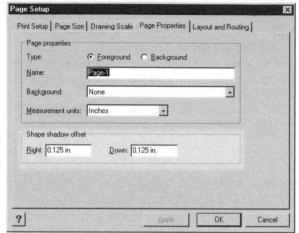

Procedures

Before presenting the general procedures for formatting, it is helpful to know about the shortcut keys. These are:

Function	Keys	Menu	Toolbar Icon
Line Color	Alt+FL	Format | Line	
Line Ends	Alt+FL	Format | Line	
Line Pattern	Alt+FL	Format | Line	
Line Weight	Alt+FL	Format | Line	
Format Corners	Alt+FC	Format | Corners	
Fill Pattern	F3	Format | Fill	
Fill Color	Alt+FF	Format | Fill	
Format Shadow	Alt+FW	Format | Shadow	

Notice that the **Format | Line** menu selection also displays **Corner** options. In the same way, the **Format | Fill** selection displays **Shadow** options.

Formatting Lines

Use the following procedure to format the look of lines, arcs, curves, rectangles, and ellipses:

1. Select a shape.

2. Select **Format | Line**. Notice that Visio displays the Line dialog box.

The Line dialog box.

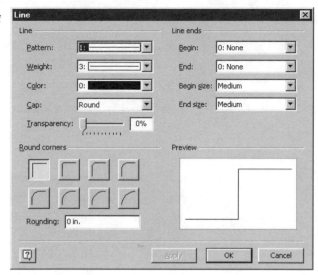

3. To change the line pattern, click on the **Pattern** list box and select one of the patterns (also known as linetypes in CAD software). When you select pattern **None**, the line becomes invisible.

   Notice that as you make selections from this dialog box, the Preview window displays the effect of the change on the line.

4. To see the effect of the change without exiting the dialog box, click **Apply**. You may need to move the dialog box aside to see the affected shapes.

5. To change the width of the lines, click the **Weight** list box and select one of the widths ranging from 1 to 17:

Weight	Points	Inches	Millimeters
I	0.24pt	0.0033"	0.085mm
3	0.72pt	0.0100"	0.254mm
5	1.20pt	0.0167"	0.425mm
9	2.16pt	0.0300"	0.672mm
13	3.12pt	0.4333"	1.10mm
17	4.08pt	0.5667"	1.44mm

6. To choose a line weight other than the pre-programmed weights, select **Custom** from the **Weight** list box. Notice that Visio displays the Custom Line Weight dialog box.

7. Type a number and follow it with a unit, such as **1 in**. Visio allows the following units:

Unit	Meaning	Unit	Meaning
"	inch	mm	millimeter; 25.4mm = 1"
in	inch	cm	centimeter
'	foot	m	meter
ft	foot	pt	point; 72.72 points = 1"
mi	miles\	p	pica; 6 picas = 1"

8. To change the color of the shape's lines, click the **Color** list box and select one of the colors.

9. If you prefer a color that is not shown, select **More Colors**. Notice that Visio displays the standard Windows Colors dialog box.

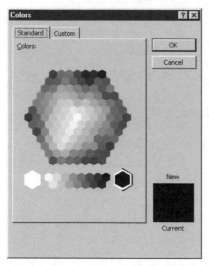

10. Select one of the colors. Click **OK** to close the Colors dialog box.

11. To change the line cap, click the **Cap** list box and select **Round** or **Square**. Notice the difference between round and square end caps. In most cases, the difference between rounded and square corners is unnoticeable, unless applied to very wide lines or seen at a very high zoom level.

12. To change the line ends (also known as *arrowheads*), click the **Begin** list box to select the beginning of the line.

13. Visio allows you to have a different line end and a different size for each end of the line. Click the **End** list box to select the ending of the line.

14. Click the **Begin size** and **End size** list boxes to select the size of the line end.

15. To round the corners of rectangles, or two or more lines, arcs, and curves, select a corner radius in the **Round corners** area.

16. As an alternative, you can specify the radius by typing a value in the **Rounding** field.

17. Click **Apply** to make changes without dismissing the dialog box.

18. Click **OK** to make the changes and dismiss the dialog box.

Applying a Fill Color and Pattern

Use the following procedure to change the fill of rectangles, circles, and ellipses, or the area created by lines, arcs, and curves:

1. Select a shape.

2. Select **Format | Fill**. Notice that Visio displays the Fill dialog box.

The Fill dialog box.

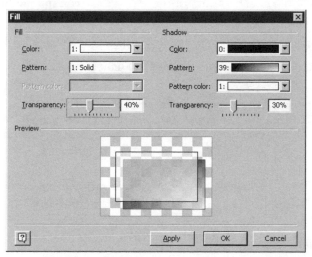

3. To change the color of the pattern lines and dots, under Fill, click the **Color** (called **Foreground** in earlier versions of Visio) list box and select one of the colors. Or, select **Custom** to choose a color from the 16.7 million available in Windows.

4. To change the pattern, under Fill, click on the **Pattern** list box and select one of the patterns. Notice that pattern #0 is None, which means the object is transparent.

5. To change the color underneath the pattern of lines and dots, under Fill, click the **Pattern Color** (called **Background** in earlier versions of Visio) list box and select a color. Notice that Visio displays the changes you make in the Preview box.

Tip: There is a difference between *no* fill and *white* solid fill: the grid lines show through the no-fill rectangle.

---

6. To give the shape a shadow, under Shadow, select a pattern from the **Pattern** list box.

7. To change the color of the shadow's pattern, under Shadow, click the **Color** list box and select one of the colors. Or, select **Custom** to choose a color from the colors available in Windows.

8. To change the color underneath the shadow pattern, under Shadow, click the **Pattern Color** list box and select one of the colors.

9. To make the fill or the shadow transparent, move the **Transparency** slider away from 0%.

10. Click **Apply** to make the changes without dismissing the dialog box.

11. Click **OK** to make the changes and dismiss the dialog box.

Tip: If a shape is not filled, or has transparency applied, the shadow "shows through." You cannot select a shape by clicking on its shadow.

Quick Formatting

To quickly format a shape, Visio provides a number of buttons that cycle though the most common formats. You find these on *two* toolbars: **Formatting** and **Format Shape**.

1. Select one or more shapes.

2. On the **Formatting** toolbar, click the arrow next to the **Line Color** button. Notice that Visio displays a small palette of colors.

Selecting a line color from the Formatting toolbar.

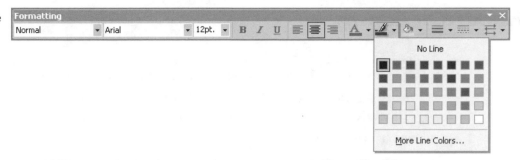

3. Select a color. Notice that the color becomes the default for the Line Color button. If you want other shapes to be the same color, you need only to select the shape, then click the Line Color button; Visio applies the color to the shape.

4. Alternatively, select **No Line** to make the object invisible or select **More Line Colors** to display the Colors dialog box.

5. A similar procedure works for changing other properties. Specifically:

   ▶ The **Formatting** toolbar changes line color, fill color, line weight, line patterns, line ends, and text.

   ▶ The **Format Shape** toolbar changes corner rounding, fill pattern, and shadow color, and applies styles. (To open this toolbar, right-click any toolbar and from the shortcut menu select **Format Shape**.)

Selecting a fill pattern from the Format Shape toolbar.

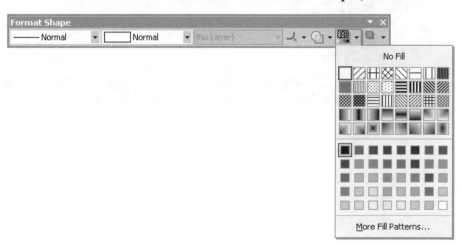

Hands-On Activity

In this activity, you use the shape formatting functions. Begin by starting Visio. Then open the **Charts and Graphs** solution found in the **Forms and Charts** folder.

1. Click the **Borders and Titles** stencil to activate it, and then drag the **Title Block Notepad** shape into the drawing from the stencil.

2. Adjust the zoom level to clearly see the shape.

The Title Block Notepad shape.

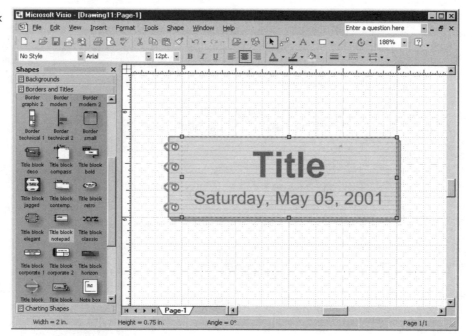

3. Click the arrow next to the **Line Color** button. Notice the color palette.

4. Select the blue color square. Notice that the shape's lines turn blue.

5. Click the arrow next to the **Line Weight** button. Notice the palette of line weights.

Changing the line weight.

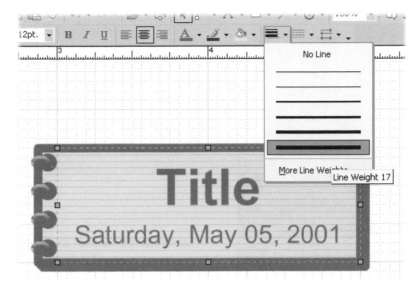

6. Select the widest line weight. Notice the shape's line becomes thicker.

7. Press **Alt+F4** to exit Visio. Click **No** in response to the Save Changes dialog box.

This completes the hands-on activity for formatting shapes in the drawing.

A text block can hold as little as a single character, or as much as many paragraphs.

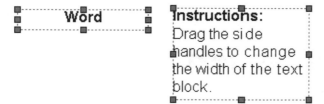

Because the text is in a block, you can position the text within the block. This is called *alignment*. Visio provides three types of alignment: top, middle, and bottom. The middle alignment is the default, which means the text is centered vertically in the text block.

Tips: To format all text in a block, you do not need to highlight it. When you select only a portion of a block of text, the changes apply to the selected portion. This allows you to apply a different look to different parts of the text.

To quickly switch between selection mode and text editing mode, press function key **F2**.

Visio 2000's Text Ruler is not available in Visio 2002.

Right-click the text to see a shortcut menu of formatting options.

Visio 2002

B	Bold
I	Italic
U	Underline
A	Increase Font Size
A	Decrease Font Size
	Horizontal Alignment ▶
	Vertical Alignment ▶
	Increase Indent
	Decrease Indent
	Bullets
	Text Ruler
A	Format Text...
	Insert Field...

Procedures

Before presenting the general procedures for formatting text, it is helpful to know about the shortcut keys. (The default values are shown in parentheses.) Note that Visio 2002 distributes the text formatting functions among two toolbars: **Formatting** and **Format Text**.

Function	Keys	Menu	Toolbar Icon
Selection-Text edit toggle	F2	...	...
Format Font:	F11	Format | Text | Text	...
Select Font Name (Arial)	...	...	Arial
Font Size (8pt)	...	...	12pt

Function	Keys	Menu	Toolbar Icon
Increase Font Size	Ctrl+Shift++	...	A˘ A˘
Decrease Font Size	Ctrl+Shift+−	...	
Bold	Ctrl+B	...	B
Italic	Ctrl+I	...	I
Underline	Ctrl+U	...	U
SMALL CAPS	Ctrl+Shift+K	...	ABC
Sub$_{script}$	Ctrl+ =	...	x₂
Super^{script}	Ctrl+Shift+ =	...	x²
Font Color	...	...	A ▾
Format Paragraph:	Shift+F11	Format | Text | Paragraph	...
Left Justify	Ctrl+Shift+L	...	▤
Center Justify (default)	Ctrl+Shift+C	...	▥
Right Justify	Ctrl+Shift+R	...	▦
Full Justification	Ctrl+Shift+J	...	...
Increase Indentation	...	...	▦
Decrease Indentation	...	...	▦
Increase Paragraph Spacing	...	...	▦
Decrease Paragraph Spacing	...	...	▦
Format Text Block	Alt+FT	Format | Text | Text Block	...
Top Alignment	...	...	▤
Middle Alignment (default)	...	...	▤
Bottom Alignment	...	...	▤
Set Tabs	Ctrl+F11	Format | Text | Tabs	...
Select Bullet	Alt+FT	Format | Text | Bullet	▤
Rotate Text	Alt+ST	Shape | Rotate Text	

Selecting All Text in a Shape

Use the following procedure to select text:

1. Click the shape containing text.

2. Press function key **F2**. Notice that Visio highlights the text by displaying it in reversed color. As an alternative, you can double-click the shape to select the text; however, double-click behavior can be changed, as described in Module 32 "Double-click Behavior," and so double-clicking might not select the text.

Selected text looks white, with a blue background.

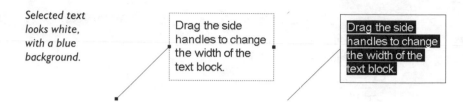

Selecting a Portion of the Text

To format part of a text block (such as a single word), use the following procedure:

1. Select the shape.

2. Press **F2**. Notice that Visio highlights all of the text.

3. Drag the cursor over the characters you want to select.

Partially selected text (left) and partially formatted text (right).

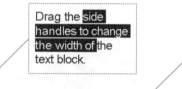

Changing the Font

Use the following procedure to change the text font:

1. Select the text.

2. Select **Format | Text**. Select the **Font** tab.

The Text dialog box.

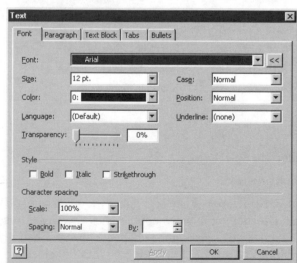

3. Click the **Font** list box to change the font (default = Arial). Notice that the list displays the names of fonts installed on your computer. A "TT" next to a font name indicates it is a TrueType font. A printer symbol means the font is installed on the printer.

4. Select a font name. If necessary, scroll down the list.

5. Click **Apply** to see the font change without leaving the dialog box.

6. To change the size of the text, click the **Size** list box. The default is 8pt. The size is measured in *pt* (short for "point"), where one point equals 1/72" or 72 points = 1 inch.

7. Select a font size. For half-inch tall text, select 36pt.

8. To change the color of the text, click the **Color** list box. The default is black. To change the background color of the text, go to the **Text Block** tab of this dialog box.

9. Select a color under **Text Background**. You can select from 12 colors and 12 shades of gray. Alternatively, select **More Colors** to display the Windows standard Colors dialog box.

10. Click the **Font** tab. You can select single or double underlining for the text. Make your selection from the Underline list box.

11. The case option can turn the text to all UPPERCASE or Initial Capitals (the first letter of every word is capitalized), which is excellent for titles. To change the case of the text, click the **Case** list box.

12. Select **Normal**, **All Caps**, **Initial Caps**, or **Small Caps**.

Applying all caps and initial caps formatting to text.

Normal text.

ALL UPPERCASE.

Initial Caps.

13. The position option moves the selected text higher (superscript) or lower (subscript), which is often used for footnotes and formulae. To change the position of the text, click the **Position** list box.

14. Select **Normal**, **Superscript**, or **Subscript**.

Applying superscript and subscript formatting to text.

Normal text

Text with superscript $x^2+y^2=z^2$

Text with subscript H_2O

15. To select the language, click the **Language** list box.

16. Select a language name. This selection has no effect on the text until you use Visio's dictionary to check the spelling.

17. To change the look of the text, select the **Style** check boxes. You may select any combination of the following: **bold**, *italic*, and ~~strikethrough~~.

Applying styles to text.

Normal text.
Boldface text.
Italicized text.
<u>Underlined text.</u>
Small Caps text.
Combination <u>*text*</u>.

18. To change the spacing between characters, make your selections from the **Scale** and **Spacing** list boxes. Selecting a value larger than 100% spreads letters apart, while a smaller value squeezes the characters together.

19. Click **Apply** to see the format changes without leaving the dialog box.

20. Click **OK** to dismiss the dialog box.

Changing the Justification of a Paragraph

Use the following procedure to change the paragraph formatting of the text block:

1. Select the text.

2. Select **Format | Text**.

3. Select the **Paragraph** tab, which controls the formatting of paragraphs of text.

The Paragraph tab of the Text dialog box.

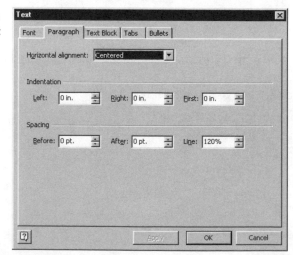

4. Click the **Horizontal Alignment** list box to change the justification, which is sometimes called "paragraph alignment" in other software.

5. Select left, center (the default), right, justify, or force justified. *Force justified* means that the last line of text in the paragraph is forced to fit the width of the paragraph.

A horizontal alignment option applies to all text in a block.

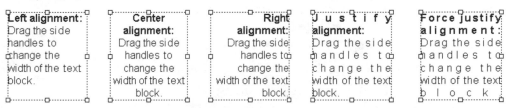

6. To change the left, right, and first line indentation of a paragraph, notice the Indentation section has three text entry boxes.

Changing the indentation of a text block.

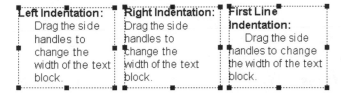

Indentation specifies how far in the text starts (left) and ends (right) from the margin:

▶ **Left** indentation "pushes" all text rightward from the left margin.

▶ **Right** indentation pushes all text leftward from the right margin.

▶ **First** indentation indents the first line. In most cases, you would use first line indentation if you want to create the look of a traditional paragraph with an indented first line. To create a *hanging indent*, type a negative number for first line indentation.

7. To set the spacing between paragraphs or change the spacing between text lines, notice the **Spacing** section has three text entry boxes. *Spacing* specifies the distance between lines of text.

Changing the spacing between lines.

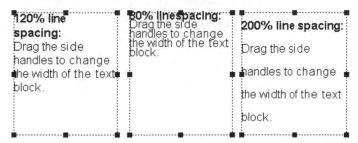

▶ **Before** spacing increases the distance between the top of the paragraph and the preceding paragraph.

▶ **After** spacing increases the distance between the bottom of the paragraph and the following paragraph.

▶ **Line** spacing sets the distance between lines of text within a paragraph, measured as a percentage of the font size; default = 120%. For example, if the font size is 8pt, the line spacing is 8pt * 120% = 9.6pt, measured from the baseline of one line of text to the baseline of the following line of text.

8. Click **Apply** to see the format changes without leaving the dialog box.

9. Click **OK** to dismiss the dialog box.

Changing the Vertical Alignment

Use the following procedure to change the vertical alignment of a text block (text within its alignment box):

1. Select the text.

2. Select **Format | Text** from the menu bar.

3. Click the **Text Block** tab, which controls the formatting of a text block.

The Text Block tab of the Text dialog box.

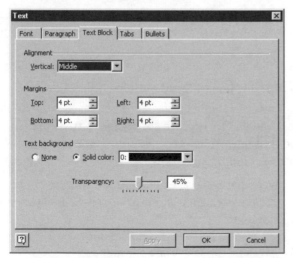

The Alignment section has three options:

▶ **Top** alignment pushes the text block to the top of its alignment box.

▶ **Middle** alignment centers the text block in its alignment box.

▶ **Bottom** alignment pushes the text block to the bottom of its alignment box.

Changing the vertical alignment of the text within its block.

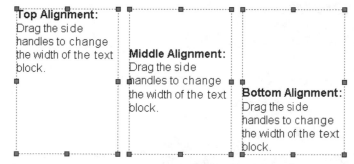

4. Notice the **Margins** section. The *margin* is the distance between a text block and its alignment box:

   ▶ The **Top** and **Bottom** margins specify the distance from the top (or bottom) of the text block to the alignment box. Type a number to increase the margin distance.

   ▶ The **Left** and **Right** margins specify the distance from the left (or right) of the text block to the alignment box. Type a number to increase the margin distance.

5. You change the color of the alignment box in the **Text Background** section:

   ▶ Click **None (Transparent)** to eliminate color from the alignment box; the default.

   ▶ Alternatively, click **Solid Color**, then select a color. The illustration below shows the difference between the two options:

Adding a background color to the text block.

No Background Color:
Drag the side handles to change the width of the text block.

Gray Background Color:
Drag the side handles to change the width of the text block.

6. Click **Apply** to see the format changes without leaving the dialog box.

7. Click **OK** to dismiss the dialog box.

Setting Tabs

Tabs make it easier to line up columns of text. Press the **Tab** key to move the cursor to the next tab setting. Use the following procedure to set the tab spacing:

1. Select the text.

2. Select **Format | Text**.

3. Click the **Tabs** tab, which controls the tab spacing. Notice that no tabs are initially set.

The Tabs tab of the Text dialog box.

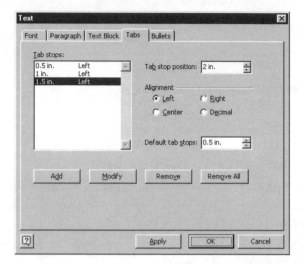

4. Type a number in the **Tab Stop Position** box.

5. Select an alignment from the **Alignment** section: left (default), center, right, or decimal. The *decimal* tab right-aligns numbers according to the position of their decimal number; it left-aligns text.

6. Click **Add** to set a tab.

7. Click **OK**. Notice the new tab setting in the Tab Stops box.

8. Click **Remove** to erase the tab.

9. Click **Apply** to see the tab changes without leaving the dialog box.

10. Click **OK** to dismiss the dialog box.

Adding Bullets to Text

A *bullet* is a small dot that starts off a paragraph of text. Using bullets can aid the readability of a list of instructions. A bullet can be any symbol, but most commonly is a dot or square.

1. Select the text.

2. Select **Format | Text**.

3. Click the **Bullets** tab. Notice that the dialog box displays seven bullet styles, as well as space for a custom bullet.

4. Click on the button with the bullet style of your liking.

5. Click **Apply** to see the tab changes without leaving the dialog box. Notice that a bullet is added to the start of every paragraph.

6. Click **OK** to dismiss the dialog box.

The Bullets tab of the Text dialog box.

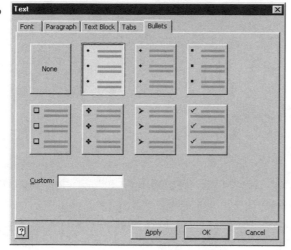

Bullets added to paragraphs of text.

No Bullets:
Drag the side handles to change the width of the text block.

- **Square Bullets:**
- Drag the side handles to change the width of the text block.

Hands-On Activity

In this activity, you use the text formatting functions. Begin by starting Visio. Then open a new drawing.

1. Right-click the toolbar. From the shortcut menu, select **Format Text**. Notice that Visio displays the Format Text toolbar.

2. Select the **Text** tool from the Standard toolbar.

3. Click anywhere in the page. Notice that Visio zooms in (to 100%) so that you can more easily read the text.

4. Type a sentence, such as **Text in Visio**.

New drawing with sample text.

Text in Visio

5. On the Format Text toolbar, click the **Increase Font Size** button three times. Notice the font size of all the text increases with each click.

Increasing the size of the text.

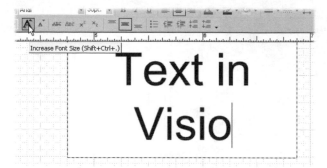

6. Click the **Font Color** button on the Formatting toolbar. Select the red color square. Notice that all the text turns red.

7. Click the **Bullets** button on the Format Text toolbar. Notice that a bullet prefixes the words.

Adding a bullet to the text.

8. Click the **Underline** button. Notice all the text becomes underlined.

Underlining the text.

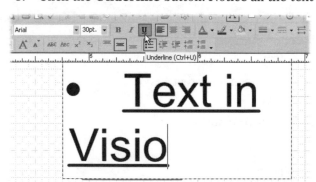

9. Click the **Bold** button on the Formatting toolbar. Notice the text becomes bolder.

10. Click the **Italic** button. Notice all the text becomes italicized.

11. Press **Alt+F4** to exit Visio. Click **No** in the Save Changes dialog box.

This completes the hands-on activity for formatting text in the drawing.

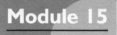

Creating and Applying Styles

Format | Define Styles, Style, Format Painter

Uses

The **Style** selection of the **Format** menu lets you apply a uniform format, called a style, to shapes. A *style* is a collection of properties saved by name. In Visio, properties are based on text, line, and fill formats. A style is based on the properties defined by the **Define Styles** selection of the **Format** menu.

In this chapter you'll learn about:

✓ **Format Painter**

✓ **Defining a style**

✓ **Applying a style**

✓ **Text style list**

✓ **Line style list**

✓ **Fill style list**

In Modules 13 "Formatting Shapes" and 14 "Formatting Text," you saw how to apply one style at a time. In this module, you learn how to apply a number of styles at once. The advantages to using a defined style include:

▶ **Faster formatting:** Since the defined style applies all properties at once, it is faster to apply a single style than to apply each property individually. As Modules 13 and 14 illustrate, shapes and text can have as many as 40 different properties.

▶ **Consistent look:** When your company defines its corporate look, using styles ensures all illustrators employ the same text, line, and fill formats.

▶ **Flexibility:** While applying a style can make everything look similar, Visio gives you the option to override the style with local formatting. *Local* is formatting applied directly.

Style definitions are saved with the drawing. Visio includes a number of predefined styles with every template. In addition, you can create your own styles. You apply a style by selecting it from the **Text, Line**, and **Fill** style lists or with the Style dialog box. Visio has two aids that help you apply styles quickly:

▶ The **Format Painter** button of the toolbar lets you copy the formatting of one shape to another.

▷ The **Formatting**, **Format Shape**, and **Format Text** toolbars have lists with the names of styles in the drawing.

The **Formatting** toolbar lists all styles stored in the drawing; "all" has a drawback, since you can't tell if the style applies to text, lines, fills, or all three. For this reason, the other two formatting toolbars are more useful. The **Format Shape** toolbar has separate lists for line and fill styles; the **Format Text** toolbar has a list for text formats.

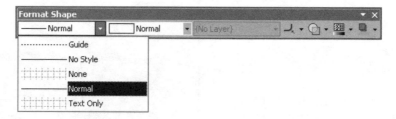

Procedures

Before presenting the general procedures for defining and using styles, it is helpful to know about the shortcut keys and icons. These are:

Function	Keys	Menu	Toolbar Icon
Format Painter	...	...	✎
Define Style	Alt+FD	Format | Define Styles	...
Apply Style	Alt+FS	Format | Style	...

Format Painter

Use the following procedure to copy properties from one shape to another:

1. Select the shape with the style you want copied.

2. Click the **Format Painter** button on the toolbar. Notice that the cursor turns into a paintbrush.

3. Select another shape to apply the style.

☞ **Tip:** To copy the style to more than one object, double-click the **Format Painter** button.

Defining a Style

Use the following procedure to create a style:

1. (*Optional*) To create a named style based on an existing shape, first select the shape.

2. Select **Format | Define Styles** from the menu bar. Notice that Visio displays the Define Styles dialog box.

The Define Styles dialog box.

3. Every style must have a name, which is how Visio identifies the style. Type a descriptive name in the **Name** text box. After you create the style, it will appear in the style list boxes on the toolbars.

4. If you want to modify an existing style, first select the style name from the **Name** list box. The list box shows the names of all styles already defined in the drawing.

5. Decide whether the style will affect text, lines, and/or fills by selecting the **Text**, **Line**, and **Fill** check boxes:

   ▶ Click **Text** to set the text properties of this style. Notice that Visio displays the Text dialog box. Refer to Module 14 "Formatting Text" for the details of changing text properties.

   ▶ Click **Line** to set the line properties of this style. Notice that Visio displays the Line dialog box. Refer to Module 13 "Formatting Shapes" for the details of changing line properties.

   ▶ Click **Fill** to set the fill properties of this style. Notice that Visio displays the Fill dialog box. Refer to Module 13 "Formatting Shapes" for the details of changing fill properties.

6. Decide whether you want this style to preserve or override local formatting. To override local formatting, keep **Preserve Local Formatting on Apply** turned off.

Tip: *Local* formatting is a change that you make manually. For example, you place some text at the default height of 8 points. Then you change the height to 12 points. The change is a *local* format. Whether you preserve or override local formatting depends on the situation: sometimes, you want to keep local formatting; other times you want to override all those changes.

---

7. Click **OK** to close the dialog box.

Applying a Style

Use the following procedure to apply a style:

1. Select one or more shapes. To select more than one shape, hold down the **Shift** key. To select all shapes on the page, press **Ctrl+A**.

2. Select **Format | Style** from the menu bar. Notice the Style dialog box.

The Style dialog box.

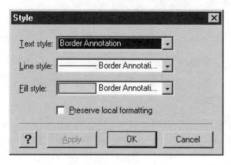

3. Select one or more styles from the three available: **Text Style**, **Line Style**, and/or **Fill Style**. For example, you could select a line and fill style together.

4. To override local formatting, keep **Preserve Local Formatting** turned off.

5. Click **Apply** to view the style changes without exiting the dialog box.

6. Click **OK** to exit the dialog box. Notice that the style list boxes on the toolbar update to reflect the selections you made in the Style dialog box.

Text Style List

Use the following procedure to apply a predefined style to text:

1. Select a text block or paragraph in the drawing.
2. Click the **Text Style** list box in the Format Text toolbar.

The Text Style list box.

3. Select one of the defined style names.
4. Notice that the text changes to match the style.

Line Style List

Use the following procedure to apply a predefined line style to a shape:

1. Select a shape in the drawing.
2. Click the **Line Style** list box in the Format Shape toolbar.

The Line Style list box.

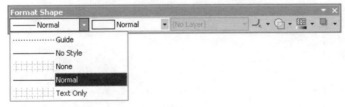

3. Select one of the defined style names.
4. Notice that the shape changes to match the line style.

Fill Style List

Use the following procedure to apply a predefined fill style to an area:

1. Select a shape in the drawing.
2. Click the **Fill Style** list box in the Format Shape toolbar.

The Fill Style list box.

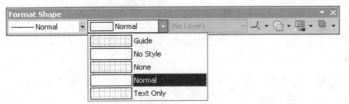

3. Select one of the defined style names.

4. Notice that the fill changes to match the style.

Hands-On Activity

In this activity, you use the text formatting functions. Begin by starting Visio.

1. Open the **Basic Diagram** solution found in the Block Diagram folder.

2. Right-click any toolbar. From the shortcut menu, select **Format Text** and **Format Shape**. Notice that Visio shows the two toolbars.

3. Select the **Borders and Titles** stencil (click its title bar to make the stencil visible).

4. Drag the **Note Box Deco** shape onto the page.

The Note Box Deco shape.

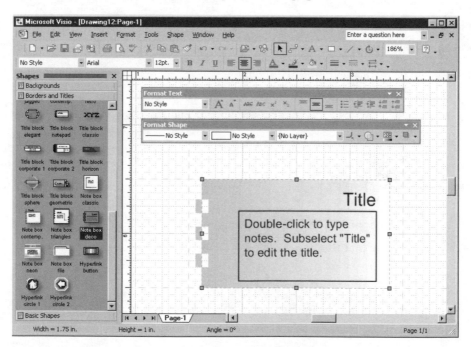

5. If necessary to see it better, zoom in to the top portion of the note box.

6. Select the shape. Notice the style lists on the toolbar: they may read "No style" or "Border Page Number" or something similar. These are the names of predefined styles for text, lines, and fills.

7. Click the **Text Style** list box. Notice the long list of style names.

8. Select **Basic** from the Text Style list box. Notice the warning dialog box Visio displays: "Text style 'Basic' also includes line and fill formatting. Do you want to apply all of the included formatting?"

This dialog box warns you that the text style is linked to line and fill formatting.

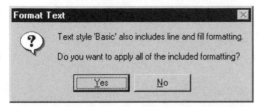

Visio is warning you that the text style also includes style elements for lines and fills. If you click **Yes**, the existing line and fill styles present in the shape will be overridden.

9. Click **Yes**. Notice that the note box shape changes its text, lines, and fill.

Applying the style changes the look of the shape.

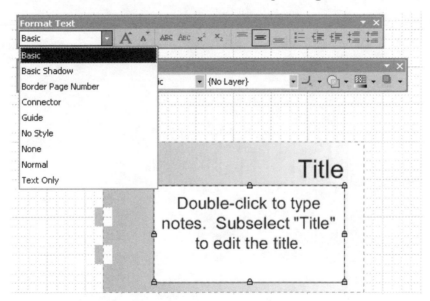

10. Press **Alt+F4** to exit Visio. Click **No** in response to the Save Changes dialog box.

This completes the hands-on activity for using styles in the drawing.

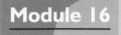

Module 16 | Aligning Shapes

Shape | Align Shapes, Distribute Shapes, Lay Out Shapes

Uses

In this chapter you'll learn about:

✓ *Aligning shapes*

✓ *Distributing shapes*

✓ *Laying out shapes*

The **Align Shapes, Distribute Shapes**, and **Lay Out Shapes** selections of the **Shape** menu automatically rearrange shapes in the drawing. Here's how they work:

▶ **Align Shapes** lines up shapes along a horizontal or vertical axis; the tool works with two or more shapes, which are aligned to the first shape selected.

▶ **Distribute Shapes** repositions three or more shapes to create an equal distance between them.

▶ **Lay Out Shapes** places shapes in a predetermined pattern, such as the pattern common to an organization chart or a flowchart.

Procedures

Before presenting the general procedures for rearranging shapes, it is helpful to know about the shortcut keys and icons. These are:

Function	Keys	Menu	Toolbar Icon
Align	F8	Shape | Align Shapes	
Distribute	Alt+SD	Shape | Distribute Shapes	
Lay Out	Alt+SL	Shape | Lay Out Shapes	...

Aligning Shapes

When you align shapes, Visio moves the shapes so that they line up vertically or horizontally. Use the following procedure to align several shapes along a baseline:

1. Select at least two shapes. This tool does not work when one or no shapes are selected.

 Tip: Notice the color of the selection handles. This is very important to obtaining the correct alignment result:

Color	Meaning
Green	First selected shape
Cyan	Other selected shapes

The first shape you select has green handles; the ensuing shapes have cyan (light blue) handles. The **Align** tool aligns the ensuing shapes to the first shape.

You might be wondering, "Which is the 'first selected' shape when I use **Ctrl+A** to select all shapes on the page?" Surprisingly, it is the *last* shape added to the page. The result is the same when you use the cursor or use the **Select Special** tool to select several shapes: the shape with the green handles is the shape that was last added to the page.

---

2. Select **Shape | Align Shapes**. Notice that each of the buttons of the Align Shapes dialog box have one green (the first selected) and two cyan (subsequent selected) rectangles.

The Align Shapes dialog box.

3. Select the type of alignment (you can select either, neither, or both types of alignment):

- ▶ **Up/Down Alignment**: Align the top, center, or bottom of the shapes to the first shape selected.

- ▶ **Left/Right Alignment**: Align the left, center, or right of the shapes to the first shape selected.

- ▶ **X** (no alignment): No alignment takes place.

4. (*Optional*) Click **Create guide and glue shapes to it** when you want Visio to create a guide line along the alignment axis and glue the shapes to it.

5. Click **OK**. Notice that Visio moves the shapes into alignment.

Tip: It is possible for some shapes to "disappear." This happens when a larger shape covers up a smaller shape.

The illustration shows unaligned shapes (right) and center-aligned shapes (left). The circle was the first shape selected, so the other shapes aligned to the center of its alignment box. The triangle disappeared since it is covered up by the square.

Unaligned shapes (right) and center-aligned with the circle shape (left).

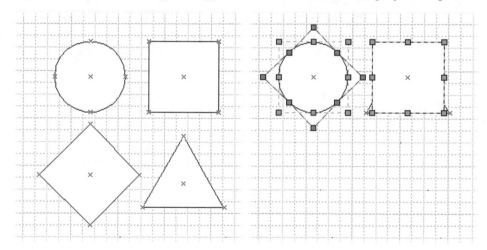

Distributing Shapes

When you distribute shapes, Visio moves the shapes so that they are evenly spaced from each other. For this reason, you must select *three* or more shapes before Visio lets you use this tool. The two outer shapes remain stationary, while the center shape(s) move to create the even spacing. Use the following procedure to distribute shapes:

1. Select at least three shapes. The order in which you select the shapes does not matter.

2. Select **Shape | Distribute Shapes**. Notice the Distribute Shapes dialog box.

The Distribute Shapes dialog box.

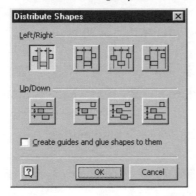

3. Select a type of distribution.

4. (*Optional*) Click **Create guides and glue shapes to them** when you want Visio to create a guideline along the alignment axis; the selected shapes will be glued to the guideline.

5. Click **OK**. Notice that the middle shape moves so that the spacing is equal between the shapes. The outer shapes (on the left and right side) remain in place. In the following illustration, three shapes were distributed horizontally.

The three shapes are equally distributed.

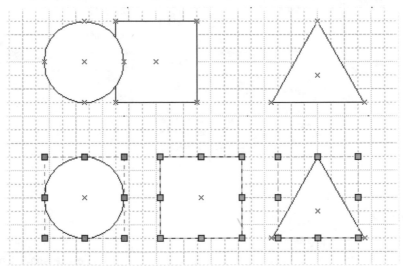

Laying Out Shapes

When you lay out shapes, Visio rearranges the connected shapes into a pattern. This tool works only with connected shapes; unconnected shapes are ignored. In most cases, you will select all shapes on the page. Use the following procedure to lay out shapes:

1. Press **Ctrl+A** to select all shapes.

2. Select **Shape | Lay Out Shapes** from the menu bar. Notice the Lay Out Shapes dialog box.

The Lay Out Shapes dialog box.

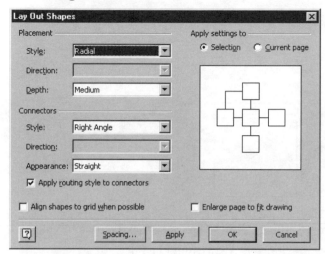

3. The **Placement** section of the dialog box determines how the shapes are placed:

    Style determines how the shapes will be laid out. Radial, for example, is meant for network diagrams. Watch the preview image to see what the style looks like.

Shapes laid out in radial style.

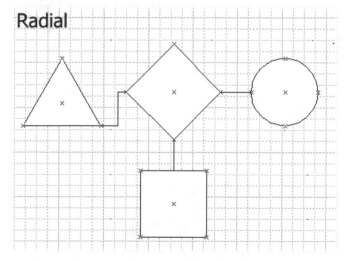

Direction specifies the direction that shapes are placed for diagrams that have a "flow," such as flowcharts, tree diagrams, and organization charts (i.e., all non-radial styles).

The same shapes laid out in flowchart style.

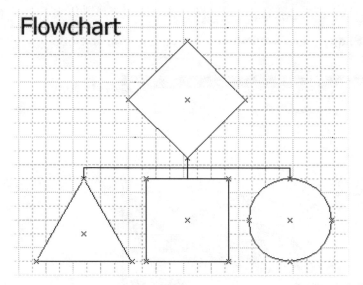

Depth determines the amount of space to leave between shapes:

▶ **Shallow** creates more of a horizontal layout.

▶ **Medium** is a combination of the Shallow and Deep options.

▶ **Deep** creates more of a vertical layout.

4. The **Connectors** section determines how the connectors are placed:

Style determines the route used to connect shapes.

Connectors laid out in center-to-center style.

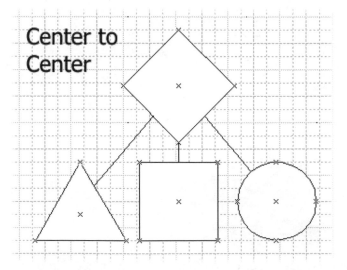

Direction specifies the direction of the routing, such as top to bottom, or left to right.

Tip: The Direction you select in the Placement and Connectors sections should match.

Shapes and connectors laid out in left-to-right style.

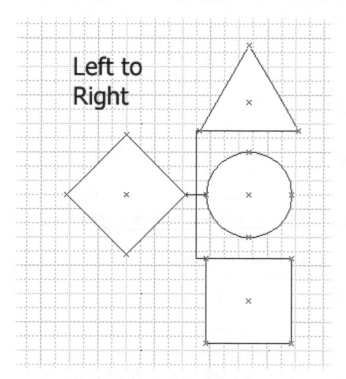

Left to Right

Apply routing style to connectors means the routing style is applied to all connectors.

5. The **Align shapes to grid when possible** option is self-explanatory.

6. The **Enlarge page to fit drawing option** enlarges the page to accommodate the shapes.

7. Click the **Spacing** button. Notice the Layout and Routing Spacing dialog box.

The Layout and Routing Spacing dialog box.

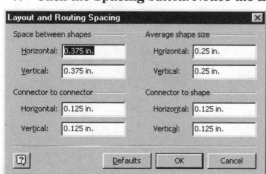

Space between shapes specifies the space between placeable shapes.

Average shape size specifies the average size of the shapes in your drawing.

Connector to connector specifies the minimum space between connectors.

Connector to shape specifies the minimum space between connectors and shapes.

8.   Click **Apply** to see the effect of the layout on the shapes and connectors in your drawing.

9.   Click **OK** to apply the layout.

Hands-On Activity

In this activity, you align, distribute, and lay out shapes. Begin by starting Visio.

1.   Open a new drawing with the **Basic Diagram** template found in the Block Diagram folder.

2.   Drag the **Triangle, Square,** and **Circle** shapes anywhere onto the page. Make no attempt to line them up.

3.   Press **Ctrl+A** to select them all.

Three shapes placed randomly on the page.

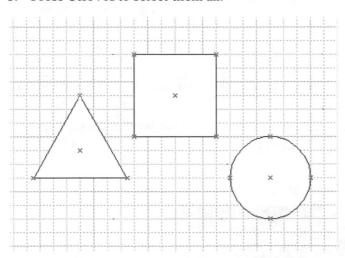

4.   From the menu bar, select **Shape | Align Shapes**. When the Align Shapes dialog box appears, click the middle button under **Up/Down alignment**.

154

5. Click **OK**. Notice that the three shapes are aligned by the center of their alignment boxes.

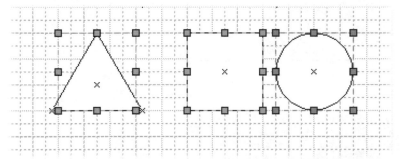

6. Let's distribute the shapes evenly. Select **Shape | Distribute Shapes**. When the Distribute Shapes dialog box appears, click the first button under **Left/Right alignment**.

7. Click **OK**. Notice that the three shapes are equally spaced.

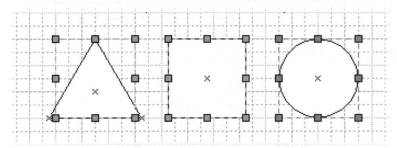

8. Let's connect the shapes. First, though, drag the **Cross** shape into the drawing.

9. From the Standard toolbar, select the **Connector** tool (or press **Ctrl+3**).

10. Use shape-to-shape (or dynamic) glue to connect the three shapes to the cross shape. (Recall that shape-to-shape glue means you place the cursor inside the shape so that the shape is surrounded by a heavy red rectangle.)

*The three
shapes are
connected to
the cross
shape.*

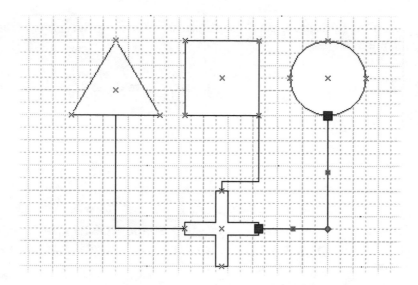

11. Let's lay out the shapes in a couple of patterns. From the menu bar, select **Shape | Lay Out Shapes.** When the Lay Out Shapes dialog box appears, select **Radial.**

12. Click **Apply.** Notice that the three shapes move to surround the cross shape.

*The four
shapes are laid
out in a radial
pattern.*

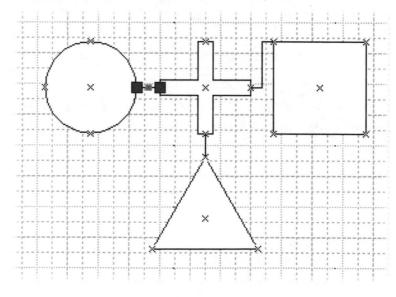

13. In the Lay Out Shapes dialog box, select **Flowchart/Tree**.

14. Click **Apply**. Notice that the cross shape moves to the head of the three other shapes.

The four shapes are laid out in a flowchart pattern.

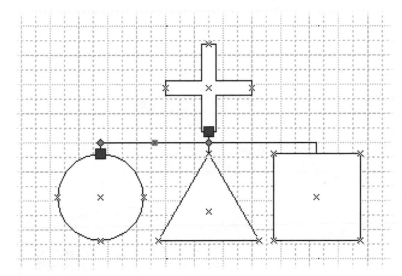

15. Click **Cancel** to exit the dialog box.

16. Press **Alt+F4** to exit Visio. Click **No** in response to the Save Changes dialog box.

This completes the hands-on activity for aligning, distributing, and laying out shapes in the drawing.

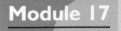 # Creating Groups

Shape | Grouping

Uses

In this chapter you'll learn about:

✓ **Creating a group from shapes**

✓ **Adding to a group**

✓ **Removing from a group**

✓ **Disbanding a group**

✓ **Converting to a group**

The **Grouping** function, found on the **Shape** menu, is used to group shapes together into a single unit. A group contains shapes and can contain other groups.

Once in a group, editing commands apply equally to all members of the group (unless you select a single member of a group). For example, when you apply the color red to lines, all shapes in the group get red lines.

You can add and remove shapes from a group. You can also convert some non-Visio objects to a group, such as a vector image placed from another program.

To edit individual lines of a group, you can open the group window or select the member you want to edit.

To break up a group, you ungroup the grouped shape.

 Caution: Many shapes that you drag into the drawing from a stencil are groups. If you ungroup them, they lose their link to the stencil. Proceed with care when ungrouping.

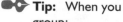 **Tip:** When you select a group, a single alignment box surrounds the group:

Grip Color	Meaning
Black box, green fill	First selected group
Black box, cyan fill	Subsequent selected groups

When you select a member of the group, the grips have a gray box:

Grip Color	Meaning
Gray box, green fill	First selected member of a group
Gray box, cyan fill	Subsequent selected members

Procedures

Before presenting the general procedures for grouping, it is helpful to know about the shortcut keys and icons. These are:

Function	Keys	Menu	Toolbar Icon
Group	Shift+Ctrl+G	Shape | Grouping | Group	
Add	Alt+SGA	Shape | Grouping | Add to Group	...
Remove	Alt+SGR	Shape | Grouping | Remove from Group	...
Convert	Alt+SGC	Shape | Grouping | Convert to Group	...
Ungroup	Shift+Ctrl+U	Shape | Grouping | Ungroup	

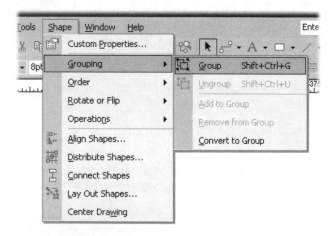

Creating a Group from Shapes

Use the following procedure to make a group:

1. Select one or more shapes.
2. Select **Shape | Grouping | Group**.

3. Notice that Visio indicates the group status by placing a single set of handles around all shapes.

Adding to a Group

Use the following procedure to add shapes to a group:

1. Select a group and one or more shapes.
2. Select **Shape | Grouping | Add to Group**.
3. Notice that Visio indicates the group status by placing a single set of handles around all shapes.

Removing from a Group

Use the following procedure to remove a shape from a group:

1. Select one or more shapes within a group.
2. Select **Shape | Grouping | Remove from Group**.
3. Notice that Visio indicates the group status by placing a single set of handles around all shapes.

Disbanding a Group

Use the following procedure to ungroup shapes:

1. Select a group.
2. Select **Shape | Grouping | Ungroup**.
3. Notice that Visio indicates the removal of group status by placing handles around all shapes within the group.
4. If the group contains nested groups, you may need to apply the Ungroup command a second time.

Tip: The **Remove from Group** and **Ungroup** tools have different effects:

▶ **Remove from Group**: A shape is removed from the group; the other shapes remain a group.

▶ **Ungroup**: All shapes are removed from the group; the group no longer exists.

Converting a Metafile to a Group

Use the following procedure to convert a pasted metafile to a Visio group:

1. Select an object that has been pasted on the page as a Picture via the **Edit | Paste Special** command. (This command does not work if the pasted object is a bitmap.)

2. Select **Shape | Grouping | Convert to Group**.

Hands-On Activity

In this activity, you use the grouping functions. Begin by starting Visio.

1. Start a new drawing with the **Directional Map** template found in the **Map** folder.

2. Select the **Metro Shapes** stencil.

3. Have fun making a subway map similar to the one shown in the following illustration. Make two subway lines. *Hint*: Place the Station shapes last, or use **Ctrl+F** to bring them to the foreground (on top of the metro track shapes).

4. Select all the metro (track) shapes.

5. Select **Shape | Grouping | Group** from the menu bar. Notice that one set of handles surround all the selected shapes.

Individual shapes (left) and a group (right).

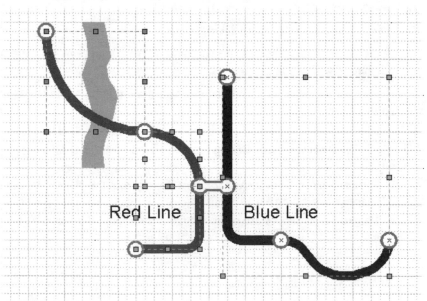

6. Select the group.

7. Change the color of the group from red to blue. Notice that the change applies to all members of the group.

8. Change the size of the group by dragging one of the handles. Notice that all shapes in the group change.

9. To select a member of the group, click it twice. The first click selects the group; the second click selects the member.

10. Select **Shape | Grouping | Ungroup**. Notice that each shape has its own set of handles again.

11. Press **Alt+F4** to exit Visio. Click **No** in response to the Save Changes dialog box.

This completes the hands-on activity for working with groups in the drawing.

Module 18 | Boolean Operations

Shape | Operations

In this chapter you'll learn about:

✓ **The Union operation**

✓ **The Combine operation**

✓ **The Fragment operation**

✓ **The Intersect operation**

✓ **The Subtract operation**

Uses

The **Operations** selection of the **Shape** menu performs *Boolean* operations on shapes. You use Boolean operations to create new shapes out of existing shapes. Very often, the order in which you select shapes is important for the outcome, as noted below.

For Boolean operations to work, the shapes must overlap. (The stacking order of overlapping shapes is not important.) In all cases, the first shape you select dictates the properties of the "Booleaned" shapes.

▸ **Union** joins all selected shapes into a single shape. The new shape takes on the attributes of the shape selected first.

▸ **Combine** is like the Union operation but removes the portions in common. The new shape takes on the attributes of the shape selected first.

▸ **Fragment** creates three new shapes from two overlapping shapes; the overlapping portion becomes an independent shape. All three shapes take on the attributes of the first selected shape.

▸ **Intersect** removes everything *except* the overlapping areas of the two shapes. **Intersect** is the opposite of the Combine operation.

▸ **Subtract** removes the overlapping portion of the second shape from the first shape. Another way of looking at it is that the overlapping portion is removed from the first shape. Selection order is crucial for the correct result.

Procedures

Before presenting the general procedures for Boolean operations, it is helpful to know about the shortcut keys. These are:

Function	Keys	Menu
Union	Alt+SNU	Shape | Operations | Union
Combine	Alt+SNC	Shape | Operations | Combine
Fragment	Alt+SNF	Shape | Operations | Fragment
Intersect	Alt+SNI	Shape | Operations | Intersect
Subtract	Alt+SNS	Shape | Operations | Subtract

The original, overlapping shapes.

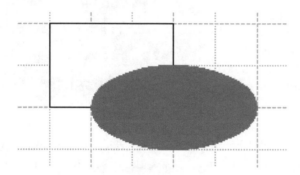

Union Operation

Use the following procedure to join two or more shapes together:

1. Select one shape. This is the shape whose properties the new shape takes on.

2. Hold down the **Shift** key and select one or more additional shapes.

3. Select **Shape | Operations | Union**. Notice that Visio creates one new shape with the outline of all selected shapes and the attributes of the first shape.

The unioned shapes.

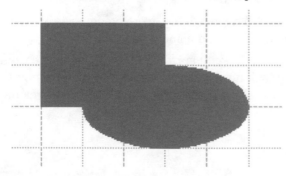

Combine Operation

Use the following procedure to join two or more shapes together, then subtract the areas in common:

1. Select one shape. This is the shape whose properties the new shape takes on.

2. Hold down the **Shift** key and select one or more additional shapes.

3. Select **Shape | Operations | Combine**. Notice that Visio creates one new shape with the outline of all selected shapes and the attributes of the first shape. Overlapping areas are removed.

The combined shapes.

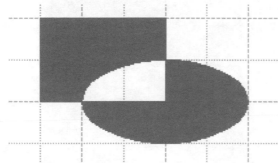

Fragment Operation

Use the following procedure to create three or more shapes from two or more shapes, where overlapping portions become independent shapes:

1. Select one shape. This is the shape whose properties the new shape takes on.

2. Hold down the **Shift** key and select one or more additional shapes.

3. Select **Shape | Operations | Fragment**. Notice that Visio creates a new fragmented shape from the overlapping portions of the original shapes. All shapes take on the attributes of the first shape. The following illustration shows the three shapes moved apart.

The fragmented shapes.

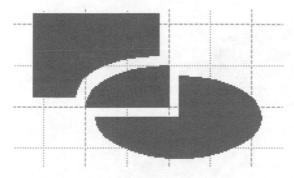

Intersect Operation

Use the following procedure to create one shape from the overlapping portion of two or more shapes:

1. Select one shape. This is the shape whose properties the new shape takes on.

2. Hold down the **Shift** key and select one or more additional shapes.

3. Select **Shape | Operations | Intersect**. Notice that Visio creates one new shape from the overlapping portions of the original shapes; the new shape takes on the attributes of the first shape.

The intersected shape.

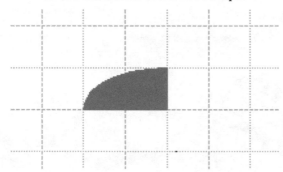

Subtract Operation

Use the following procedure to subtract one shape from another shape:

1. Select one shape. This is the shape whose properties the new shape takes on.

2. Hold down the **Shift** key and select one or more additional shapes.

3. Select **Shape | Operations | Subtract**. Notice that Visio creates one new shape by removing the second shape and the overlapping portions of the second shape from the first shape.

The subtracted shape.

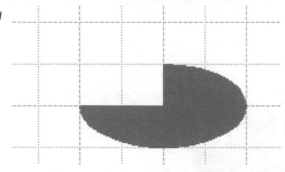

Hands-On Activity

In this activity, you use the Boolean operations. Begin by starting Visio.

1. Open a new drawing using the **Basic Diagram** solution found in the **Block Diagram** folder.

2. Drag the **Triangle** shape into the drawing.

3. Drag the **Circle** shape into the drawing, half overlapping the triangle.

4. Apply a diagonal fill pattern to the circle. This will help you see how the properties of one shape are applied to another, as a result of Boolean operations.

The white triangle and the striped circle.

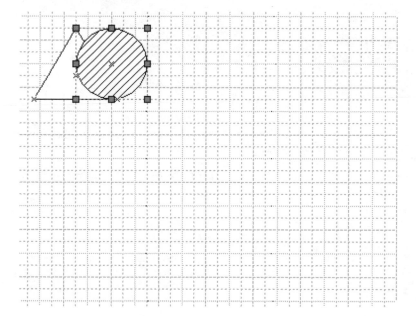

5. Select both shapes.

6. Make five copies of the originals. (Recall that you can make copies by (1) selecting both shapes; (2) holding down the **Ctrl** key; and (3) dragging the shapes to a new location.) Remember to use the **Shift** key to force the movement to horizontal and vertical. Use the **F4** key to repeat an action. You should have a total of six pairs of shapes, on which we will perform Boolean operations.

The six pairs of shapes.

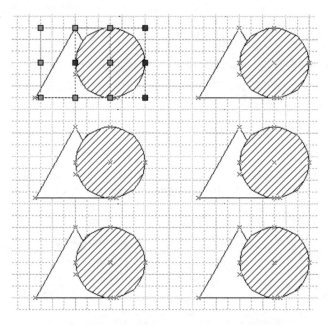

7. Select the first circle, then the triangle. Remember to hold down the **Shift** key when selecting the triangle.

8. Select **Shape | Operations | Union**. Notice that the two shapes become a single shape, which takes on the fill pattern of the circle.

The unioned shape.

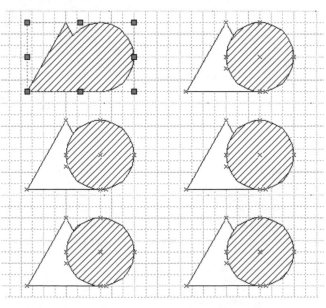

9. Select the second circle, then the triangle.

10. Select **Shape | Operations | Combine**. Notice the two shapes become a single shape that takes on the fill pattern of the circle — except for the area in common.

The combined shape.

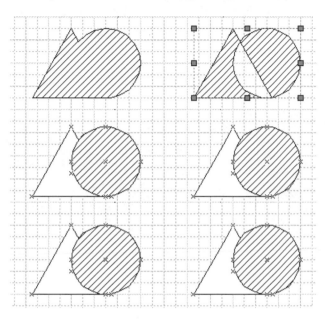

11. Select the third circle, then the triangle.

12. Select **Shape | Operations | Fragment**. Notice that the two shapes become three shapes and take on the fill pattern of the circle. (For clarity, the illustration shows the three shapes moved apart.)

The fragmented shapes.

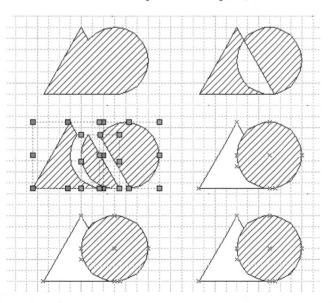

13. Select the fourth circle, then the triangle.

14. Select **Shape | Operations | Intersect**. Notice that the two shapes become a single shape — consisting of the area in common — which takes on the fill pattern of the circle.

The intersected shape.

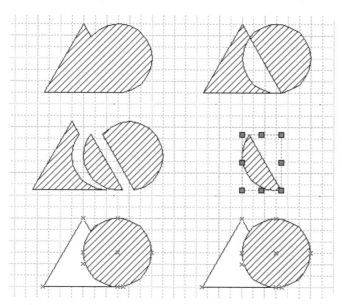

15. Select the fifth circle, then the triangle.

16. Select **Shape | Operations | Subtract**. Notice that the triangle is removed from the circle.

The subtracted shape.

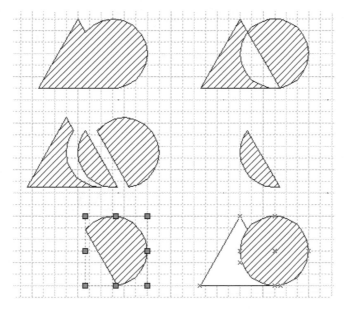

17. To show the importance of selection order, this time select the sixth triangle, then the circle.

18. Select **Shape | Operations | Subtract**. Notice that the circle is removed from the triangle. Since the triangle was selected first, the resulting Boolean shape takes on the attributes of the triangle.

The other subtracted shape.

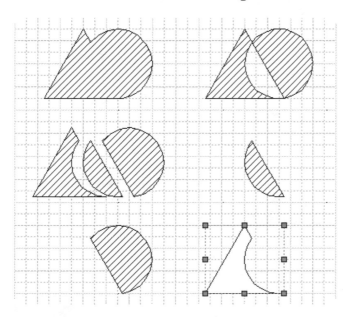

19. Press **Alt+F4** to exit Visio. Click **No** in response to the Save Changes dialog box.

This completes the hands-on activity for Boolean operations. Being familiar with the five operations makes it easier to create many interesting (and sometimes unique) new shapes.

Previewing Before Printing

File | Print Preview

> **In this chapter you'll learn about:**
> ✓ **Print Preview**

Uses

Before you print your drawing, you
should always do a print preview. *Print preview* means that Visio displays your drawing on a white rectangle that represents the paper. By previewing the drawing, you see how it will print, and then you can make the appropriate changes to orientation, paper size, and so on. This action takes only a few seconds, and saves you a lot of wasted paper.

The **Print Preview** selection of the **File** menu lets you see how the drawing will appear on the paper, before committing to printing.

Procedures

Before presenting the general procedure for print preview, it is helpful to know the following shortcuts.

Function	Keys	Menu	Toolbar Icon
Print Preview	...	File	Print Preview	🔍

Once in print preview mode, the following shortcut keys are available:

Function	Keys	Menu	Toolbar Icon
Print dialog box	Ctrl+P	File	Print	Print...
Page Setup dialog box	...	File	Print Setup	Setup...
Whole Page	Ctrl+W	View	Whole Page	🔳
Zoom Out	Shift+F6	View	Zoom Out	🔍
Zoom In	Alt+F6	View	Zoom In	🔍
Close	Ctrl+F4	...	Close
Help	F1	Help	Visio Help	?

Print Preview

Use the following procedure to preview the drawing before printing:

1. Select **File | Print Preview**.

2. Notice that Visio displays the drawing on a white background, representing the sheet of paper. The light gray edging represents the printer margins. If any portion of the drawing extends into the margin, that part will not be printed.

Visio in print preview mode. The white rectangular area represents the printable portion of the paper; the light gray area is the paper's unprintable margin.

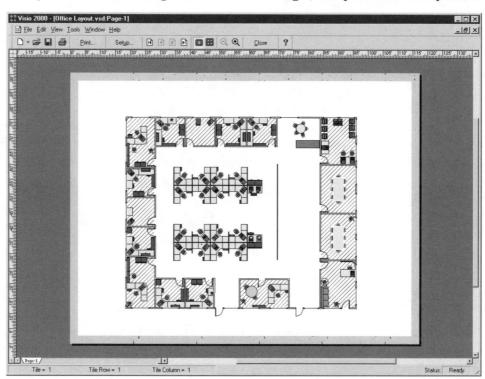

3. Notice that the Print Preview window has its own toolbar:

The Print Preview toolbar.

The buttons, from left to right, are:

New Drawing, **Open**, and **Save** icons: You can open new and existing Visio drawings from print preview mode; the drawings, however, are opened in the Visio drawing window, not in print preview.

Print Page: Prints the drawing.

Caution: The **Print Page** button is a shortcut that immediately prints the drawing to the current printer. Do not click this button unless you know all settings are correct. In fact, I never click this icon, which I consider dangerous.

Usually, you use print preview to see how your drawing is going to print. Then you make adjustments and preview the drawing again. When you preview a drawing for the last time, and don't need to make any more adjustments, you simply click the **Print Page** button.

Print: Displays the Print dialog box. (See Module 20 "Printing Drawings.")

Setup: Displays the Page Setup dialog box. (See Module 4 "Setting Up Pages and Layers.")

First Tile, Previous Tile, Next Tile, Last Tile: These buttons perform double-duty; they work for multi-page drawings and tiled drawings:

▶ When the drawing contains more than one page, these buttons display the first, previous, next, and last pages of a multi-page drawing.

▶ When the drawing is tiled, these buttons take you from tile to tile. The **Previous Tile** and **Next Tile** buttons move left to right, then top to bottom. The status line reports which tile you are looking at. For example:

Tile = 2 Tile Row = 1 Tile Column = 2

 Tip: Most office printers and fax machines are limited to printing on letter-size paper (8.5" x 11", also known as "A-size" paper), as well as legal-size paper (8.5" x 14"). Tiling allows you, if somewhat awkwardly, to use the printer or fax to create an engineering-size printout, such as D-size (22" x 34"). Hey, why not using Visio and tiling to create Happy Birthday and Bon Voyage banners?

Using Visio to create celebratory banners; this banner is nine sheets of paper wide.

Happy 43rd Birthday, Heather!

Single Tile and **Whole Page:** When the drawing is larger than one sheet of paper, Visio tiles the drawing. *Tiling* means that the drawing will be printed on enough sheets of paper to print the full drawing, which you can tape together. Visio can tile to a maximum of 2,500 sheets of paper, limited to 50 sheets horizontally and 50 vertically — not that you would probably ever want to tape together that many sheets! Click the **Single Tile** button to see one sheet of a multi-tile printout; click the **Whole Page** button to show all sheets.

Zoom Out and **Zoom In**: The **Zoom Out** button displays the whole page; the **Zoom In** button displays the drawing in full size.

Tip: You never need to use the zoom buttons. That's because the cursor becomes the zoom tool in print preview mode. Click the drawing to examine it full size; click the drawing again to return to the full-page view.

Close and **Help**: **Close** takes you back to the Visio drawing screen, which it calls "normal view." If you have more than one print preview window open, all are closed. The **Help** button brings up the help window.

4. Select **File | Print** to print the drawing.

5. Or, click the **Close** button on the toolbar to return to the drawing without printing.

Hands-On Activity

In this activity, you use the print preview function. Begin by starting Visio.

1. Select **File | New | Browse Sample Drawings**.

2. From the Browse Sample Drawings dialog box, go to the **Organization Chart** folder and double-click **Organization Chart.Vsd**. Wait while Visio loads the four-page drawing.

3. Select **File | Print Preview**. Notice that Visio displays the drawing in a window with a gray background as shown on the following page.

4. Move the cursor over the drawing. Notice the cursor is a magnifying glass with a + sign. This indicates Visio is in zoom mode.

5. Click the drawing. Notice that Visio enlarges the view.

6. Notice that the cursor's + sign has changed to a – sign. This indicates Visio is ready to zoom out to the full-page view.

7. Click the drawing.

8. Notice Visio reduces the view.

9. Click **Close** on the Print Preview toolbar to return to the drawing.

10. Press **Alt+F4** to exit Visio. Click **No** in response to the Save Changes dialog box.

This completes the hands-on activity for print preview.

*The
Organization
Chart drawing
in Visio's print
preview mode.*

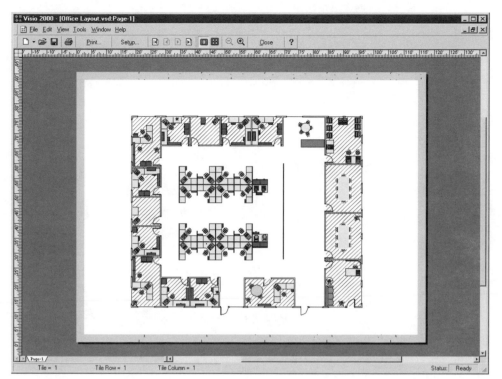

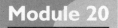

Module 20 *Printing Drawings*

File | Print

Uses

In this chapter you'll learn about:

✓ **Printing drawings**

✓ **Tiling drawings**

✓ **Transmitting faxed drawings**

✓ **E-mailing drawings as attachments**

✓ **Printing to file**

You can share your drawings with others by printing them, pasting them into other programs, and saving them as Web pages. While you can gain satisfaction from creating the drawing, there is a certain amount of pleasure to be gained from showing off your work to co-workers, friends, and family — in serious black and white, or in brilliant color! Visio provides several ways to output your drawing, which can be done on paper or electronically.

Printing on paper:

▶ **Office printer:** The **Print** selection of the File menu displays a dialog box that allows you to control how the diagram is printed. In most cases, you will want Visio to print the diagram to fit the standard letter-size paper on a laser or inkjet printer.

▶ **Engineering plotter:** In some cases, you may want to produce accurate scale drawings on engineering-size paper, such as 22" x 34" or larger. Visio can print to large printers and plotters that handle this size of media; or, it can tile a print so that a large drawing is printed on two or more letter-size sheets.

Outputting electronically:

▶ **Fax transmission:** Windows does not limit you to printing to one particular printer. If your computer is connected to a fax modem, you can send the Visio drawing as a fax.

▶ **E-mail attachment:** If your computer is hooked up to an e-mail system, you can attach the drawing to an e-mail message with the **File | Send To** command.

181

▶ **Web display**: For displaying the Visio drawing on a Web site, it can be published as a static, raster GIF image, or as an interactive, vector VML file. (See Module 36 "Creating a Web Document.")

▶ **Printing to file**: In some cases, it may make sense to print the drawing to a file on disk. This is an alternative method of exporting the drawing. (See Module 29 "Exporting Drawings.")

Tip: Before you print the drawing, always select **File | Print Preview** to ensure the drawing will be printed to your satisfaction. (See Module 19 "Previewing Before Printing.")

Procedures

Before presenting the general procedures for printing, it is helpful to know about the shortcut keys. These are:

Function	Keys	Menu	Toolbar Icon
Print	Ctrl+P	File | Print	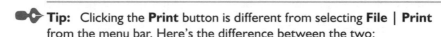
Page Setup	Alt+FU	File | Page Setup	...
E-mail	Alt+FD	File | Send To	...

Tip: Clicking the **Print** button is different from selecting **File | Print** from the menu bar. Here's the difference between the two:

▶ Clicking the **Print** button on the toolbar causes Visio to immediately print the drawing, without displaying a dialog box. This may result in wasted paper, since you don't get a chance to check things, like the printer model and the number of copies. Only click this button if you are sure the print will be completed correctly.

▶ Selecting **File | Print** from the menu bar displays the Print dialog box, which gives you a chance to check the printer's parameters before committing to placing the drawing on paper.

Printing Drawings

Use the following procedure to print the drawing to your office printer:

1. Select **File | Print**. Notice the Print dialog box.

The Print dialog box provides basic control over the printing of a Visio drawing.

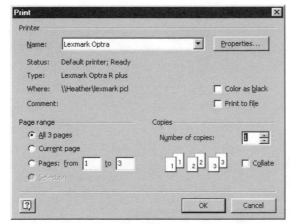

2. Select the name of the printer from the **Name** list box.

3. Click the **Properties** button to change the characteristics of the printer, such as resolution and paper orientation. Click **OK** to return to the Print dialog box.

4. Click **Color as black** to ensure all shapes are printed on a monochrome printer (one that is incapable of printing color or shades of gray).

5. If the drawing consists of more than one page, select which pages you want printed in the **Page range** area:

   All: Prints all pages in the drawing (the default).

   Current Page: Prints the currently displayed page.

   Pages: When the drawing consists of more than one page, specifies the range of pages to print.

   Selection: Prints the selected objects of the current page.

6. Type the number of copies in the **Number of copies** text box.

7. Click **OK** to begin printing; as an alternative, you can click **Cancel** to dismiss the dialog box without printing the drawing.

Tiling Drawings

When your drawing is larger than a single sheet of paper, Visio can tile the print so that a large drawing is printed on two or more sheets. Since the drawing is larger than the paper, the print is *tiled*. Use the following procedure to print the drawing on several sheets of paper:

1. Select **File | Page Setup** from the menu bar.

2. When the Page Setup dialog box appears, click the **Print Setup** tab. In this tab, you specify the number of sheets of paper Visio should spread the drawing over. For most office printers, set the following options to print a drawing on two or more sheets of paper. For example, to print the drawing on nine (3 x 3) sheets of paper:

   ▶ Paper size: **Letter 8½ x 11 in**

   ▶ Paper orientation: **Portrait**

   ▶ Fit to: 3 **sheets across**

                         3 **sheets down**

Click **OK**.

The Page Setup dialog box.

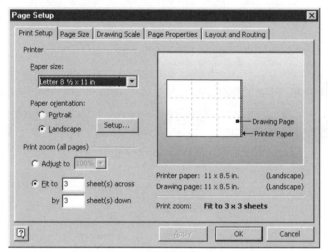

Tip: Only use the method outlined above if the accuracy of scale is not important. When you have a large, scaled drawing and you don't specify the number of sheets you want your drawing to fit on, Visio still tiles the drawing. If the drawing must be plotted at a specific scale, use the following method via the Page Setup dialog box:

Step 1: Select the size of paper used by the printer (Print Setup tab).

Step 2: Select the size of the drawing page (Page Size tab).

Step 3: Specify the drawing scale, so that the drawing covers the page (Drawing Scale tab).

Transmitting Faxed Drawings

Windows does not limit you to printing to one particular printer. If your computer is connected to a fax modem, you can send the Visio drawing as a fax. Just like with any other printer, you can fax a drawing tiled over several pages.

 Note: Unlike other printers, drawings cannot be faxed in color — colors will be converted to shades of gray. For this reason, avoid using backgrounds with drawings you intend to fax.

Use the following procedure to fax the drawing:

1. Select **File | Print**. Notice the Print dialog box.

2. To fax the drawing, click the **Name** list box, and select the **Microsoft Fax** or other fax "printer" from this list.

3. To be more economical, faxes are usually sent at 200 dpi (dots per inch resolution) and in monochrome (just black and white). A Visio drawing, however, contains much detail. To improve the quality of the faxed drawing, click the **Properties** button.

4. When the Fax Properties dialog box appears, click the **Graphics** tab. Select the following options.

   ▶ Dots per inch (dpi): **300 dpi**
   ▶ Grayscale — Halftoning: **Patterned Grays**
   Click **OK**.

Selecting the options for optimal fax transmission of a Visio drawing.

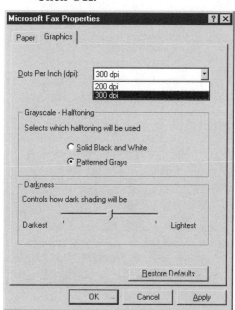

5. Back in the Visio Print dialog box, select the pages you want printed, then click **OK**. Notice that Visio spends a few moments converting the drawing to fax format.

6. Notice that your fax software's dialog box appears. The look of the dialog box will vary, depending on the brand of fax software installed on your computer. Fill in the required information, then send the fax on its way.

The fax software provided with Microsoft Windows.

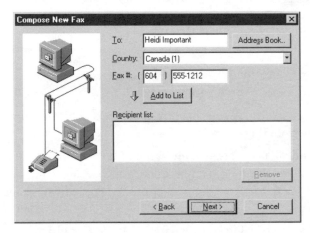

E-Mailing Drawings as Attachments

If your computer is hooked up to an e-mail system, you can attach the drawing to an e-mail message. Use the following procedure to e-mail the drawing:

1. Select **File | Send To** from the menu bar. Notice that you may have several options:

   ▶ **Mail Recipient (as Attachment)**: A message appears with your drawing attached.

   ▶ **Routing Recipient**: Displays the Routing Slip dialog box. Select a recipient by clicking the **Address** button, then click **OK**. This option is useful when you want to send the drawing via the addresses stored in the Address Book provided with Windows.

   ▶ **Exchange Folder**: Displays the Send to Exchange Folder dialog box; select a folder. The drawing is saved in the folder so that you can later open the drawing from within Microsoft Exchange.

 Caution: If your computer is not set up to handle Microsoft Mail, the Send To command may not work correctly. In that case, you can use this work-around: from the Explorer window, drag the VSD file into the e-mail message.

Drag the file from Explorer into your e-mail message.

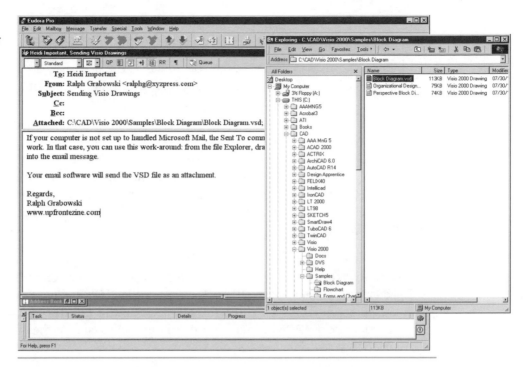

To display the Visio drawing on a Web site, it can be published as a GIF image or as a vector VML file. See Module 36 "Creating a Web Document."

Printing to File

There are some cases where it makes sense to print the drawing to a file on disk:

▶ When you need to translate the drawing to a file format not found in the Visio Save As dialog box. One common example is converting the file to HPGL (short for Hewlett-Packard graphics language), which can be imported into another drawing or CAD program. Printing to disk is an alternative method of exporting the drawing. (See Module 29 "Exporting Drawings.")

▶ When you want to print the drawing but you have no access to the printer. Print the file to a disk, then carry the disk to the computer with the printer. There are three options. First, you can use the DOS command by typing the following:

C:\> **copy /b d:\filename.prn prn**

where

copy	The DOS command that copies the print file to the printer.
/b	Ensures the **Copy** command does not stop sending the print file before the end of the file.

d:	Name of the drive containing the print file.
filename.prn	Name of the print file.
prn	Name of the port to which the printer is attached; you may use **ltp1** for the first parallel port or **lpt2** for the second parallel port.

Or, if the machine you are printing from has an application installed that can open a PostScript file, you can use the Send To command in Explorer by right-clicking on the file, selecting Send To from the shortcut menu, then selecting a printer from the secondary menu. The application associated with the PRN file extension will open, load the file, and print it. You can also drag the file to a printer icon on the desktop or to the desired printer in the Printers folder in Explorer.

Use the following procedure to print the drawing to a file:

1. Ensure that the required Windows printer driver is installed on your computer. To add a printer, such as an HP plotter (for creating HPGL files), from the **Start** menu, select **Settings | Printers**, then click the **Add Printer** icon. Follow the instructions of the Add Printer Wizard; it is not necessary for the printer to be attached to your computer.

2. In Visio, select **File | Print** from the menu bar.

3. Click the Name list, and select the appropriate printer.

4. Click **Print to file** to save the drawing in a file.

5. Click **OK**. Notice that Visio displays the Print to File dialog box.

6. Enter the filename and select the folder for the file. Notice that you must provide the extension to the filename; use the following standards:

    HP Plotter: **HPG** or **PLT**

    PostScript: **PS** or **EPS**

    Others: **PRN**

7. Click **OK**. Visio saves the drawing as a print file on disk.

Hands-On Activity

In this activity, you use the print function. Ensure Visio is running.

1. Select **File | New | Browse Sample Drawings**. Notice the Browse Sample Drawings dialog box.

2. From the **Flowchart** folder, double-click the **Basic Flowchart.Vsd** drawing file.

3. Select **File | Print**. Notice the Print dialog box.

4. Click **OK**. Notice the Printing message box, which tells you of the progress in sending the drawing to the printer. Wait for the printer to print the drawing.

5. Press **Alt+F4** to exit Visio. Click **No** in the Save Changes dialog box.

This completes the hands-on activity for printing.

Module 21 | *Undoing and Redoing*

Edit | Undo, Redo

Uses

In this chapter you'll learn about:

✓ **Undoing an action**

✓ **Redoing an undo**

✓ **Multiple undo levels**

When you make a mistake, such as deleting a shape, **Undo** returns the deleted shape. Visio remembers the actions you performed, so that repeating the Undo command reverses each action, one at a time. To help you remember what the next undo action will be, the **Edit** menu follows **Undo** with the action, such as Undo Move Object.

The Edit menu allows you to undo and redo one action at a time.

If you change your mind, the **Redo** command undoes the **Undo**. Like Undo, Visio remembers as many Redo actions as Undo actions. Naturally, you can undo a redo.

Visio 2002 allows you to undo and redo more than one action at a time. To view the list of all actions stored in the undo list, click the small arrow to the right of the Undo button on the toolbar.

The Undo button allows you to undo more than one action at a time.

Some actions cannot be undone, such as saving, printing, and certain shape operations. When the action cannot be undone, the Edit menu shows Can't Undo instead of Undo.

Procedures

Before presenting the general procedures for undoing and redoing, it is helpful to know about the shortcut keys. These are:

Function	Keys	Menu	Toolbar Icon
Undo	Ctrl+Z	Edit | Undo	↺
Redo	Ctrl+Y	Edit | Redo	↻ ▾

 Tip: When first installed on your computer, Visio is set up for 20 levels of undo and redo. That means Visio remembers the last 20 actions you performed. You can change the number of levels via the **Tools | Options** command. In the Options dialog box, on the General tab, look for **Undo levels**. The default value of **20** can be reduced to **0**, or increased to **99**. The higher the number of levels, the more memory Visio uses to store the actions to be undone.

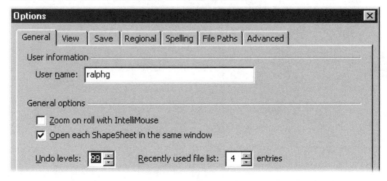

The Options dialog box allows you to change the number of undo levels.

Undoing an Action

Use the following procedure to undo the most recent action:

1. Select **Edit | Undo** or press **Ctrl+Z**.

2. If necessary, select **Edit | Undo** again.

Redoing an Undo

Use the following procedure to redo the undo:

1. Select **Edit | Redo** or press **Ctrl+Y.**

Multiple Undo Levels

Use the following procedure to undo more than one action:

1. Click the arrow button to the right of the **Undo** button. Notice that Visio displays a list of actions.

2. Holding down the mouse button, slide the cursor down the list. Notice that Visio highlights the actions and reports the number of undo actions, such as **Undo 4 Actions**.

3. Release the mouse button. Notice that Visio instantly changes the drawing back to its previous state.

 Note: You cannot pick and choose the actions to undo; undo and redo work in sequential order only.

Hands-On Activity

In this activity, you use the undo and redo functions. Begin by starting Visio. Then start a new document with the **Basic Diagram** template:

1. Drag the **Star 5** shape from the Basic Shapes stencil to the center of the page.

2. Drag the **Square** shape from the stencil to a location above the star.

3. Select **Edit | Undo Drop On Page**. Notice that the square disappears from the page.

4. Drag the **Circle** shape from the stencil to on top of the **Star.**

5. Select gray fill from the **Fill Color** list box to turn the circle gray.

6. Press **Ctrl+A** to select all objects in the drawing.

7. Select **Shape | Operations | Combine**. Notice that the star shape is "punched" out of the gray circle.

*Punching the
star out of the
circle.*

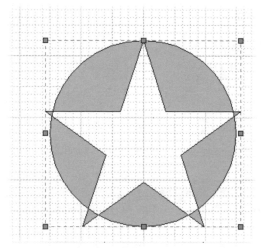

8. Click the arrow to the right of the **Undo** button on the toolbar. Notice that Visio displays a list in reverse order of all the actions that can be undone.

   Some actions are not recorded, such as selecting all objects (the **Ctrl+A** of step 6), adding and removing the square shape (steps 2 and 3), nor any pan and zoom operations you may have performed.

9. Select three undo actions, so that you see **Undo 3 Actions**. Notice that the circle and star return to their former states.

The undo list.

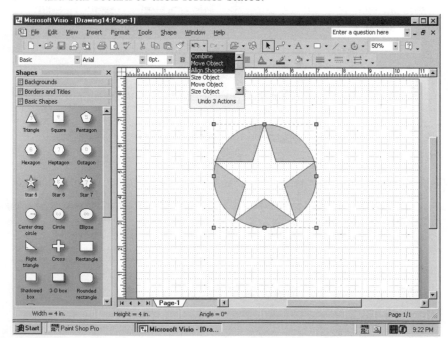

10. Click the arrow to the right of the **Redo** button on the toolbar. Notice that Visio displays a list in reverse order of the actions you undid.

The redo list.

11. Select two redo actions, so that you see **Redo 2 Actions**. Notice that the circle reappears, shaded in gray.

12. Press **Alt+F4** to exit Visio. Click **No** in response to the Save Changes dialog box.

This completes the hands-on activity for the undo and redo operations.

Help

Help | Microsoft Visio Help

Uses

> **In this chapter you'll learn about:**
> ✓ **Microsoft Visio help**

The **Help** menu displays an expanded version of the printed documentation provided with the Visio 2002 package. Via the Help menu, you access information helpful to you in these areas:

▶ **Microsoft Visio Help**: Assistance in using Visio menus, toolbars, and other program features.

▶ **Developer Reference**: Information for programming Visio's ShapeSheet and VBA (Visual Basic for Applications).

▶ **Visio on the Web**: Access to the Visio Web site at www.microsoft.com/office/visio via your computer's default Web browser. The Knowledge Base section of the Support area can be helpful when you have a specific problem.

▶ **Office on the Web**: Access to the Microsoft Office Web site at officeupdate.microsoft.com and its Assistance Center.

▶ **Detect and Repair**: Detects problems with Visio 2002 and attempts to repair them.

The online help gives specific details, whereas the printed documentation gives a general overview. I find it is faster to find online help on a specific topic, rather than searching the printed index and flipping through pages.

*Visio on the
Web.*

Visio 2002 adds an Ask a Question tool, which is a shortcut to the help system's Answer Wizard. This technology attempts to answer your question by analyzing the words in your question.

*Where can I
find help?*

When you select **Help | Microsoft Visio Help**, Visio opens a second window next to Visio. Click the **Show** button to search for documentation via the Contents, Index, and Answer Wizard functions. **Contents** lists help topics in logical order; the **Index** lists topics in alphabetical order; and the **Answer Wizard** searches for information based on words you type in.

As an alternative to using the Help menu, you can click for help directly within Visio itself. Here are some examples:

Almost all dialog boxes include a **Help** button (shown by a ?), which displays help for the options of that dialog box. That means you don't need to search the online help for how to use that dialog box.

Click the dialog box's ? button to display context-sensitive help.

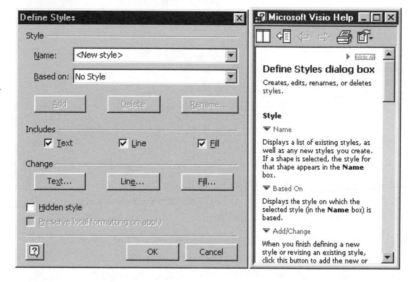

The help for toolbar buttons and menu items is less comprehensive. Pause the cursor over a toolbar button to display the yellow tooltip (a one- or two-word description). When you press **F1** while holding down a toolbar button or menu item, the Visio Help window displays the general Visio Help item.

Help for toolbar buttons is displayed by a tooltip.

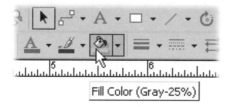

Procedures

The shortcut keys for help are as follows:

Function	Keys	Menu	Toolbar Icon
Help	F1	Help | Microsoft Visio Help	**?**

Hands-On Activity

Begin by starting Visio with no document open.

Finding a general help topic

1. Select **Help | Microsoft Visio Help**. Notice that Visio displays a new Help window that positions itself next to the Visio window. If necessary, Visio makes itself smaller to make room for the new window.

2. Notice the blue text; this text is linked to other help topics. Click the blue phrase **Keyboard Shortcuts** under **Help Topics**. Notice that the help text changes. Click on the blue underlined text for more information about a particular topic.

Click the blue underlined text to go to related information.

3. Click **Back** on the toolbar to return to the previous topic.

Finding a help topic using the tabs

1. If necessary, click the button labeled **Show**. Notice that the window widens to show three tabs: Contents, Index, and Answer Wizard.

2. Click the **Index** tab in the Microsoft Visio Help window. Notice that it displays an alphabetical list of topics in the left pane.

3. Type the word **flowchart** in the **Type in the keywords to find** field. Notice that the left pane displays many topics starting with the word "flowchart."

3. Click the **Create a Basic Flowchart** phrase. Notice that the Visio Help window displays related help in the right pane.

This completes the hands-on activity for using help.

Module 23 · *Drawing Tools*

Pencil, Line, Arc, Freeform, Rectangle, Ellipse

In this chapter you'll learn about:

✓ *Drawing with the Pencil tool*

✓ *Drawing with the Line tool*

✓ *Drawing with the Arc tool*

✓ *Drawing with the Rectangle tool*

✓ *Drawing with the Ellipse tool*

✓ *Drawing closed objects*

✓ *Adding segments to an object*

✓ *Moving the vertex*

Uses

Most of the time when you create a drawing with Visio, you work with shapes. You drag shapes into the drawing, position them, resize them, copy them, and so on. Sometimes, however, the thousands of shapes provided with Visio 2002 are not enough. You may want to create your own shapes, or need to draw a one-of-a-kind object, like a squiggly line.

For these reasons, Visio includes a basic set of six drawing tools. These tools are found on the **Standard** toolbar — and not on any menu. The tools draw straight and curved lines, circles and arcs, rectangles, and ellipses. Many of the Visio drawing tools are dual purpose: a different object is created depending on how you move the mouse or hold down a key.

Tool	Draws	Special Action
Pencil	Straight line	Move mouse in a straight line.
	Circular arc	Move mouse in a curve.
	Line at 45-degree increments	Hold down **Shift** key.
Line	Straight line	
	Line at 45-degree increments	Hold down **Shift** key.
Arc	Elliptical arc	
	Line	Move mouse in horizontal or vertical direction.
Rectangle	Rectangle	
	Square	Hold down **Shift** key.

Tool	Draws	Special Action
Ellipse	Ellipse	
	Circle	Hold down **Shift** key.
Freeform	NUBS curve	

The only tool that isn't dual purpose is the **Freeform** tool (also called the **Spline** tool), which draws NUBS curves. *NUBS* is short for non-uniform Bezier spline and should not be confused with the more common NURBS curve (non-uniform *rational* Bezier spline) found in computer-aided design software.

Another way of looking at the drawing tools is to list them by the objects they draw:

To draw a...	Use this tool...
Line	Line tool
	Pencil tool, and move mouse in a straight line
Constrained line	Line tool, and hold down **Shift** key
	Pencil tool, and hold down **Shift** key
	Arc tool, and move mouse in a horizontal or vertical direction
Circular arc	Pencil tool, and move mouse in a curve
Curve	Freeform tool
Circle	Ellipse tool, and hold down **Shift** key
Elliptical arc	Arc tool
Ellipse	Ellipse tool
Rectangle	Rectangle tool
Square	Rectangle tool, and hold down **Shift** key
Spline	Freeform tool

The **Pencil** tool also creates new vertices and allows you to move the vertices, as described later in this module.

 Tip: So that you know where an open object, such as a line or arc, starts and ends, Visio uses these symbols:

Symbol	Meaning
x	Starting point of a line or arc
□	Midpoint (control point)
+	Ending point

X marks the start, and + marks the end of open objects; the small square marks the midpoint.

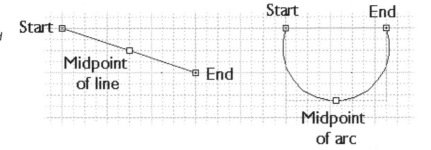

After you draw a line or arc, notice that there is a small x where you began drawing and a small + where you stopped drawing. To connect one line or arc to another, start drawing from the endpoint. Visio automatically connects the two. The control point is used to change the radius of arcs and splines.

Procedures

Before presenting the general procedures for drawing, it is helpful to know the shortcut keys. These are:

Function	Keys	Toolbar Icon
Arc tool	Ctrl+7	⌐
Ellipse tool	Ctrl+9	○
Line tool	Ctrl+6	/
Pencil tool	Ctrl+4	✎
Rectangle tool	Ctrl+8	□
Spline tool	Ctrl+5	∿

Visio 2002 combines the six drawing tools into two *flyout* toolbars. One flyout contain the drawing tools for closed objects (Rectangle and Ellipse); the other contains the drawing tools for open objects (Line, Arc, Freeform, and Pencil). To access a tool, follow these steps:

1. Click the small arrow next to the **Rectangle** or **Line** tool.

2. Move the cursor down to the tool you want.

3. Click the tool's button.

Visio 2002 drawing tools are found in two flyouts.

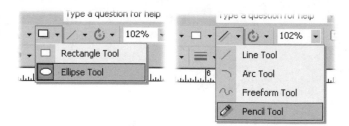

Drawing with the Pencil Tool

Use the following procedure to draw a line or a circular arc with the Pencil tool:

1. Click the **Pencil** tool.
2. Drag (hold down the button and move the mouse) to draw with the Pencil tool.
3. Move the mouse in a straight line to draw a straight line at any angle.
4. Hold down the **Shift** key to draw a line in 45-degree increments.
5. Or, slowly move the mouse in the shape of an arc and the Pencil tool draws a circular arc. You cannot draw a circle with this tool.

The Pencil tool draws straight lines and round arcs.

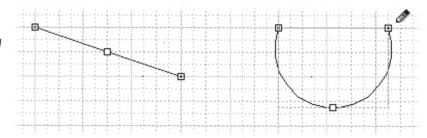

Tip: To draw a line in *45-degree increments* means that Visio draws the line at one of the 45-degree angles — 0, 45, 90, 135, 180, 225, 270, and 315 degrees — nearest to the angle your mouse is moving. The following illustration shows lines drawn at 45-degree increments.

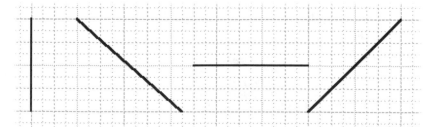

Holding down the Shift key locks line drawing to 45-degree increments.

Drawing with the Line Tool

Use the following procedure to draw a line with the Line tool:

1. Click the **Line** tool.

2. Drag to draw a line at any angle with the Line tool.

3. Hold down the **Shift** key to draw a line in 45-degree increments.

The Line tool draws straight lines.

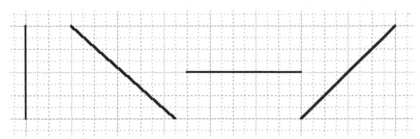

Drawing with the Arc Tool

Use the following procedure to draw an elliptical arc or a line with the Arc tool:

1. Click the **Arc** tool.

2. Drag to draw an elliptical arc with the Arc tool.

3. Or, move the mouse in a horizontal or vertical direction to draw a horizontal or vertical line.

The Arc tool draws elliptical quarter-arcs and straight lines.

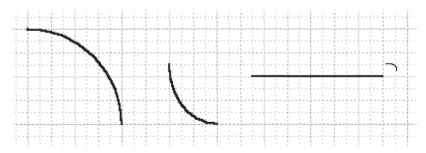

 Note: The arcs drawn by the Arc and Pencil tools may seem the same, but they have a couple of differences. The Arc tool draws a quarter elliptical arc, while the Pencil tool draws a circular arc that isn't necessarily a quarter of a circle.

Drawing with the Rectangle Tool

Use the following procedure to draw a rectangle or a square with the Rectangle tool:

1. Click the **Rectangle** tool.

2. Drag diagonally to draw a rectangle with the Rectangle tool. By default, the rectangle has a white fill.

3. Or, hold down **Shift** key to draw a square.

The Rectangle tool draws rectangles and squares.

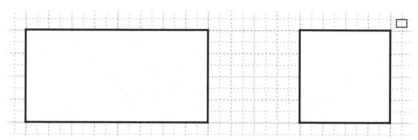

Drawing with the Ellipse Tool

Use the following procedure to draw an ellipse or a circle with the Ellipse tool:

1. Click the **Ellipse** tool.

2. Drag diagonally to draw an ellipse with the Ellipse tool. By default, the ellipse has a white fill.

3. Or, hold down the **Shift** key to draw a circle.

The Ellipse tool draws ellipses and circles.

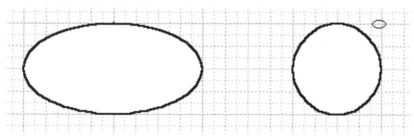

 Tip: As you draw with the Rectangle or Ellipse tools, keep an eye on the status line. Visio reports the rectangular size of the object, such as:

Width = 1.25 in Height = 4.5678 in

For the other drawing tools, the status line reports the current x- and y-coordinates, such as:

X = 2.345 in Y = 10 in

Drawing Closed Objects

The types of objects drawn with the tools discussed in this chapter fall into two categories: open and closed. An *open object* is like a line, arc, or open spline. A *closed object* is like a circle, rectangle, or square.

Visio lets you create closed objects using the Line, Arc, and other open object tools. For example, you would use these tools to create shapes that look like a triangle, the letter D, and so on. You cannot, however, easily convert a closed object (drawn with the Rectangle and Ellipse tools) into open objects — without getting into the ShapeSheet, which is beyond the scope of this book (see *Learn Microsoft Visio 2002 for the Advanced User*, also from Wordware Publishing).

 Tip: You will find it easier to draw a closed object when snap is turned on (which it normally is). If you find it difficult to connect to the ends, select **Tools | Snap & Glue** from the menu bar. In the Snap & Glue dialog box, ensure the following options are set:

▶ Currently active: **Snap**

▶ Snap to: **Shape geometry**

Use the following procedure to draw a closed object in the shape of a triangle:

1. Click the **Line** tool.

2. Hold down the **Shift** key, then click and drag to create a line at a 45-degree angle.

3. Ensure the cursor is over the endpoint of the line. When the cursor is over the endpoint, it changes to look like a small + sign.

4. Click and drag to create the horizontal base of the triangle. Notice that each endpoint of the two line segments has changed, from a small square to a small diamond, called a *vertex*.

5. Hold down the **Shift** key, then click and drag to create the last 45-degree segment of the triangle.

Carefully connect the endpoints of line segments to create a triangle.

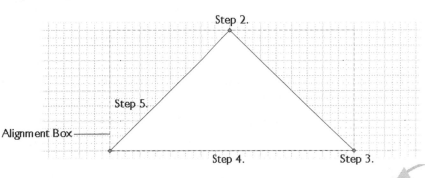

> **Note:** As soon as you release the mouse button, notice that the triangle is filled with white, and is surrounded by a green, dashed rectangle called the *alignment box*. These two indicators tell you that you have successfully created a closed object.

Adding Segments to an Object

Once you have drawn an object, you can add additional segments along the existing lines and arcs making up the objects. This works with any open or closed object drawn with any of the drawing tools. You add a segment by inserting a vertex. Here's how:

1. Select one of the open drawing tools (**Pencil**, **Line**, **Arc**, or **Freeform**).

2. Click anywhere on the object to select it.

3. Between two existing vertices, hold down the **Ctrl** key and click on the line at the point at which you want to add the vertex. It is not important that you click at a precise location, since the new vertex can be later moved to the correct location. Notice the new vertex at your click point, resulting in two segments where previously there was just one.

4. While the vertex is selected, you can use the Pointer tool to adjust the location of the vertex.

Adding a vertex to a segment.

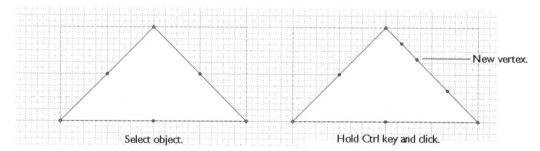

Select object.   Hold Ctrl key and click.   New vertex.

Moving the Vertex

With the vertex added, you can now drag it to a different location. Follow this procedure:

1. Select the **Pencil** tool and select the shape. Notice that the vertices and control points are displayed.

2. Move the pencil cursor over the new vertex.

3. When the cursor changes to a four-headed arrow, drag the vertex.

*Dragging the
newly added
vertex to a
new location.*

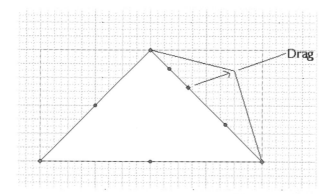

Hands-On Activity

In this activity, you use the drawing tools. Begin by starting Visio. Then start a new document with no template.

1. Click the **Pencil** tool button. Notice that the cursor looks like a tiny pencil with a small crosshair at the "pencil" tip.

2. Drag across the page (hold down the button, move the mouse, let go of the button). Notice that Visio has drawn a line (or an arc, depending on your mouse movement).

Tip: While holding down the mouse button for the Pencil tool, carefully examine the cursor. It has changed to a + marker, along with either (1) a short straight line; or (2) a small arc. The straight line means Visio has sensed your mouse movement to be in a straight line; Visio accordingly draws a straight line.

The small arc means Visio has sensed your mouse movement to be curved; Visio accordingly draws an arc. If the arc looks to you like a straight line — even though Visio shows the arc indicator — it probably is a straight line.

---

3. Using the Pencil tool is tricky. Practicing drawing lines with the Pencil tool by moving the mouse straight.

4. Practicing drawing arcs with the Pencil tool by moving the mouse in a curve. I find it easier by moving the mouse slowly and in an exaggerated curving motion.

5. Hold down the **Shift** key while drawing with the Pencil tool. Notice how Visio constrains the line to 45 or 90 degrees; if you are drawing an arc, holding the **Shift** key constrains the curvature of the arc.

Lines and arcs drawn with the Pencil tool.

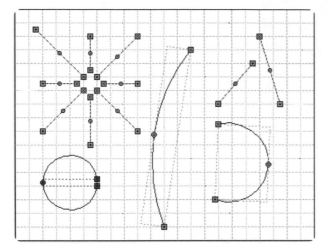

6. Select one of the arcs you have drawn.

Note: Notice that the lines and arcs have three green squares, called *handles*. At one end, the green square has a small x in it. That handle is Visio's reminder of where you began drawing the line or arc.

At the other end, the green square has a small + in it. That is where you ended drawing the line or arc.

At the center, the third green square is empty. This handle shows you the center of the line or arc. It also functions as a *control point*. When you grab it and move it toward the midpoint of the other two handles, an arc straightens out into a line. Moving the midpoint of a line moves the line.

7. Drag the center handle back and forth. Notice how the arc changes its curve.

8. Press **Ctrl+A** to select all objects in the drawing.

9. Press **Delete** to delete all objects.

10. Select the **Rectangle** tool.

11. Drag to draw a rectangle. Notice the rectangle is filled with white.

12. Select gray from the **Fill Color** list box.

13. Hold the **Shift** key while dragging with the Rectangle tool to draw a square.

Drawing rectangles and squares with the Rectangle tool.

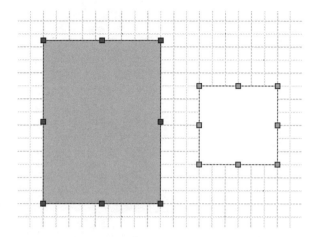

14. Press **Alt+F4** to exit Visio. Click **No** in response to the Save Changes dialog box.

This completes the hands-on activity for using the drawing tools. While just using stencil shapes and connector tools can create many Visio drawings, it is helpful to be familiar with the drawing tools.

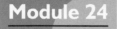

Module 24 *Placing Text and Fields*

Text Tool
Insert | Field

> **In this chapter you'll learn about:**
> ✓ **Placing text**
> ✓ **Inserting a text field**

Uses

You can add text to the drawing in
two ways: to an existing shape
(double-click the shape), or anywhere in the drawing via the **Text** tool. Once the text
is placed, you can change the size, font, color, etc., as described in Module 14 "Formatting Text."

A *field* is a piece of text attached to a shape that automatically updates itself. For
example, the Date/Time field displays the current date and time, making it a time
stamp. Some fields update themselves each time the drawing is opened; other fields
update when the attached shape changes.

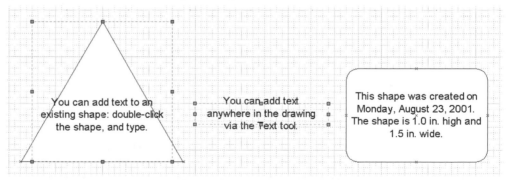

You can add text to an
existing shape: double-click
the shape, and type.

You can add text
anywhere in the drawing
via the Text tool.

This shape was created on
Monday, August 23, 2001.
The shape is 1.0 in. high and
1.5 in. wide.

*Text can be added to any shape (at left); or standing free in the drawing (center). Text fields, such as date
and geometry data, automatically update themselves (at right).*

Caution: There are some shortcomings you should be aware of in how Visio 2002 handles text. Visio does not automatically resize the alignment box to fit the text (see the center figure on the previous page). To partially overcome this limitation, Visio 2002 updates the text as you adjust the alignment box.

Text can only be flowed into a rectangular frame; you cannot, for example, flow text in a triangular or circular frame. The problem is illustrated by the text in the triangle shape, shown at left in the previous figure.

Procedures

Before presenting the general procedures for placing text and fields, it is helpful to know about the shortcut keys. These are:

Function	Keys	Menu	Toolbar Icon
Add text to shape	F2 (*)	...	...
Text tool	Ctrl+2	...	A
Insert field	...	Insert | Field	...

(*) As an alternative, you can double-click shapes (not groups) to add text, provided the double-click behavior has been set to edit text.

Placing Text

Use the following procedure to add text to a page:

1. Select the **Text** tool from the toolbar.

2. Click on the page at the location you want the text. As an alternative, you can click and drag a rectangle that defines a *text box* to hold the text.

 Note: When you use the Text tool to click the position for the text, Visio creates an invisible rectangle shape to hold the text. What appears to be the alignment box for the text is actually the alignment box of the rectangle.

3. Begin typing.

4. Select the **Pointer** tool when finished typing.

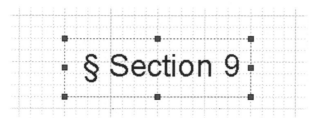

*This text was produced by using the keyboard shortcut **Ctrl+Shift+6**, and then typing **Section 9**.*

5. Resize and position the text block by dragging on the handles.

6. By default, the text is 8pt Arial font, and is centered horizontally and vertically relative to the alignment box. Format the text, as described in Module 14.

 Note: Visio lets you include special characters in the text. These characters are ones that you cannot normally type at the keyboard:

Special Character		Keystroke
'	(beginning single-quote)	Ctrl+[
'	(ending single-quote)	Ctrl+]
"	(beginning double quote)	Ctrl+Shift+[
"	(ending double quote)	Ctrl+Shift+]
•	(bullet)	Ctrl+Shift+8
–	(en dash)	Ctrl+=
—	(em dash)	Ctrl+Shift+=
-	(discretionary hyphen)	Ctrl+hyphen
-	(nonbreaking hyphen)	Ctrl+Shift+hyphen
/	(nonbreaking slash)	Ctrl+Shift+/
\	(nonbreaking backslash)	Ctrl+Shift+\
§	(section)	Ctrl+Shift+6
¶	(paragraph)	Ctrl+Shift+7
©	(copyright)	Ctrl+Shift+C
®	(registered trademark)	Ctrl+Shift+R

A *discretionary hyphen* shows Visio where to hyphenate a word, if necessary, such as *dis-cretionary*; the hyphen is normally invisible. A *nonbreaking hyphen* tells Visio not to hyphenate the word at the hyphen, such as "on-line." The *nonbreaking slash* is useful for fractions, such as "11/32." See Appendix A for a list of all keyboard shortcuts, including command shortcuts.

●━ᴥ **Tip:** You can place text in the drawing from any other Windows appli-
cation. Copy the text to the Clipboard (using **Ctrl+C**), then switch to
Visio. Press **Ctrl+V** (you don't need to select the Text tool first) and
Visio places the text in the center of the drawing.

If the text was formatted in the other application, Visio faithfully
mimics the formatting, including font, size, bolding, and so on. If you
don't want the text formatting copied, follow these steps:

▶ Select **Edit | Paste Special** from the menu bar.

▶ Select **Unformatted Text** from the Paste Special dialog box.

▶ Click **OK**.

For more information on using the Clipboard with Visio, see Module 12
"Cutting, Copying, and Pasting."

Inserting a Text Field

Use the following procedure to insert a text field:

1. Select a shape.

2. Select **Insert | Field**. Notice the Field dialog box.

*The Field
dialog box
allows you to
select and
format fields.*

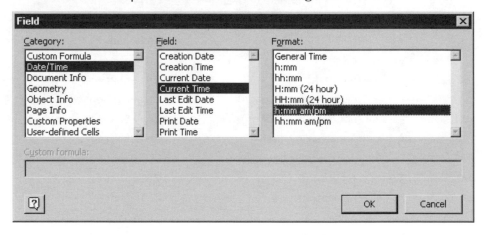

3. Select a **Category**:

   Custom Formula: Allows you to enter a formula that would be valid in a
   ShapeSheet cell.

   Date/Time: Displays the current date and time, or the date and time the drawing was created, last edited, or most recently printed. The date and time are
   based on your computer's clock.

   Document Info: Displays the data stored in the Properties dialog box (**File |
   Properties**), such as title, author, and keywords.

Geometry: Displays the height, width, and rotation angle of the shape.

Object Info: Displays the data recorded by the Special dialog box (**Format | Special**), and stored in the ShapeSheet.

Page Info: Displays the page number, number of pages, and name of the background shape.

Custom Properties: Displays the shape's custom property data as defined by the Custom Properties dialog box (**Shape | Custom Properties**).

User-defined Cells: Displays the data stored in the shape's Value cell of the User-defined Cells section of the ShapeSheet.

4. Select an item in the **Field** column. The variety of fields available differs, depending on the category selected. In some cases, such as Custom Properties and User-defined Cells, the Field column is blank until you define those items.

5. Select an item in the **Format** column. The formats available vary, depending on the field selected.

6. Click **OK**. Notice that Visio adds the field to the shape.

The current date in mm/dd/yy format.

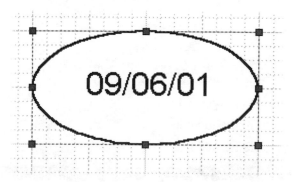

 Note: Visio allows you to insert some text fields without needing to access the Field dialog box. Use the following keystrokes to insert these fields as you type:

Text Field Functions	Keystroke
Rotation angle of text	Ctrl+Shift+A
Height of text	Ctrl+Shift+H
Width of text	Ctrl+Shift+W

Hands-On Activity

In this activity, you use the text and field functions together. Begin by starting Visio. Then open any template.

1. Select the **Text** tool.

2. Click anywhere on the page.

3. Type **This drawing was created on:**.

Typing text in the drawing with the Text tool.

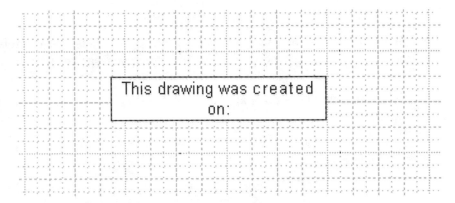

4. Select **Insert | Field**. Notice the Field dialog box.

5. Select **Date/Time** from the Category list.

6. Select **Creation Date** from the Field list.

7. Select **Long Date** from the Format list.

Selecting the long format for the creation date.

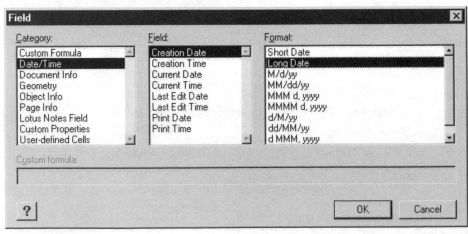

8. Click **OK**. Notice the date text placed in the drawing. (The date displayed in your drawing depends on the date you perform this task.)

The text together with date field.

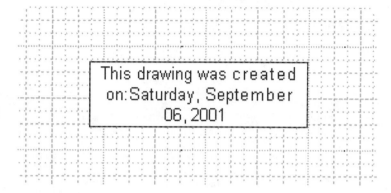

Creating a Dimension Line

One useful application of text and fields is geometry that mimics the dimension lines used in CAD (computer-aided design) drawings. You can have the dimension display the length or the angle of the line.

1. Click the **Line** tool.
2. Draw a line at any angle on the lower half of the page.
3. Select **Insert | Field**, ensuring that the line is still selected.
4. Select **Geometry** from the Category list.
5. Select **Angle** from the Field list.
6. Select **Degrees** from the Format list.

Selecting degrees for the angle field.

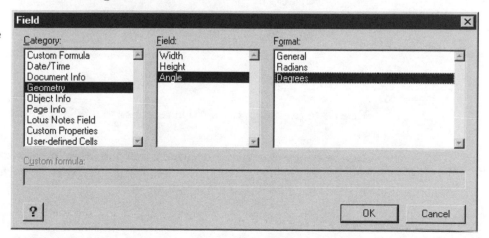

7. Click **OK** to close the Field dialog box.

8. If necessary, zoom in to better read the text. Notice the text "27.65 deg." (The text displayed in your drawing may differ from the illustration below, depending on the angle at which you drew the line.)

The line reports its rotation angle, just like a dimension line.

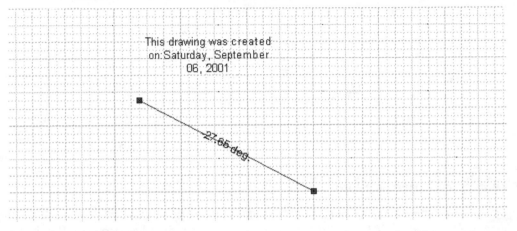

9. Click the **Pointer** tool.

10. Move an endpoint of the line to change its angle. Notice that the text automatically updates itself (to "6.84 deg." in my drawing).

When rotated, the line updates its rotation angle.

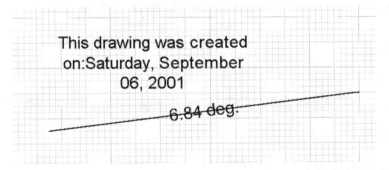

11. Press **Alt+F4** to exit Visio. Click **No** in response to the Save Changes dialog box.

This completes the hands-on activity for placing text and inserting fields. While text is important for annotating the drawing, the field feature is a very powerful way to display information that automatically updates itself.

Spelling

Tools | Spelling

Uses

> **In this chapter you'll learn about:**
>
> ✓ **Spell checking**

The **Spelling** function, found on the
Tools menu, is used to check the
spelling of words in the current drawing. You can have Visio check the spelling of
words in the entire drawing, on a specific page, or of selected text. You may add
words to the Visio dictionary, such as trademarked names, personal names, and
words particular to your discipline.

 Caution: The spell checker does not check correct word usage.
Instead, it looks for words it does not recognize (i.e., words it does not
find in its lengthy word list). The speller has no way of knowing whether
a correctly spelled word is used incorrectly, such as using "weather"
instead of "whether."

Procedures

Before presenting the general procedures for spelling, it is helpful to know about the
shortcut keys. These are:

Function	Keys	Menu	Toolbar Icon
Spell Check	F7	Tools | Spelling	✓

Spell Checking

Use the following procedure to check the spelling of all words in the current page:

1. Select **Tools | Spelling**.
2. When Visio finds a word it does not recognize, it displays the Spelling dialog box.

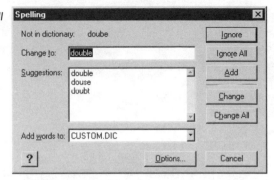

When the spell checker doesn't recognize a word, it displays this dialog box.

3. Click **Ignore** to have the speller skip the word; click **Ignore All** to ignore every instance of this word.

4. Click **Change** to select the word the speller guesses might be correct; click **Change All** to change all instances of the word.

5. Click **Add** to add the word to the speller's word list.

6. Click **Options** to display the Options dialog box.

The Options dialog box for the spell checker.

7. In the **Search** section, select if you want selected text checked, all text on the current page, or all text of all pages.

    The **Check spelling as you type** option finds spelling errors as you enter text in the diagram.

    The **Ignore words with numbers** option does not spell check words containing a number, which are often dimensions and angles.

    The **Custom dictionary** section lets you maintain different custom dictionaries for different disciplines. Click **Add** to select a dictionary.

8. Click **OK**.

9. Click **OK** in the Visio dialog box when the spell check is complete.

The spell checking process is complete.

Hands-On Activity

In this activity, you use the spell checking function. Begin by starting Visio. Then open any template.

1. Select the **Text** tool.

2. Type the following sentences:

   How to save Visio dramings.
   A tutorial by R. H. Grabowski.

   Notice the spelling error "dramings" and the uncommon surname "Grabowski."

A sentence with a deliberate spelling error and an uncommon surname.

How to save Visio dramings.
A tutorial by R. H. Grabowski.

3. Select **Tools | Spelling** or press function key **F7**. Notice the Spelling dialog box shows "dramings" is not in its dictionary.

4. Click **Change**.

5. Notice that the Spelling dialog box now shows that "Grabowski" is not in its dictionary. Click **Add** to add the word to the Custom.Dic dictionary file. Visio gives no indication it has done so.

6. Visio displays a dialog box to indicate the spelling check is complete. Click **OK**. Notice that the spelling is correct in the drawing.

*The misspelling
is corrected.*

How to save Visio drawings.
A tutorial by R. H. Grabowski.

7. Press **Alt+F4** to exit Visio. Click **No** in response to the Save Changes dialog box.

This completes the hands-on activity for spell checking text.

Module 26 | *Finding and Replacing Text*

Edit | Find, Replace

Uses

> **In this chapter you'll learn about:**
>
> ✓ **Finding text**
>
> ✓ **Replacing text**

The **Find** and **Replace** selections of the **Edit** menu are used to find and replace text in the current drawing. You can have Visio search:

▶ The selected text block

▶ The entire page

▶ All pages of the current drawing

Visio's find function finds *all* instances of a word or phrase, which the human eye easily misses. This is particularly useful when your drawing spans several pages.

Another example is when another company buys yours, and you have to change the name in all your drawings. Or, perhaps you have a standard set of drawings that you provide to a variety of clients; the replace function lets you change all instances of the client name. (It would be an embarrassment to have the client's name wrong.)

With Visio 2002, you can use the find and replace functions on text stored in custom properties, shape names, and user-defined cells.

Procedures

Before presenting the general procedures for finding and replacing text, it is helpful to know about the shortcut keys. These are:

Function	Keys	Menu	Toolbar Icon
Find	Ctrl+F	Edit | Find	...
Replace	...	Edit | Replace	...
Repeat	F4	Edit | Repeat	...

Finding Text

Use the following procedure to find text:

1. Select **Edit | Find** to display the Find dialog box.

The Find dialog box finds text in the drawing.

2. Type the word or phrase to find in the **Find what** text box.

3. Click **Special** to insert a special character.

Click Special to display the list of characters that cannot be typed.

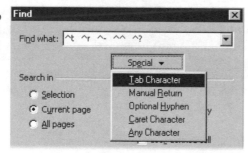

 Note: Visio lets you search for some special characters that cannot be typed at the keyboard. For example, you cannot press the **Tab** key to search for tabs in text (pressing **Tab** take you to the next field in the dialog box). For this reason, Visio provides a list box to insert special characters. Or, you can type these special characters:

Special Character	Meaning
^t	Tab
^r	Return (end of paragraph)
^-	Discretionary hyphen
0^^	Caret (^) symbol
^?	Any character

A *discretionary hyphen* shows Visio where to hyphenate a word, if necessary, such as *hy-phenate*; the hyphen is normally invisible.

4. The **Search in** section lets you choose where to search for the phrase:

    Selection: The currently selected text.

    Current page: The currently visible page (the default).

    All pages: All pages of the drawing.

    You can also select one or more of the following:

    Shape text: Always on, since all text in a drawing is in a shape.

    Custom property: Data stored in custom properties.

    Shape name: The name of the shape itself.

    User-defined cell: Data stored in user-defined ShapeSheet cells.

5. Click **Match case** to find a phrase that matches the same pattern of upper- and lowercase characters. When turned off (the default), the case is not matched. Searching for "visio" finds "Visio," "VISIO," and "visio." When on, the case is matched; searching for "visio" finds "visio" but not "VISIO" or "Visio."

6. Click **Find whole words only** to find a phrase that matches the same set of words. Searching for "visio" finds "Visio" but not "vision." When turned off (the default), the exact wording is not matched. Searching for "visio" finds "Visio" and "vision."

7. The **Match character width** option is meant for the Japanese Kanji version of Visio.

8. Click **Find Next** to find the next occurrence of the word or phrase.

9. When you are done finding words, click the **Cancel** button. When Find or Replace can't find or replace any more text, the Cancel button becomes the Close button.

Tip: If you are not sure of the spelling, or want to search for variants of a word (such as Tool and Tools), use the ^? *wildcard* character. The ^? searches for any single character. In this example, you would ask Visio to search for tool ^?.

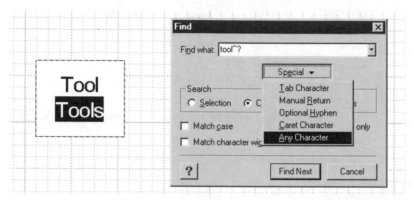

The ^? wildcard character matches any single character.

Replacing Text

The procedure for replacing text is similar to that of finding text:

1. Select **Edit | Replace**.

The Replace dialog box.

2. Type the word or phrase to find in the **Find what** text box.
3. Type the replacement word or phrase in the **Replace with** text box.
4. Click **Special** to insert a special character, as described earlier.
5. Click **Replace** to replace the next occurrence of the word or phrase.
6. Or, click **Replace All** to replace all occurrences of the word.

7. When you are done replacing words, click the **Cancel** or **Close** button.

Hands-On Activity

In this activity, you use the find function. Begin by starting Visio.

1. From the menu bar, select **File | New**, then select **Browse Sample Drawings**.

2. From the Organization Chart folder, double-click on the **Organization Chart.Vsd** drawing. Notice that this is a two-page drawing, showing an organization chart. You want to find "Laura Jennings" but are not sure where she is in the company structure.

3. Select **Edit | Find**. Notice the Find dialog box.

4. In the **Find what** text box, type **Laura Jennings**.

5. Click the **All Pages** button in the Search in area to search all pages of this drawing.

Searching for Laura Jennings.

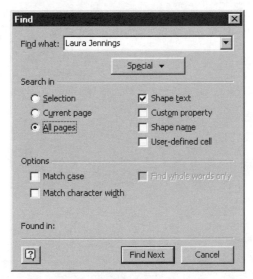

6. Click **Find Next**. Notice that Visio takes you directly to the page with Laura Jennings' name, and highlights the text block.

Found her!

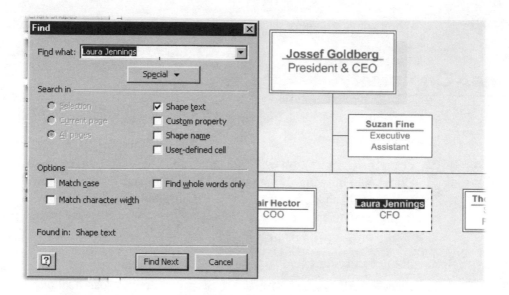

7. Click **Cancel** to close the Find dialog box.

This completes the hands-on activity for finding text in a drawing.

Module 27 *Dimensioning*

Uses

Architects and engineers use dimensions to indicate the exact measurement of distances and angles. Specifying the distance with a label is much more accurate than measuring the paper with a ruler. Dimensions are usually used in building plans, which indicate distances, such as the length of a wall or the width of a door.

> **In this chapter you'll learn about:**
> ✓ **Automatically dimensioning a wall shape**
> ✓ **Manually dimensioning any shape**
> ✓ **Changing the dimension line**
> ✓ **Changing the extension line**
> ✓ **Changing the dimension text**

Visio 2002 comes with many dimension shapes for placing dimensions that measure horizontal, vertical, and radial distances.

Examples of a horizontal dimension (at left) and a vertical dimension (center).

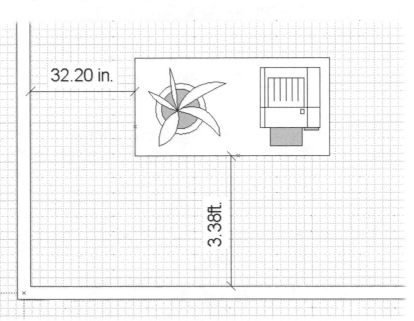

Most dimension shapes measures linear distances, such as the horizontal distance between two points or the vertical distance between two points. The dimension is made up of five parts:

The parts of a dimension. At left is the default dimension, as drawn by Visio; at right is a dimension that has been modified by the author.

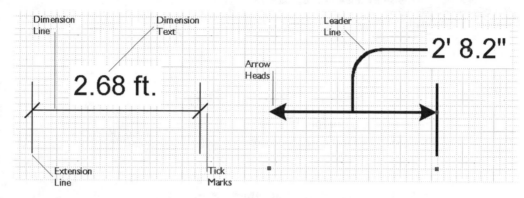

Dimension line shows the distance being measured. You may change the color and line weight of the dimension line; changing it to another line pattern is not usually done in dimensioning.

Dimension text explicitly states the distance. You can choose from Visio's many different dimension formats, such as imperial and metric units, and a varied number of decimal places. The text can be placed anywhere relative to the dimension line.

Leader line matches the dimension text to the dimension, in cases where the text is not right next to the line.

Arrowheads (look like tick marks and called *line ends* by Visio) indicate the ends of the dimension line. Visio has dozens of line ends available, plus you can define your own line end.

Extension lines extend from the dimension line down to the points being measured. These lines can be any length you desire, including zero length. In some cases, it is not uncommon to have just one extension line. As with dimension lines, you may change the color and line weight of the extension line; changing it to another line pattern is not usually done in dimensioning.

The dimension has five control points that affect the look of the dimension. The control handles change the length of the extension lines, the length and angle of the dimension line, and the position of the text. You learn more about using these control points later in this module.

The control points allow you to change the size and alignment of the dimension.

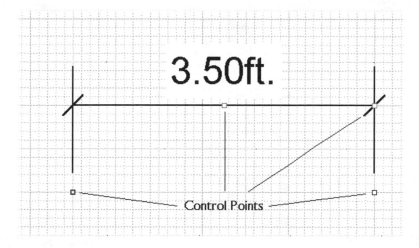

Procedures

The dimensioning "function" is not found on any menu or toolbar, nor are there are any shortcut keys for dimensioning in Visio. For best results, start with the **Office Layout** template (choose the **Building Plan** folder, and then the **Office Layout** drawing type; then click **OK**). You can create dimensions by using two methods:

Automatic dimensioning: Right-click a wall shape, and select **Add a Dimension** from the shortcut menu.

Manual dimensioning: Drag the a dimension shape into the drawing, and attach it to the shape(s) being dimensioned.

Automatically Dimensioning a Wall Shape

1. With Visio already running, from the menu bar select **File | New | Building Plan | Office Layout**. Notice that Visio opens a new drawing and several stencils.

2. Drag the **Wall** shape into the drawing. Notice that the shape looks like a long, narrow rectangle.

3. Right-click the wall shape. Notice the shortcut menu.

4. From the shortcut menu, select **Add a Dimension**. Notice that Visio immediately adds a horizontal dimension.

Select Add a Dimension to automatically dimension a wall shape.

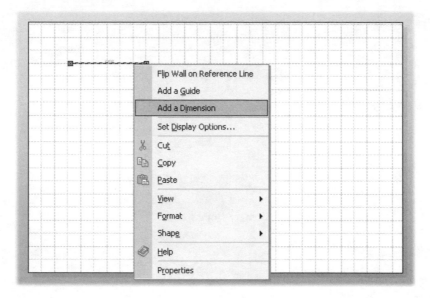

Tip: When a drawing contains many wall shapes, you can dimension them all at one time. Select all walls (hold down the **Shift** key while selecting them). Right-click one of the walls, and select **Add a Dimension**. Visio places a dimension on all walls you selected.

Manually Dimensioning Any Shape

1. With Visio already running, from the menu bar select **File | New | Building Plan | Office Layout**. Notice that Visio opens a new drawing and layout-related stencils.

2. Click the **Cubicles** stencil to activate it, and then drag the **Panel** shape into the drawing.

3. Click the **Walls, Doors and Windows** stencil to activate it, and then drag the **Controller Dimension** shape into the drawing.

4. Attach an end of the dimension line to one end of the **Panel** shape. When you let go of the mouse button, notice that you see the dimension line at an angle.

5. Drag the free end of the dimension line to the other end of the panel. Notice that the dimension text updates itself to reflect the length of the dimension line.

Attaching the Dimension Line shape to another shape.

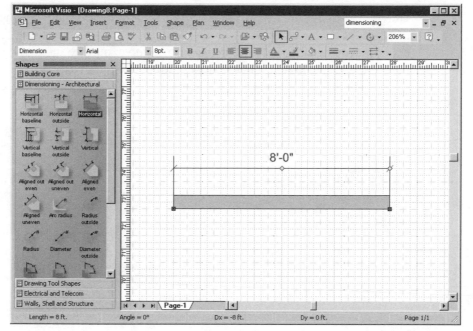

🔑 **Tip:** You can create your own dimension lines. Recall from Module 24 "Placing Text and Fields" that you can insert a field in a shape that automatically updates as the shape changes. Here's how to create a custom dimension shape:

1. Draw a line with the Line tool.
2. Use **Format | Line** to add arrowheads at both ends.
3. Use **Insert | Field** to attach a **Geometry | Width | General Units** field to the line. (Substitute **Height** for vertical dimensions and **Angle** for angular dimensions.)
4. Use **Format | Text** to make the font a legible size.
5. Once the dimension line looks good to you, use **Format | Define Styles** to create text and line styles for the named dimension.

As an alternative, you can take the dimension shape provided with Visio and format it. See Module 13 "Formatting Shapes."

Changing the Dimension Line

To change the angle and length of the dimension line, move either of two control handles located at the base of the extension lines. (The following notes do not apply to one specific dimension called the Controller Dimension, which updates automatically when the attached shape is stretched.)

1. Drag a control handle back and forth, horizontally, to lengthen and shorten the dimension. Notice that the dimension text updates itself. When the dimension becomes too small, first the dimension lines move outside the extension lines; then the dimension text moves outside the extension lines.

2. Rotate the dimension to make the dimension vertical or at an angle. Notice that the text rights itself when the dimension goes upside down.

Two control handles determine the angle and length of the dimension line.

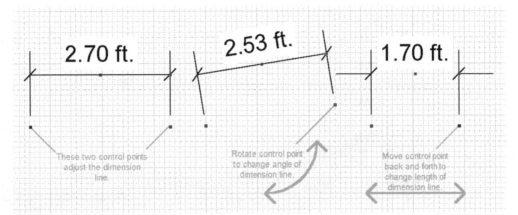

Changing the Extension Line

To change the length of both extension lines, move the single control handle located at the end of the dimension line. An option on the shortcut menu allows you to select additional options for extension lines.

1. Drag the control handle up and down to change the length of the extension lines.

2. When you drag the control handle to the other side of the shape, the dimension relocates to that side.

One control handle determines the length of both extension lines.

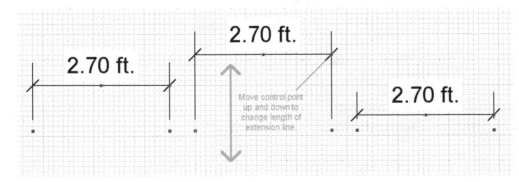

3. Right-click the dimension and select **Extension Lines** from the shortcut menu. Notice that Visio displays the Custom Properties dialog box.

 Caution: Do *not* select the **Define** button of the Custom Properties dialog box, unless you are familiar with ShapeSheet programming. Unintentional changes to parameters in the Define Custom Properties dialog may ruin the look of your fine drawing.

4. From the dialog box, you can select whether you want both, neither, end only, or begin only extension line displayed.

This dialog box determines which extension lines are displayed.

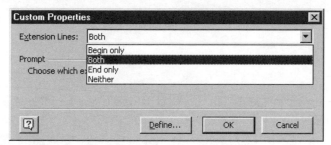

5. Make a selection and click **OK**. One or both extension lines may disappear, depending on which option you selected.

Changing the Dimension Text

To change the position of the dimension text, move the control handle located in the center of the text. Options on the shortcut menu allow you to set additional options for dimension text.

1. Drag the control handle around to move the location of the dimension text.

2. When you drag the text far away from the dimension line, notice the leader line that appears as shown in the illustration on the following page. The *leader* line shows which dimension the text belongs to.

3. Right-click the dimension, and select **Reset Text Position** from the shortcut menu. Notice that Visio moves the dimension text to its original position over the dimension line.

One control handle determines the position of the dimension text.

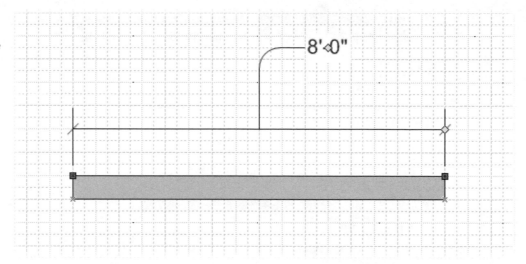

4. To rotate the dimension text, use the **Text Block** tool. (The Reset Text Position option does not apply to the angle of the text.)

5. To change the display format of the text, right-click the dimension and select **Precision & Units** from the shortcut menu. (The *display format* is the format that Visio displays the text in; it does not affect the measured accuracy of the dimension.) Notice that Visio displays a Custom Properties dialog box.

This dialog box controls the display format of the dimension text.

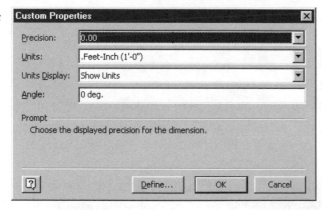

▶ **Precision:** Determines the number of decimal places displayed by the dimension text. Select from 0 through 4 decimal places. For example, selecting 0 precision means that a dimension 2.85 long is displayed as 3.

▶ **Units:** Determines the units in which the dimension text is displayed. You can select from Use Drawing Page's Units or one of nine other imperial and metric units. Selecting a metric unit automatically converts the dimension's value. For example, selecting cm units means that a dimension 1 unit long is displayed as 2.54.

▶ **Units Display:** Toggles between turning the display of dimension text on and off.

▶ **Angle:** Rotates the dimension line and text.

6. Once you have made changes to the dimension's display format, you can make that the style for all dimensions on the page. Right-click the dimension, and select **Set as Page Default** from the shortcut menu.

Rotating the angle of the dimension.

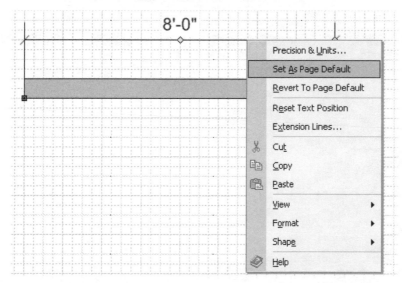

Notice that the text of all other dimensions changes to match the one you modified. In addition, when you now drag dimension shapes into the page, their text resembles the one that you modified.

7. If you accidentally "over modify" some dimension text, you can quickly return it to the default settings of the page. Right-click the dimension, and select **Revert to Page Default** from the shortcut menu.

Hands-On Activity

In this activity, you use the dimensioning functions.

1. Start Visio.

2. Select **File | New**, then select **Building Plan** and **Office Layout**.

3. Click **OK**. Notice that Visio opens a new drawing and the office layout stencils. The page has been set up for floorplan designs. Its orientation is landscape, and its scale is 1/2"=1' (i.e., each half-inch on the page represents one foot in the real world).

The new drawing with the office layout stencils.

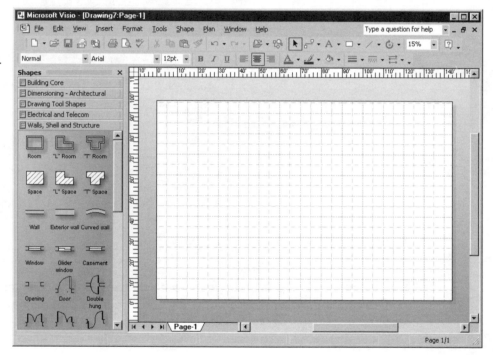

4. From the **Walls, Shell and Structure** stencil, drag the **Wall** shape onto the page. Notice the gray text that reports the length of the wall. This text appears only when the wall is selected.

5. Drag three more **Wall** shapes onto the page, connecting them together to create a square room. To make a wall shape vertical, drag the free end around until it connects with another wall end. Notice that Visio automatically *miters* (or joins) the ends of the walls, so that it looks like one continuous, four-sided wall shape.

Four wall shapes dragged onto the page, forming a square room.

Length indicator.

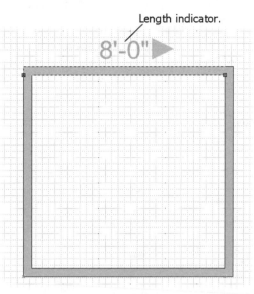

8'-0"

6. Here you automatically dimension a wall. Select a horizontal wall. Right-click and select **Add a Dimension** from the shortcut menu. Notice that Visio automatically places a horizontal dimension along the wall.

To automatically dimension a wall object, right-click and select Add a Dimension.

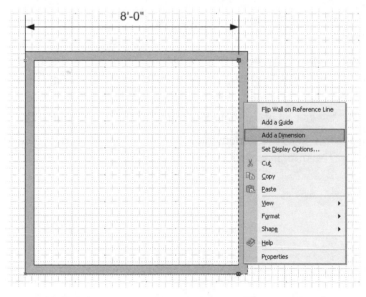

8'-0"

Flip Wall on Reference Line
Add a Guide
Add a Dimension
Set Display Options...
Cut
Copy
Paste
View ▶
Format ▶
Shape ▶
Help
Properties

Tip: Dimensions should always, if possible, be located outside the walls of a room. If the dimension appears on the "wrong" side (inside the room), use the control handle on the extension line to drag the dimension to the other side of the wall.

7. In this step, you automatically dimension two walls at the same time. Hold down the **Shift** key and select a vertical wall and the remaining horizontal wall. Right-click and select **Add a Dimension** from the shortcut menu. Notice that Visio automatically places dimensions along both walls.

Automatically dimensioning two wall objects at the same time.

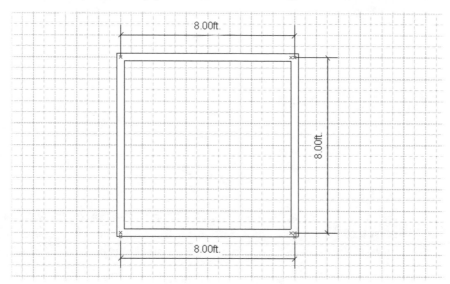

8. In the final steps of this activity, you manually dimension the remaining vertical wall. From the **Dimensioning - Architectural** stencil, drag the **Vertical Dimension** shape onto the page.

9. Attach the lower end of the dimension line to the lower end of the vertical wall.

10. Drag the free end of the dimension line to the upper end of the vertical wall. Notice that the dimension clicks into place.

To manually dimension an object, attach the Dimension Line shape to the object.

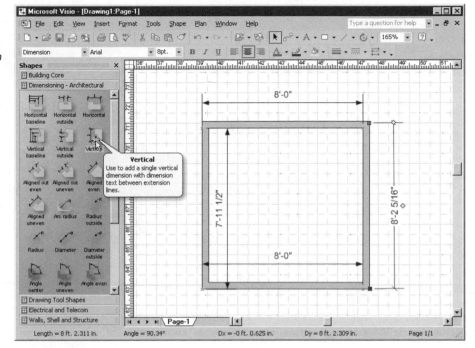

11. Press **Alt+F4** to exit Visio. Click **No** in response to the Save Changes dialog box.

This completes the hands-on activity for dimensioning.

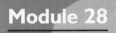

Module 28 *Inserting Objects*

Insert | Object
Crop Tool

In this chapter you'll learn about:

✓ **Inserting a picture**

✓ **Using the Crop tool**

✓ **Inserting a new object**

✓ **Inserting an object from a file**

✓ **Placing a linked object**

✓ **Editing an object within Visio**

Uses

The insert functions, found on the **Insert** menu, are used to insert objects created by other Windows applications. From the Insert menu, Visio 2002 inserts specific kinds of objects — VBA controls, CAD drawings, Microsoft clip art, Microsoft charts, images from a file, raster images from scanners and digital cameras — as well as objects from any other application.

In general, you only view the inserted object (technically, Visio displays a raster or metafile image of the object). Visio allows you to perform limited editing on inserted objects, such as moving, copying, and cropping. While Visio cannot change the contents of the object, Visio can apply formatting to its frame, such as adding a shadow.

To edit the inserted object, you double-click the object and Visio launches the originating application, which then allows you to edit the object. You usually see the originating application's menu bar (and perhaps some toolbars) replace the Visio menus.

The options of the **Insert** menu item, as they relate to this chapter, are:

▶ **Insert | Control:** Inserts a VBA control. *VBA* is short for Visual Basic for Applications, which is not covered in this book.

▶ **Insert | Picture | Clip Art:** Inserts clip art from the Microsoft collection (not covered in this book).

▶ **Insert | Picture | Chart:** Inserts a chart created by Microsoft Chart (not covered in this book).

▶ **Insert | Picture | Data Map:** Inserts a map created by Microsoft MapPoint software (not covered in this book).

▶ **Insert | Picture | Equation:** Inserts an equation created by Microsoft's equation editor (not covered in this book).

▶ **Insert | Object:** Inserts an object from any OLE-aware Windows application installed on your computer, including Paintbrush, PowerPoint, WordPad, Netscape Navigator, Excel, Media Clip, and AutoCAD.

▶ **Insert | Picture | From Scanner or Camera:** Uses the industry-standard TWAIN interface to directly import raster images from a scanner, digital camera, or similar input device.

▶ **Insert | CAD Drawing:** Inserts a drawing created by a CAD (computer-aided design) program. (See Module 37 "Importing CAD Drawings" for details.) Visio 2002 supports:

File Extension	*Application File Format Notes*
DGN	File format created by Bentley Systems' MicroStation CAD software; short for "design."
DXF	The file format invented by Autodesk for accessing data stored in its proprietary DWG format, and often used for exchanging drawings among CAD programs; short for "drawing interchange format."
DWG	The file format created by several CAD packages, including AutoCAD, IntelliCAD, and VDraft; short for "drawing."

▶ **Insert | Picture | From File:** Inserts a picture in any of these file formats:

File Extension	*Application File Format Notes*
AI	File format created by Adobe Illustrator, a vector-based drawing program.
BMP	The Windows standard raster format; short for "bitmap."
CDR	CorelDraw v3, 4, 5 is a popular Bezier-based drawing program; short for "Corel drawing."
CGM	A file format that mixes vector and raster; short for "computer graphics metafile."
CMX	The file format of clip art included with the CorelDraw package.
DIB	The "devic- independent bitmat" variant of the Windows bitmap file format.
DRW	File format created by Micrografx Designer v3.1; short for "drawing."
DSF	The Micrografx Designer v6 (now called iGrafx) format, a diagramming product similar to Visio; short for "designer format."

EMF	The Windows 95/98 standard format for mixed raster and vector illustrations; short for "enhanced metafile."
EMZ	Compressed enhanced metafile.
EPS	A mixed raster-vector file format designed for PostScript-compatible printers, and understood by some software programs; short for "encapsulated PostScript."
GIF	The most common raster format used on the Internet for smaller images due to its high level of loss-less compression (invented by CompuServe); short for "graphic interchange format."
IGS	A constantly shifting vector file format designed by a committee of CAD (computer-aided design) software companies, and meant for exchanging drawings between CAD systems (now largely superceded by STEP/PDES); short for "initial graphics exchange specification."
JPG	Another popular format for displaying raster images on the Internet for larger images due to its very high levels of compression; also known as JPEG format, and short for "Joint Photographic Experts Group."
PCT	The image file format standard on Macintosh computers; short for "picture."
PCX	One of the earliest raster formats for personal computers, invented by ZSoft for its PC Paint software; short for "personal computer raster."
PNG	For a time, the GIF format became less popular due to royalty issues over its compression engine; the "portable network graphics" format was created as an alternative royalty-free, high-compression raster file format for use on the Internet.
PS	A vector file format designed for PostScript-compatible printers, and understood by some software programs; short for "PostScript."
TIF	The most-popular raster file format for desktop publishing, and invented by Microsoft and Adobe; short for "tagged image file format."
WMF	This Windows 3.x standard for mixed raster and vector illustrations was based on CGM; short for "Windows metafile."

Note: You can import additional file formats using the **File | Open** command. (See Module 3 "Opening Existing Drawings.") If a vector-based graphic appears jagged after being inserted in Visio, it may appear smoother by importing it with the **File | Open** command. Visio documentation notes that this may occur with files created by Adobe

Illustrator (AI), CorelDraw (CDR), encapsulated PostScript (EPS), and Micrografx Designer (DRW).

Using one of the Insert commands on a "foreign" file differs from using the Open command:

Open Command	Insert Command
Translates the file into Visio format	Keeps the object in its original format
Displays the translated object	Displays a raster or metafile image of the object
Slower	Faster
Cannot be linked	Can be linked back to source application
Editable by Visio	Not editable by Visio; edited by the source application with the result seen in Visio

When you insert an object, you can instruct Visio to maintain a link back to the original file. Whenever that file is updated, the image in Visio is also updated.

Procedures

Before presenting the general procedures for inserting objects, it is helpful to know about the menu keystrokes. These are:

Function	Keys	Menu	Toolbar Icon
Insert picture	Alt+IP	Insert | Picture	…
Insert OLE object	Alt+IO	Insert | Object	…
Insert VBA control	Alt+IC	Insert | Control	🔧
Insert CAD drawing	Alt+ID	Insert | CAD Drawing	…
Insert clip art	Alt+IPC	Insert | Picture | Clip Art	…
Insert chart	Alt+IPH	Insert | Picture | Chart	…
Insert digital image	Alt+IPS	Insert | Picture | From Scanner or Camera	…
Crop object	…	…	🔲

Inserting a Picture

Use the following procedure to insert a picture file into the Visio drawing:

1. Select **Insert | Picture | From File**. Notice that Visio displays the Insert Picture dialog box.

The Insert Picture dialog box.

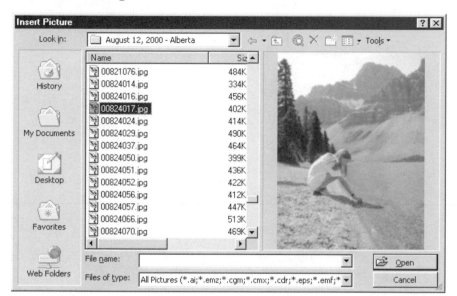

2. Select the drive and folder that contains the picture you want to insert. Notice that the dialog box provides a preview of the picture you select.

3. Click **Open**.

4. Depending on the file type selected, Visio may display an Import dialog box, which displays options specific to the file type. If required, change the type of Color Translation:

Color Translation	Meaning
Normal	Keep colors the way they appear in the file.
Inverse	Invert all colors, giving you a negative image.
Inverse Grays Only	Invert only black, white, and gray colors.
Gray Scale	Convert all colors to shades of gray.
Inverse Gray Scale	Convert all color to shades of gray, then invert them.

  ▶ If required, change the **Retain Background** option. When turned on, Visio draws a background rectangle in the image's background color.

  ▶ If required, set up the **Emulate Line Styles**. When turned on, Visio translates thick lines into polygons to help preserve visual accuracy.

5. Click **OK**. Notice that Visio places the picture in the center of the drawing, with green handles. You can move and resize the picture object, just like a Visio shape.

The picture is placed in the center of the Visio page.

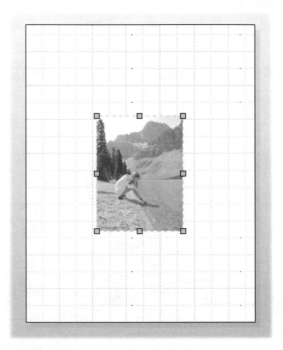

Using the Crop Tool

Use the following procedure to crop a picture in the Visio drawing:

1. Select the picture object. Notice that Visio places handles around the picture.

2. Click the **Crop** tool button; the tool may be "hidden" in the Rotation tool flyout.

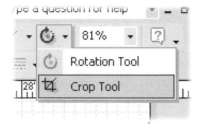

3. Move the cursor over any of the handles. Notice that the cursor changes to a double-headed arrow.

4. Drag the handle inward to crop the picture.

The Crop tool "cuts off" a portion of the picture.

5. Let go of the mouse button; Visio displays the smaller image. You can crop a picture object wider or narrower. When cropping wider, you don't see any more than what was present in the original image. The wider crop does, however, affect the placement of fill and shadow.

6. While the Crop tool is active, you may grab the center of the image and move it around.

Inserting a New Object

Use the following procedure to insert a new object:

1. Select **Insert | Object**. Notice that Visio displays the Insert Object dialog box.

The Insert Object dialog box in Create New mode.

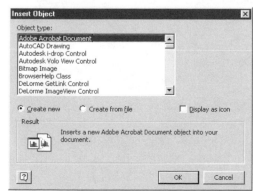

2. Click the **Create new** radio button. Notice the list of software names in the Object type list box.

3. Select a software program name from the Object type list box.

4. Click **OK**. Notice that Windows launches the application within Visio.

5. You can now create the new document within the application.

6. The method of exiting the application and returning to Visio varies. In some cases, select **File | Exit & Return to filename.vsd** when you are ready to return to Visio with the object. In other cases, simply pressing the **Esc** key works.

7. Notice the object is placed in the center of the Visio page.

Placing a Linked Object

One problem with placing an object in Visio is that, after a period of time, it may no longer be up to date. For this reason, Visio allows you to insert a *linked* object. Whenever the source application makes a change to the original file, the object in Visio is also updated. Use the following procedure to insert a linked object:

1. Select **Insert | Object**. Notice that Visio displays the Insert Object dialog box.

2. Click the **Create from file** radio button.

3. Type the name of the file; if you do not know it, click the **Browse** button to find it.

4. Click the **Link to file** check box.

The Insert Object dialog box in Create from File mode, with the Link to File option turned on.

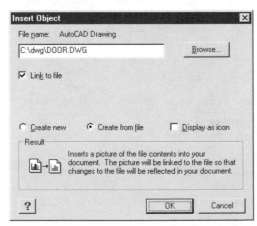

5. Click **OK**. Notice that Windows launches the application (called the *source* application) with the file you specified. At the same time, the file appears in Visio, centered in the drawing.

6. A linked object looks no different from an unlinked object. To check if the object is linked:

    ▶ Right-click the object.

    ▶ Notice the words "Linked Object" on the shortcut menu.

    Although the menu may read **Link Drawing Object | Convert**, the option *cannot* convert drawing objects to Visio shapes; see the following section for the workaround solution.

7. You may exit the source application. Notice the object remains in Visio.

Editing an Object Within Visio

It is possible to edit an inserted object in Visio, once the object has been converted to Visio format. (Although the Convert option appears to be available on the object's shortcut menu, it does not work.) The workaround described here works for vector pictures, not bitmap or raster pictures.

1. Select the object.

2. Right-click the object. Notice the shortcut menu.

3. From the shortcut menu, select **Shape | Ungroup**. Notice that Visio displays the Convert To Group dialog box during the conversion process. Despite the name of the dialog box, Visio is *not* converting the object to a group; rather the object is converted to lines and arcs.

The Convert To Group dialog box would be better named "Ungroup Object."

 Note: If the picture is complex, it may take several minutes to ungroup the object. During the ungrouping process, Visio converts each vector (line or arc) to the nearest equivalent Visio object. The link (if any) back to the source application is lost. All lineweights change to the thinnest value.

4. The converted picture now consists of hundreds, or even thousands, of line and arc segments. I recommend that you group together this collection. Press **Ctrl+A** to select all shapes in the drawing, then press **Ctrl+G** to group the shapes together. (See Module 17 "Creating Groups.")

Collecting the shapes into a group.

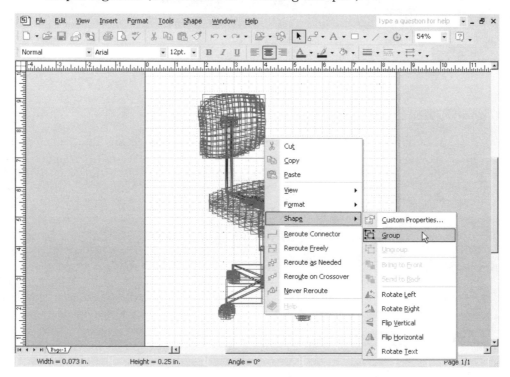

 # Exporting Drawings

File | Save As

Uses

The export function, found on the Save As dialog box accessed from the **File** menu, converts the Visio drawing into other file formats. Visio drawings need to be converted since no other software program reads Visio files. You can export the current Visio page or selected shapes; you cannot export more than one page at a time (with the exception of exporting a multi-page Visio drawing in HTML format).

> **In this chapter you'll learn about:**
>
> ✓ **Export options**
> ✓ **Exporting to AI and EPS**
> ✓ **Exporting to BMP and DIB**
> ✓ **Exporting to CGM**
> ✓ **Exporting to GIF**
> ✓ **Exporting to IGS**
> ✓ **Exporting to JPG**
> ✓ **Exporting to PCX**
> ✓ **Exporting to PICT**
> ✓ **Exporting to PNG**
> ✓ **Exporting to TIF**

 Caution: When Visio saves the drawing in another file format, it translates the drawing. This can have significant implications, since translations are never perfect.

▶ When saving in a raster format, all Visio shapes are lost; indeed, when you see the raster image, it looks like a "grainy" photograph (the raster portion of the illustration has been exaggerated to show the effect).

▶ When saving in a vector format or metafile format, shapes are usually saved as a similar object. For example, a line in Visio becomes a line in the other format; in some cases, however, there may be no exact match — or any match at all. For example, Visio almost exclusively uses the elliptical arc; older versions of AutoCAD, for example, have no native elliptical arc. In these cases, data may be changed or missing altogether.

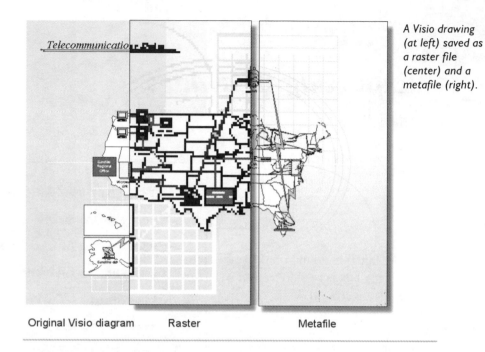

A Visio drawing
(at left) saved as
a raster file
(center) and a
metafile (right).

Original Visio diagram   Raster   Metafile

When you select File | Save As, Visio displays the Save As dialog box. In the Save as type list, you can select from the following file formats:

The Save As dialog box's supported file types.

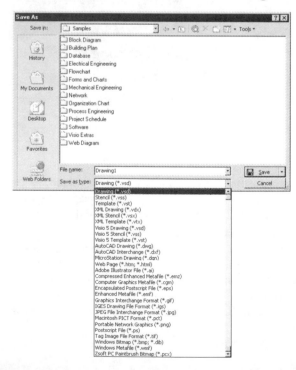

Save File As	Extension	Notes
Visio Formats		
Visio 5 Drawing	VSD	Older version of Visio
Visio 5 Stencil	VSS	Older version of Visio
Visio 5 Template	VST	Older version of Visio
Vector Formats		
Adobe Illustrator	AI	Also saves in EPS format.
AutoCAD Drawing	DWG	Created by AutoCAD, IntelliCAD, and other CAD (computer-aided design) systems.
AutoCAD Interchange	DXF	Drawing interchange format; used to access the data stored in DWG files and to exchange drawing files between CAD programs.
MicroStation Drawing	DGN	Created by Bentley Systems' MicroStation.
IGES Drawing File Format	IGS	Short for "initial graphics exchange specification"; used to exchange drawing files between CAD programs; superceded by the PDES/STEP format.
PostScript File	PS	Commonly used in desktop publishing; designed to be a printer language.
Metafile Formats		
Computer Graphics Metafile	CGM	Saves in many flavors of CGM.
* Compressed Enhanced Metafile	EMZ	Compressed version of EMF.
Encapsulated PostScript File	EPS	Commonly used in desktop publishing; also saves in AI format.
Enhanced Metafile	EMF	Standard for vector files in Windows 95/98; improves on WMF format.
Macintosh PICT Format	PCT	Picture format standard on Macintosh computers.
Windows Metafile	WMF	Standard for vector files in Windows 3.x; based on CGM format.
* XML Drawing	VDX	XML version of Visio diagram.
* XML Stencil	VSX	XML version of Visio stencil file.
* XML Template	VTX	XML version of Visio template file.
Raster Formats		
⌐ Graphics Interchange Format	GIF	Commonly used for small images on Web sites; lossless compression.
⌐ JPEG File Interchange Format	JPG	Commonly used for large images on Web sites; lossy compression.
ZSoft PC Paintbrush Bitmap	PCX	The first commonly used raster file format.
⌐ Portable Network Graphics	PNG	Designed to replace GIF on Web pages.
Tag Image File Format	TIF	Commonly used for desktop publishing.

Save File As	Extension	Notes
Windows Bitmap	BMP, DIB	Standard for raster files in Windows; suffers from lack of compression.

Notes:

 Indicates the format is suitable for use on the Internet. Two vector formats meant for Web use were dropped by Visio 2002: Autodesk's DWF (drawing Web format) and Microsoft's VML (vector markup language).

* Indicates format new to Visio 2002.

Exporting in DWF and HTML formats is described in Module 35.

Importing AutoCAD DWG and DXF files is described in Module 37.

> **Tip:** When you have a choice of file formats and options, in general it is better to:
>
> ▶ Use a vector format since Visio is a vector format. Raster formats lose "resolution," which is a measure of accuracy.
>
> ▶ Use compression to reduce the file size of raster formats. Compression reduces the size of the file without losing any data.
>
> ▶ Not use compression when the receiving software cannot read it or when the format does not have the option.

Procedures

Before presenting the general procedures for exporting Visio files, it is helpful to know about the shortcut key. It is:

Function	Keys	Menu	Toolbar Icon
Export	F12	File | Save As	...

Export Options

Many output formats display a dialog box of options, called Output Filter Setup (VS*, V*X, EMF, DWG, DXF, EMZ, and WMF do not display the options). The content of this dialog box varies, depending on features supported by the file format and the translator. The following sections describe the options of the Output Filter Setup dialog boxes.

Some of the dialog boxes allow you to save the settings by name, called *profiles*. In this way you can have several settings. For example, you might want low-resolution color output for a Web graphic, but a high-resolution grayscale output for desktop publishing work. Profiles allow you to save settings by name, without needing to reselect the options.

With Visio open and a drawing loaded:

1. Select **File | Save As** from the menu bar. Notice the Save As dialog box.

2. In the **Save as type** list, select a file format such as AI.

3. Click **Save**. After a moment, Visio displays the Output Filter Setup dialog box specific to the file format you selected.

4. Select the options in the dialog box, then click **New**. Notice the New Profile Menu dialog box.

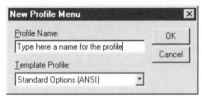

5. Type a name in the **Profile Name** text box. This name will appear in the Profiles list box the next time you see the Output Filter Setup dialog box.

6. Click **OK** twice. Notice that Visio's translator spends a few moments saving the drawing to disk in the translated format.

Exporting to AI and EPS

Convert the Visio drawing to AI (Adobe Illustrator) and EPS (Encapsulated Post-Script) formats:

The dialog box for exporting the drawing in AI or EPS format.

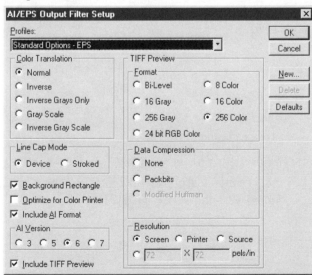

Color Translation:

▶ **Normal:** Keep the colors as they are in the Visio drawing.

▶ **Inverse:** Invert the colors (the picture looks like the strip of negatives from color film).

▶ **Inverse Grays Only:** Invert only white, black, and grays; keep other colors as they are.

▶ **Gray Scale:** Change the colors to levels of gray.

▶ **Inverse Gray Scale:** Change the colors to levels of gray and make a negative.

Line Cap Mode:

▶ **Device:** Use the line style and width capabilities of the display and printer driver.

▶ **Stroked:** Thick and patterned lines are drawn as polygons to more closely represent how they appear in the Visio drawing.

Other Options:

▶ **Background Rectangle:** Places a rectangle around the drawing as a border.

▶ **Optimize for Color Printer:** Optimized export format for color printers.

▶ **Include AI Format:** Include data for Adobe Illustrator format.

▶ **AI Version:** Select from version 3, 5, 6, or 7.

▶ **Include TIFF Preview:** Includes a small raster image for use within desktop publishing software, which cannot display AI and EPS formats.

TIFF Preview:

▶ **Bilevel:** Reduce the image to black and white; creates a smaller file size.

▶ **16 Gray:** 16 shades of gray.

▶ **256 Gray:** 256 shades of gray.

▶ **8 Color:** 8 colors.

▶ **16 Color:** 16 colors.

▶ **256 Color:** 256 colors; the default.

▶ **24 Bit RGB Color:** 16.7 million colors.

Data Compression for the preview image:

▶ **None:** No compression creates a larger file but may be necessary for some applications that cannot read compressed TIFF files.

▶ **Packbits:** Best suited to black and white images.

▶ **Modified Huffman:** Best suited for gray images.

Resolution for the preview image:

▶ **Screen:** Use the screen resolution, typically 72 dpi (dots per inch) or 96 dpi.

▶ **Printer:** Use the printer's resolution, typically 300 dpi or 600 dpi; use this for the best quality hardcopy.

▶ **Source:** Let the destination application figure out the best resolution to use.

▶ **Custom:** Specify any resolution; default = 72 x 72 dpi. Visio recommends that the resolution range between 32 dpi and 400 dpi.

Exporting to BMP and DIB

Convert the Visio drawing to BMP (bitmap) or DIB (device-independent bitmap) raster file format using the following dialog box.

The dialog box for exporting the drawing in BMP or DIB format.

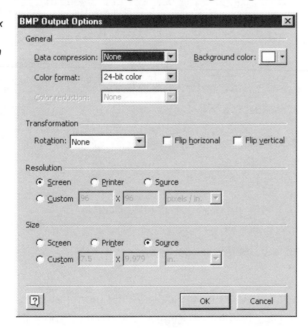

The Profiles and Color Translation features have been removed in Visio 2002.

General options:

▶ **Data compression:** Determines whether the BMP and DIB files will be compressed. While the file size is greatly reduced using RLE (short for "run length encoding"), most applications cannot read compressed BMP files. Therefore, leave the choice at None.

▶ **Color format:** Specifies the number of colors stored in the image:

Color Format	Number of Colors
24-bit color	16.7 million colors (full color)
16-bit color	65,536 colors
256 Color	256 colors
16 Colors	16 colors
Bi-level	2 colors (black and white)

Fewer colors results in a smaller file size, but may cause some colors to change.

▶ **Color reduction:** When you choose less than 24-bit color, you can have Visio "fake" fewer colors by one of several means. You may need to experiment with each setting to see which produces the best result for your diagram.

Visio's color reduction options.

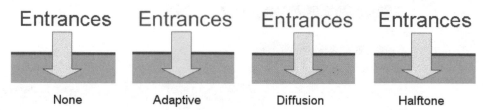

None   Adaptive   Diffusion   Halftone

▶ **Background color:** Normally white, but you can choose another color to be the underlying color.

Transformation options:

▶ **Rotation:** Rotate the image by 90 degrees left or right.

▶ **Flip horizontal:** Mirror the image.

▶ **Flip vertical:** Mirror the image upside-down.

Resolution:

▶ **Screen:** Use the screen resolution, typically 72 dpi (dots per inch) or 96 dpi.

▶ **Printer:** Use the printer's resolution, typically 300 dpi or 600 dpi; use this for the best quality hardcopy.

▶ **Source:** Let the destination application figure out the best resolution to use.

▶ **Custom:** Specify any resolution; default = 72 x 72 dpi. Visio recommends that the resolution range between 32 dpi and 400 dpi.

Size:

▶ **Screen:** Use the screen size as the image size.

▶ **Printer:** Use the printer's page size.

▶ **Source:** Let the destination application figure out the best size to use.

▶ **Custom:** Specify a size; default = 6.67 x 5 inches.

Exporting to CGM

Convert the Visio drawing to CGM (short for "computer graphics metafile") format:

The dialog box for exporting the drawing in CGM format.

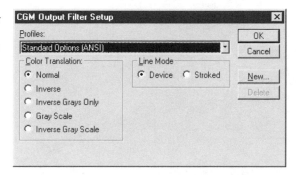

Color Translation format:

▶ **Normal:** Keep the colors as they are in the Visio drawing.

▶ **Inverse:** Invert the colors (the picture looks like the strip of negatives from color film).

▶ **Inverse Grays Only:** Invert only white, black, and grays; keep other colors as they are.

▶ **Gray Scale:** Change the colors to levels of gray.

▶ **Inverse Gray Scale:** Change the colors to levels of gray and make a negative.

Line Mode:

▶ **Device:** Use the line style and width capabilities of the display and printer driver.

▶ **Stroked:** Thick and patterned lines are drawn as polygons to more closely represent how they appear in the Visio drawing.

Exporting to GIF

Convert the Visio drawing to GIF (short for "graphics interchange format").

The Profiles and Color Translation features have been removed in Visio 2002.

General options:

▶ **Data format:** Interlace is useful for the Internet, since it shows parts of the image in the Web browser before the entire image has been delivered over the (relatively slow) telephone lines. Non-interlace means the entire image is displayed at once.

The dialog box for exporting the drawing in GIF format.

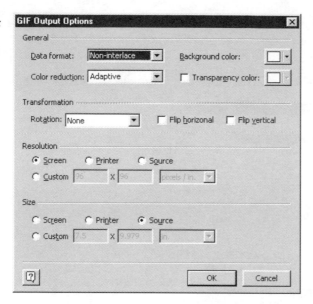

▶ **Color reduction:** GIF saves images in 256 colors, but a Visio diagram can contain as many as 16.7 million colors. This option allows you to experiment with each setting to see which produces the best result for your diagram.

▶ **Background color:** Allows you to specify a different background color for the image:

▶ **Transparency color:** Allows other images or text "underneath" the GIF image to show through the color selected as transparent.

Transformation options:

▶ **Rotation:** Rotate the image by 90 degrees left or right.

▶ **Flip horizontal:** Mirror the image.

▶ **Flip vertical:** Mirror the image upside-down.

Resolution and **Size:**

▶ **Screen:** Use the screen resolution, typically 72 dpi (dots per inch) or 96 dpi.

▶ **Printer:** Use the printer's resolution, typically 300 dpi or 600 dpi; use this for the best quality hardcopy.

▶ **Source:** Let the destination application figure out the best resolution to use.

▶ **Custom:** Specify any resolution; default = 72 x 72 dpi. Visio recommends that the resolution range between 32 dpi and 400 dpi.

Exporting to IGS

IGS is a file format commonly used by high-end CAD systems to exchange drawings. Typically, these CAD packages must translate the IGS file to their own format. Convert the Visio drawing to IGS (short for "initial graphics exchange specification"):

The dialog box for exporting the drawing in IGS format.

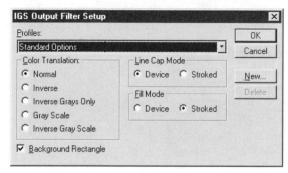

Color Translation format:

▶ **Normal:** Keep the colors as they are in the Visio drawing.

▶ **Inverse:** Invert the colors (the picture looks like the strip of negatives from color film).

▶ **Inverse Grays Only:** Invert only white, black, and shades of gray; keep other colors as they are.

▶ **Gray Scale:** Change the colors to levels of gray.

▶ **Inverse Gray Scale:** Change the colors to levels of gray and make a negative.

Background Rectangle:

▶ Draws a rectangle around the extents of the drawing.

Line Cap Mode:

▶ **Device:** Use the line style and width capabilities of the display and printer driver.

▶ **Stroked:** Thick and patterned lines are drawn as polygons to more closely represent how they appear in the Visio drawing.

Fill Mode:

▶ **Device:** Use the fill capabilities of the display and printer driver.

▶ **Stroked:** Filled areas are drawn as polygons to more closely represent how they appear in the Visio drawing.

Exporting to JPG

JPG is popular for very large images because it does a terrific job of compressing files. JPG can make the file size smaller than any other file format; the drawback is that it is a *lossy* compression, which means some of the image may be distorted due to the compression process. JPG (or JPEG) is short for "Joint Photographic Experts Group." Convert the Visio drawing to JPG format using the following dialog box:

The dialog box for exporting the drawing in JPG format.

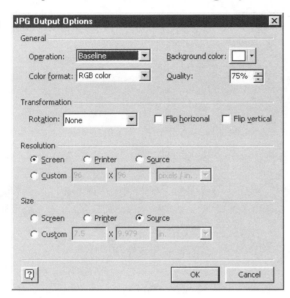

The profiles and Color Translation features have been removed in Visio 2002.

General options:

▷ **Operation:** Select from baseline or progressive (similar to non-interlace and interlace).

▷ **Color format:** Select from monochrome, YCC color, RGB (red, green, blue) color, or CMYK (cyan, magenta, yellow, black) color. Here are some examples of the color created by the RGB system:

R (Red)	G (Green)	B (Blue)	Meaning
0	0	0	Black
255	0	0	Red
0	255	0	Green
0	0	255	Blue
191	191	191	Medium Gray
255	255	255	White

The RBG method allows you to specify 16.7 million colors by varying the amount of red, green, and blue in 256 increments.

▶ **Background color:** Normally white, but you can choose another color to be the underlying color.

▶ **Quality:** The JPG term for "compression." The higher the quality (closer to 100%), the lower the compression but the larger the file size.

Transformation options:

▶ **Rotation:** Rotate the image by 90 degrees left or right.

▶ **Flip horizontal:** Mirror the image.

▶ **Flip vertical:** Mirror the image upside-down.

Resolution and **Size:**

▶ **Screen:** Use the screen resolution, typically 72 dpi (dots per inch) or 96 dpi.

▶ **Printer:** Use the printer's resolution, typically 300 dpi or 600 dpi; use this for the best quality hardcopy.

▶ **Source:** Let the destination application figure out the best resolution to use.

▶ **Custom:** Specify any resolution; default = 72 x 72 dpi. Visio recommends that the resolution range between 32 dpi and 400 dpi.

Exporting to PCX

Convert the Visio drawing to PC Paintbrush file format:

The dialog box for exporting the drawing in PCX format.

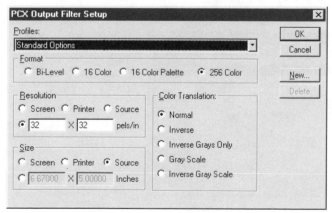

Format options:

▶ **Bi-Level:** Convert Visio drawing colors to black or white.

▶ **16 Color:** Reduce Visio drawing colors to 16 colors of the Windows standard.

▶ **16 Color Palette:** Reduce Visio drawing colors to 16 colors to the best approximation of the original.

▶ **256 Color:** Retain all Visio drawing colors.

Resolution and **Size:**

▶ **Screen:** Use the screen resolution, typically 72 dpi (dots per inch) or 96 dpi.

▶ **Printer:** Use the printer's resolution, typically 300 dpi or 600 dpi; use this for the best quality hardcopy.

▶ **Source:** Let the destination application figure out the best resolution to use.

▶ **Custom:** Specify any resolution; default = 72 x 72 dpi. Visio recommends that the resolution range between 32 dpi and 400 dpi.

Color Translation format:

▶ **Normal:** Keep the colors as they are in the Visio drawing.

▶ **Inverse:** Invert the colors (the picture looks like the strip of negatives from color film).

▶ **Inverse Grays Only:** Invert only white, black, and shades of gray; keep other colors as they are.

▶ **Gray Scale:** Change the colors to levels of gray.

▶ **Inverse Gray Scale:** Change the colors to levels of gray and make a negative.

Exporting to PICT

Convert the Visio drawing to Macintosh PICT (short for picture) file format:

The dialog box for exporting the drawing in PICT format.

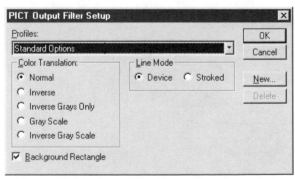

Color Translation format:

▶ **Normal:** Keep the colors as they are in the Visio drawing.

▶ **Inverse:** Invert the colors (the picture looks like the strip of negatives from color film).

- ▶ **Inverse Grays Only**: Invert only white, black, and shades of gray; keep other colors as they are.
- ▶ **Gray Scale**: Change the colors to levels of gray.
- ▶ **Inverse Gray Scale**: Change the colors to levels of gray and make a negative.

Background Rectangle draws a rectangle around the extents of the drawing.

Line Cap Mode:

- ▶ **Device**: Use the line style and width capabilities of the display and printer driver.
- ▶ **Stroked**: Thick and patterned lines are drawn as polygons to more closely represent how they appear in the Visio drawing.

Exporting to PNG

PNG was invented to replace GIF, which requires royalty payments under certain situations. Convert the Visio drawing to PNG (short for "portable network graphics") format using the following dialog box.

The dialog box for exporting the drawing in PNG format.

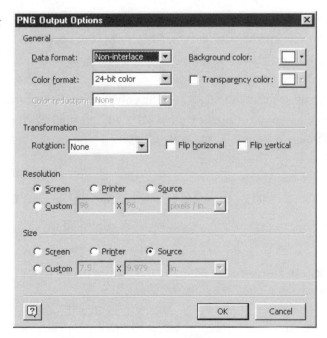

The Profiles and Color Translation features have been removed in Visio 2002.

General options:

▶ **Data format:** Interlace shows parts of the image before the entire image is loaded. Non-interlaced means the entire image is displayed at once.

▶ **Color format:** PNG can save images in as many as 16.7 million (full color) or as few as two (monochrome) colors.

▶ **Color reduction:** This option allows you to experiment with each setting to see which produces the best result for your diagram.

▶ **Background color:** Allows you to specify a different background color for the image:

▶ **Transparency color:** Allows other images or text "underneath" the GIF image to show through the color selected as transparent.

Transformation options:

▶ **Rotation:** Rotate the image by 90 degrees left or right.

▶ **Flip horizontal:** Mirror the image.

▶ **Flip vertical:** Mirror the image upside-down.

Resolution and **Size:**

▶ **Screen:** Use the screen resolution, typically 72 dpi (dots per inch) or 96 dpi.

▶ **Printer:** Use the printer's resolution, typically 300 dpi or 600 dpi; use this for the best quality hardcopy.

▶ **Source:** Let the destination application figure out the best resolution to use.

▶ **Custom:** Specify any resolution; default = 72 x 72 dpi. Visio recommends that the resolution range between 32 dpi and 400 dpi.

Exporting to TIF

Convert the Visio drawing to TIF (short for "tagged image file format").

The Profiles and Color Translation features have been removed in Visio 2002.

General options:

▶ **Data compression:** Determines whether the TIF is compressed. The file size is greatly reduced using compression, such as LZW.

▶ **Color format:** Specifies the number of colors stored in the image: 24-bit color, 16-bit color, 256 color, 16 colors, or bi-level. Fewer colors results in a smaller file size, but may cause some colors to change.

▶ **Color reduction:** When you choose less than 24-bit color, you can have Visio "fake" fewer colors by one of several means. You may need to experiment with each setting to see which produces the best result for your diagram.

The dialog box for exporting the drawing in TIF format.

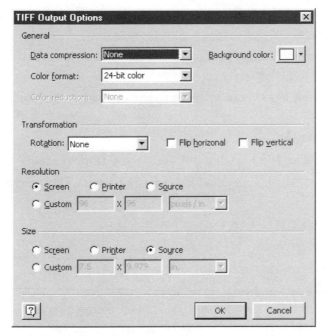

> **Background color:** Normally white, but you can choose from another color to be the underlying color.

Transformation options:

> **Rotation:** Rotate the image by 90 degrees left or right.
> **Flip horizontal:** Mirror the image.
> **Flip vertical:** Mirror the image upside-down.

Resolution:

> **Screen:** Use the screen resolution, typically 72 dpi (dots per inch) or 96 dpi.
> **Printer:** Use the printer's resolution, typically 300 dpi or 600 dpi; use this for the best quality hardcopy.
> **Source:** Let the destination application figure out the best resolution to use.
> **Custom:** Specify any resolution; default = 72 x 72 dpi. Visio recommends that the resolution range between 32 dpi and 400 dpi.

Size:

> **Screen:** Use the screen size as the image size.
> **Printer:** Use the printer's page size.
> **Source:** Let the destination application figure out the best size to use.
> **Custom:** Specify a size; default = 6.67 x 5 inches.

Hands-On Activity

In this activity, you use the export functions. Begin by starting Visio. Use **File | New | Browse existing files**.

1. Open the document **Perspective Block Diagram.Vsd** supplied in the **Block Diagram** folder.

2. Select **File | Save As**.

3. Click on the **Save as type** list box and select the **GIF** file format.

4. If necessary, type a filename in the **Filename** text box and select the destination subdirectory.

5. Click **Save**. Notice the GIF Output Options dialog box.

6. Select options, as necessary.

7. Click **OK**. Visio converts the drawing and saves it in GIF format.

8. Let's bring the exported Visio drawing in to a raster editor. Start Windows Paintbrush (or another raster editor) by double-clicking on its icon in the Windows desktop or from the Windows Start menu.

9. Select **File | Open** from the menu bar and open **Perspective Block Diagram.Gif**. Notice the raster version of the Visio drawing.

10. Press **Alt+F4** to exit Paintbrush.

11. Click on Visio and press **Alt+F4** to exit Visio. Click **No** in response to the Save Changes dialog box.

This completes the hands-on activity for exporting Visio drawings in other file formats.

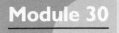 **Special Selections**

Edit | Select by Type

Uses

In this chapter you'll learn about:

✓ *Using Select by Type*

Usually, you click a shape to select it.

To select more than one shape, you hold down the **Shift** key while clicking the shapes. To select all shapes on the page, you press **Ctrl+A**. But what about the case when you don't want to select everything, yet need to select specific object types in the drawing? Or what about a situation in which you want to select all guidelines? The answer is the **Select by Type** selection of the **Edit** menu. It lets you select shapes on the basis of *what* they are, or by the name of the *layer* they reside on. You can choose shapes and objects in either of two categories: shapes and other objects in the drawing, or by layer name:

The Select by Type dialog box.

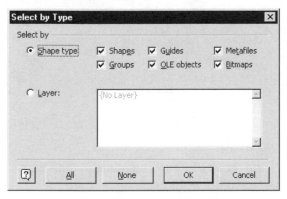

The **Shape Type** options are:

Shapes: Selects all shapes on the current page.

Groups: Selects all grouped objects on the page.

Guides: Selects all guidelines and guide points on the page.

OLE Objects: Selects all linked and embedded objects.

Metafiles: Selects all objects pasted in WMF format.

Bitmaps: Selects all objects pasted in BMP format.

All: Selects all shape types.

None: Selects no shape types.

The **Layer** options are:

Layer: Selects all objects assigned to a specific layer name; hold down **Ctrl** to select more than one layer.

All: Selects all layers.

None: Selects no layers.

This command was known as Select Special in Visio 2000 and earlier.

Procedures

Before presenting the general procedures for special selections it is helpful to know about the shortcut keys. These are:

Function	Keys	Menu	Toolbar Icon
Select	...	...	▸
Select by Type	Alt+EB	Edit | Select by Type	...
Select All	Ctrl+A	Edit | Select All	...

Using Select by Type

Use the following procedure to select objects:

1. Select **Edit | Select by Type**. Notice the Select by Type dialog box.

2. Choose **Shape Type** or **Layer**.

   ▸ Within the **Shape Type** area, select any combination of shapes, groups, guides, OLE objects, metafiles, or bitmaps.

   ▸ Or, within the **Layer** area, select a layer name from the list box.

3. Click **OK**. Notice that Visio highlights the objects that match your search criteria.

Hands-On Activity

In this activity, you use the special selection function. Begin by starting Visio and choosing **File | New | Browse existing file**.

1. Open the document **Basic Network Diagram.Vsd** found in the **Network** folder.

*The Basic
Network
Diagram
drawing.*

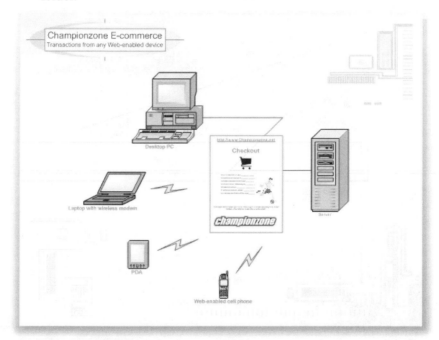

2. Select **Edit | Select by Type**. Notice the Select by Type dialog box.
3. Ensure the **Shape type** radio button is turned on (has a dot in the center).
4. Click **None** to turn off all options.
5. Click **Shapes** to turn on the option.

*The Select by
Type dialog box
is set up to
select just
shapes.*

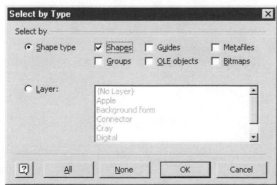

6. Click **OK**. Notice that the selected shapes are surrounded by handles. Some objects that appear to be shapes are not selected; these are groups.

Shapes are selected in this drawing.

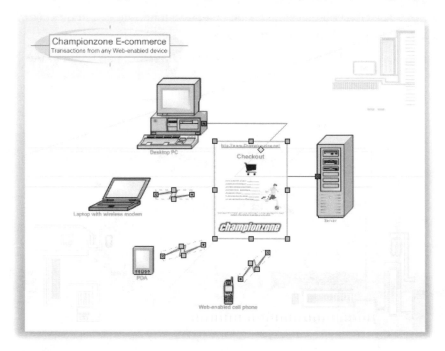

7. Select **Edit | Select by Type** again.

8. Click the **None** button to remove all selected options.

9. Click **Groups**.

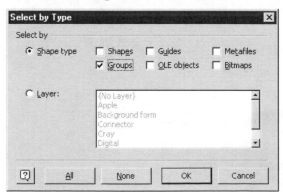

10. Click **OK**. Notice that this time the groups are selected and surrounded by handles.

All groups are selected in this drawing.

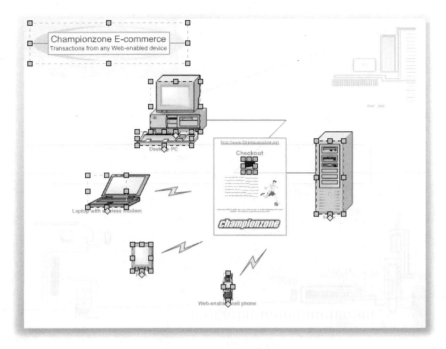

11. Click anywhere on the page to deselect the shapes.

12. Press **Alt+F4** to exit Visio. Click **No** in response to the Save Changes dialog box.

This completes the hands-on activity for special selections.

Drawing Explorer

View | Drawing Explorer

Uses

Visio provides you with three ways to view the drawing. One is the drawing page, which you have been working with all through this book. Another view is the underlying ShapeSheet, as discussed in detail in *Learn Microsoft Visio 2002 for the Advanced User* (also from Wordware Publishing). The third view is the Drawing Explorer.

The Drawing Explorer allows you to view the drawing hierarchically, in much the same manner as the File Explorer provided by Windows. Instead of showing you drives, folders, and files, though, the Visio Drawing Explorer shows you foreground and background pages, shapes, layers, styles, masters, fill patterns, line patterns, and line ends. You can add, delete, edit, and highlight objects in your drawing. As you do, the Drawing Explorer updates the drawing — and vice versa.

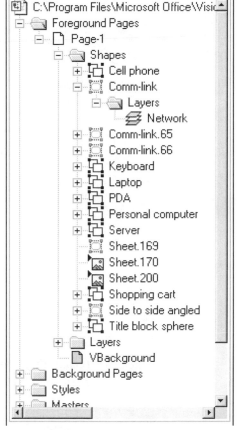

Drawing Explorer.

Procedures

Before presenting the general procedures for navigating the Drawing Explorer, it is helpful to know about the shortcut keys. These are:

Function	Keys	Menu	Toolbar Icon
Drawing Explorer	Alt+VD	View | Drawing Explorer	🔲
🗁 Rename	F2	...	...
🗁 Undo renaming	Esc	...	...

Note: 🗁 Indicates the function operates within Drawing Explorer only.

Navigating the Drawing Explorer

The Drawing Explorer presents a different interface to the Visio user.

The user interface of the Drawing Explorer.

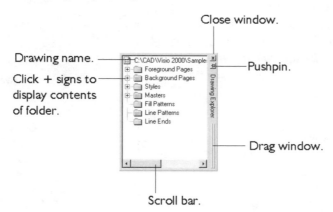

The Drawing Explorer window normally stays open. You can have it roll open and closed when the cursor passes over it. Click the pushpin (so that it no longer looks pressed down) to minimize the window.

The window is normally docked to the side of the Visio drawing area. Drag the window's title bar away to make the window float. When floating, double-click the title bar to re-dock the window.

Click the + (plus) sign to open a folder. When the folder is open, the + is replaced by a – (minus) sign; click the – sign to close the folder.

When the window is too small to display all its data, horizontal and vertical scroll bars appear. Click the scroll bars to see the data that isn't in view.

The Drawing Explorer window shows the content of each drawing, using the following hierarchical structure:

Drawing filename: The full pathnames of drawings currently open in Visio. Within each drawing are the following folders:

▶ **Foreground Pages** and **Background Pages**: The pages used in the drawing; every drawing has at least one foreground page. Within each page are the following folders:

▶ **Shapes**: The names of shapes on the page; when a "shape" is a group, then additional **Shapes** and **Layers** folders appear within it.

▶ **Layers**: The names of the layers on the page.

▶ **Styles**: The names of text styles, if any.

▶ **Masters**: The names of master shapes used in the drawing.

▶ **Fill patterns**: The names of fill pattern styles, if any.

▶ **Line patterns**: The names of line pattern styles, if any.

▶ **Line ends**: The names of line end styles, if any.

The Drawing Explorer has a multitude of shortcut menus associated with it. You can right-click any item in the window and get a context-specific shortcut menu. The following illustration shows a shortcut menu.

A shortcut menu in the Drawing Explorer.

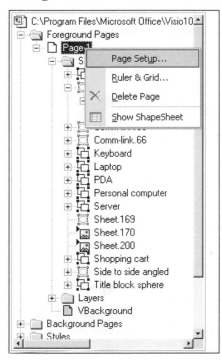

When an option on a shortcut menu has an ellipsis (…), this means the option displays a dialog box. For example, **Page Setup** displays the Page Setup dialog box.

Tip: When you move the cursor over a rollout window set to AutoHide, you can hear a sound as the window opens and closes. To add the sounds to Visio rollout windows, from the Windows taskbar, select **Start | Settings | Control Panel | Sounds**. In the Events | Windows list, select **Restore Up** or **Restore Down**. In the Sound area, select a WAV file from the **Name** list. Test the sound in the Preview area. Click **OK** to dismiss the dialog box.

When the sound becomes annoying, you can return to the Sounds Properties dialog box, and select **(None)** for the sound.

Hands-On Activity

In this activity, you use the Drawing Explorer. Begin by starting Visio.

1. In the Open dialog box, select **Block Diagram.Vsd**, which you can find in the Visio 2002\Samples\Block Diagram folder.

2. Open the Drawing Explorer:

The Block Diagram drawing with Drawing Explorer.

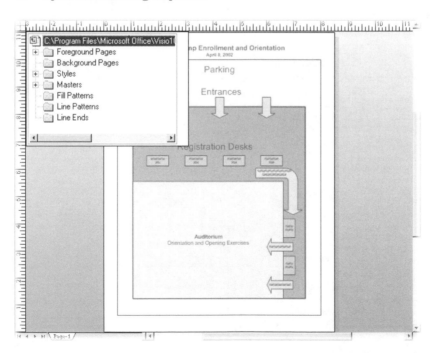

> ▷ If you do not see Drawing Explorer, select **View | Drawing Explorer Window** from the menu bar.

> ▷ If you see just the title bar of Drawing Explorer, it is "rolled up." Move your cursor over the title bar to "roll out" the window.

> ▷ To keep the Drawing Explorer window from rolling up, click the pushpin icon.

3. Open the **Foreground Pages** folder by clicking the + next to the folder. Notice that it contains a single page, called Page-1.

4. Open **Page-1**. Notice it contains a pair of folders called Shapes and Layers.

5. Open the **Shapes** folder. Notice it contains a long list of shape names, such as Box and Box.14.

6. Select the **Box** shape. Notice that a shape is highlighted in the drawing.

Selecting a shape in Drawing Explorer highlights the shape in the drawing.

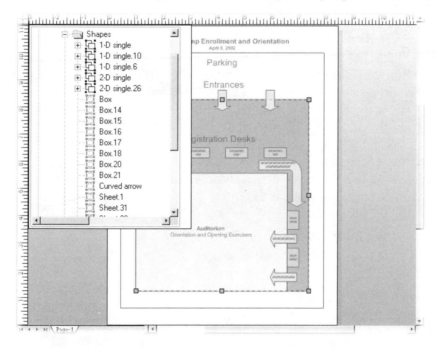

7. Notice the + next to **1-D single**. This indicates the "shape" is actually a group. Click the + to open the group. Notice that another Shapes folder appears

8. Click the + to see the name of the shapes, such as Sheet.5, in the group.

Right-clicking masters brings up a shortcut menu.

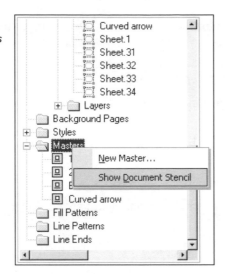

9. Scroll down the Drawing Explorer. Right-click **Masters**, and select **Show Document Stencil** from the shortcut menu. Notice that Visio opens a green stencil called Document Stencil. This stencil is special because it shows all the masters used by the drawing. (Recall that when you drag a shape into a page, the shape is a copy of the *master* stored in the stencil.)

10. Press **Alt+F4** to exit Visio. Click **No** in response to the Save Changes dialog box.

This completes the hands-on activity for using the Drawing Explorer.

Using the Drawing Explorer to display the masters used by the drawing.

Module 32 | Double-click Behavior

Format | Behavior | Double-Click

Uses

In this chapter you'll learn about:

✓ **Double-click tab options**

✓ **Assigning double-click action to a shape**

Many software programs perform an action when you double-click an object. For example, double-clicking in Word usually selects a word; double-clicking an icon on the Windows desktop opens the program or document. In Visio, double-clicking a Visio shape lets you edit the shape's text.

Other programs, however, usually don't let you change the double-click action. Visio does. You can choose from as many as ten options from the **Double-Click** tab of the Behavior dialog box.

The Double-Click tab governs the action of a double-click.

> **Behavior**
>
> Behavior Double-Click Placement
>
> When shape is double-clicked
> - ⦿ Perform default action
> - ○ Perform no action
> - ○ Edit shape's text
> - ○ Open group in new window
> - ○ Open shape's ShapeSheet
> - ○ Custom
> - ○ Display help: [   ]
> - ○ OLE verb:
> - ○ Run macro: [_organization Chart Wizard ▾]
> - ○ Go to page: [Page-1 ▾]
>   - ☐ Open in new window
>
> [?]   [OK]   [Cancel]

Tip: To double-click, press the left mouse button twice quickly. If nothing happens, it could be you are double-clicking too slowly — or too fast. Here's how to check your double-click speed: From the Windows taskbar, select **Start | Settings | Control Panel | Mouse**. In the **Buttons** tab, look for the option that allows you to adjust and test your double-click speed.

Testing your double-click speed (at left); defining the middle button as the double-click button (at right).

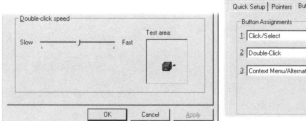
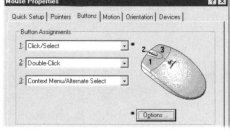

If you have a three-button mouse, you may find it useful to define the center button to execute a double-click. When reconfigured like this, you press the middle button once, but the computer interprets it as a double-click; I find this saves a lot of wear on my index finger! (If your computer's mouse does not include software for defining the function of buttons, you may be able to download such software from the mouse vendor's Web site.

The Double-Click tab's options are:

Perform default action:

▷ For a *shape*, allows editing of the shape's text block.

▷ For a *group*, opens the group in a new window.

▷ For an *OLE object*, launches the linked application.

Perform no action:

▷ Nothing happens when you double-click.

Edit shape's text:

▷ Goes into text editing mode.

▷ Applies to shapes only; other objects are ignored.

Open group in new window:

▷ Displays the group in an independent window for editing.

▷ Applies to groups only.

Open shape's ShapeSheet:

▶ Displays the numbers that control the look and size of the shape in a spreadsheet-like interface.

▶ This option is useful for developers who work with the ShapeSheet.

Custom:

▶ Performs a custom (user-defined) behavior.

▶ Available only when the object's ShapeSheet contains an action defined in the **EventDblClick** cell of the **Events** section.

Display help:

▶ Displays a topic from an HLP help file.

▶ The help filename and topic must be specified in the following formats: **filename.hlp!keyword** or **filename.hlp!#Number.**

Metaname	Meaning
filename.chm	Name of a Windows help file, such as Shape.Chm.
!keyword	Index term associated with the help topic, such as "Basic Shape."
!#number	Numeric ID referenced in the map section of the help project file.

OLE verb:

▶ Typically executes a command like Edit or Open.

▶ Applies to an inserted object only.

Run macro:

▶ Runs one of the macros installed with Visio.

▶ The name of the macro program can be selected from the list box.

▶ This option was called "Run Add-on" in previous versions of Visio.

Go to page:

▶ Switches to another page in the drawing.

▶ The name of the page can be selected from the drop-down list.

Open in new window:

▶ Opens the page, shape, group, OLE object, etc., in a new window.

▶ This option applies to some of the double-click options listed above.

Caution: The option of the **Double-Click** tab apply only to the shape you select. In fact, you cannot access the Double-Click tab unless you first select a shape. You cannot assign double-click behavior to a page.

Procedures

Use the following procedure to change the double-click action assigned to a shape:

1. Select the shape.
2. From the menu bar, select **Format | Behavior**.
3. In the **Behavior** dialog box, select the **Double-Click** tab.
3. Click an option from the **Double-Click** tab.
4. Click **OK**.
5. Double-click on the shape to test the action.

Hands-On Activity

In this activity, you use one of the double-click functions. Begin by starting Visio.

1. Open a new, blank drawing.
2. Open the **Symbols.Vss** stencil file from the **Visio Extras** folder.
3. Drag the **Coffee** shape into the drawing.

The Coffee shape from the Symbols stencil.

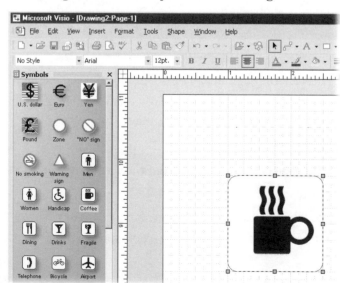

4. Double-click the Coffee shape. Notice that Visio switches to text mode; this is the shape's default action.

5. Select the Coffee shape to get out of text editing mode.

6. From the menu bar, select **Format | Behavior** and select the **Double-Click** tab. Notice that **Perform default action** is selected.

7. Select **Open group in new window.**

The Double-Click tab with the Open group in new window option selected.

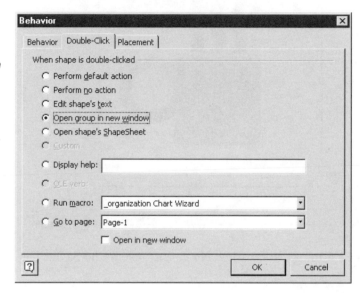

8. Click **OK.**

9. Double-click on the coffee cup. Notice that the group is displayed in a separate window.

The Double-Click tab with the Open group in new window option selected.

10. Press **Alt+F4** to exit Visio. Click **No** in response to the Save Changes dialog box.

This completes the hands-on activity for changing the double-click action assigned to a shape.

Module 33 *Behavior*

Format | Behavior, Special

In this chapter you'll learn about:

✓ **The Behavior dialog box**

✓ **The Placement tab**

✓ **The Special dialog box**

Uses

The **Behavior** and **Special** selections of the **Format** menu change how shapes and groups act and display. The Behavior dialog box controls the behavior of each shape; the Special dialog box displays basic information, and lets you attach data to the shape.

The Behavior Dialog Box

The Behavior dialog box controls the interaction, highlighting, resize, and group behaviors:

The Behavior tab of the Behavior dialog box.

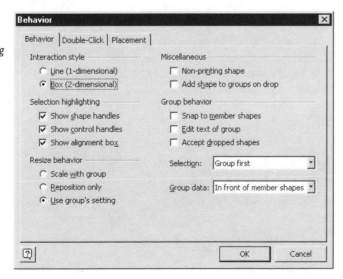

Interaction style: Visio treats lines as one-dimensional, while nearly all other shapes are treated as two-dimensional. By selecting **Line** for a 2D shape, you change how the shape reacts to resizing and rotation.

  ▶ **Line (1-dimensional):** Shape can stretch and move, but cannot be widened.

  ▶ **Box (2-dimensional):** Shape can also be widened.

Selection highlighting: Determines which of three indicators — shape handles, control handles, and alignment box — display when an object is selected, as the illustration below shows.

  ▶ **Show shape handles:** Displays handles when the shape is selected.

  ▶ **Show control handles:** Displays control handles.

  ▶ **Show alignment box:** Displays the alignment box.

Shape handles, control handles, and alignment box.

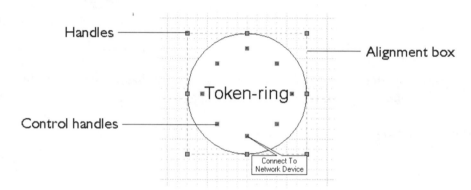

🔗 **Tips:** The control handles allow you to change specific aspects of a shape without affecting the shape overall. For example, in the door shape, one control handle changes the width of the door, while the other control handles changes the angle of the swing.

Control handles can be identified by their tooltips.

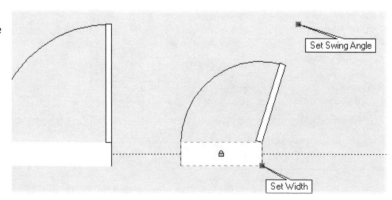

When the handle looks like a padlock, the shape cannot be resized.

Padlocks indicate the shape is locked.

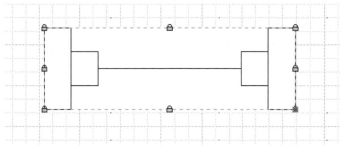

Resize behavior: These three settings affect a shape only when it is part of a group:

▶ **Scale with group**: The shape scales with the group.

▶ **Reposition only**: The shape can be moved but cannot be scaled.

▶ **Use group's setting**: The shape reacts the same way as the group.

Miscellaneous:

▶ **Non-printing shape**: The shape is not printed.

▶ **Add shape to groups on drop**: When a shape is dropped on a group, the shape is added to the group.

Group behavior: Controls the behavior of groups and their components.

▶ **Selection**: Specifies what happens when you select a group.

Group only specifies that individual shapes within the group cannot be selected.

Group first specifies that the first click selects the group; a second click selects the shape.

Members first specifies that individual shapes are selected; click the bounding box to select the group.

▶ **Group data**: Determines the group's display order of text and shapes created with drawing tools:

Hide hides the group's text and shapes, except for connection points and control handles.

Behind member shapes displays the group's components behind the drawing tool-created shapes.

In front of member shapes displays the group's components in front of the drawing tool-created shapes.

▶ **Snap to member shapes:** Determines whether shapes within the group can be snapped and glued to.

▶ **Edit text of group:** Determines whether group text can be edited.

▶ **Accept dropped shapes:** The group incorporates the shape dropped onto the group.

The Placement Tab

A shape becomes *placeable* when you glue a dynamic connector shape to it. Placeable shapes are detected by dynamic connectors, and are included in automatic layouts.

The Placement tab.

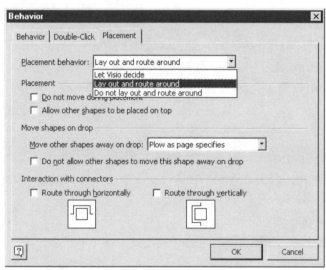

Placement behavior: Determines how the selected 2D shape interacts with dynamic connectors:

▶ **Let Visio decide:** The shape is placeable depending on the type of connector glued to the shape.

▶ **Layout and route around:** The 2D shape is always placeable.

▶ **Do not lay out and route around:** The 2D shape is never placeable.

Placement: Determines the behavior of the selected 2D shape during the Lay Out Shapes command.

▶ **Do not move during placement:** The shape does not move.

▶ **Allow other shapes to be placed on top:** Other shapes can be placed on top of the selected shape.

Move shapes on drop:

▷ **Move other shapes away on drop**: Determines whether other shapes *plow* (automatically move out of the way) when a shape is dropped in the drawing.

Plow as page specifies: Shapes move out of the way based on the page's setup.

Plow no shapes: Shapes do not move out of the way.

Plow every shape: All shapes move out of the way.

▷ **Do not allow other shapes to move this shape away on drop**: The selected shape does not move when another shape is dropped on the page, regardless of the setting of the Move other shapes away on drop option.

Interaction with connectors:

▷ **Route through horizontally**: Dynamic connectors are allowed to can go through the selected 2D shape horizontally.

▷ **Route through vertically**: Dynamic connectors are allowed to can go through the selected 2D shape vertically.

The Special Dialog Box

The Special dialog box displays some basic information about the shape and lets you attach data to the shape. The data fields, such as **Data 1,** contain a field, which can be inserted with the **Field** command (see Module 24 "Placing Text and Fields").

The Special dialog box.

ID specifies the number assigned by Visio to the shape; the first shape created in the drawing is 1, etc.

Master is the name of the shape's master; the name is displayed only if the shape is an instance of a master.

Type specifies the type of shape, such as group, etc.

Name specifies the shape's name up to 31 characters long.

Help specifies the help reference, in the format of *filename*.chm!*keyword* or *file-name*.chm!*#number*.

Copyright displays copyright information.

Data 1, **Data 2**, and **Data 3** allow you to enter up to 64KB of data for the shape.

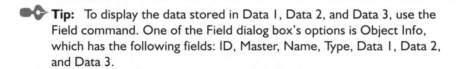 **Tip:** To display the data stored in Data 1, Data 2, and Data 3, use the Field command. One of the Field dialog box's options is Object Info, which has the following fields: ID, Master, Name, Type, Data 1, Data 2, and Data 3.

Hands-On Activity

In this activity, you use the behavior functions. Begin by starting Visio.

1. Open a new, blank drawing.

2. Open the **Basic Network Shapes.Vss** stencil file, which is found in the **Network** folder.

3. Drag the **Ethernet** shape into the drawing. Notice its handles (small green squares at the corners of the shape) and alignment box (green dashed rectangle surrounding the entire shape). The three "handles" on the word "Ethernet" are control handles.

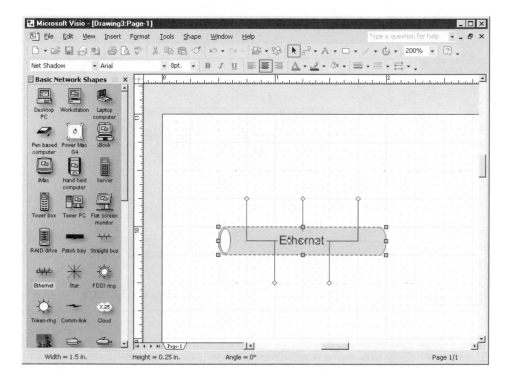

4. Select **Format | Behavior** from the menu bar. In the Behavior dialog box, ensure the **Behavior** tab is showing.

5. Turn off all three **Selection highlighting** options.

Turning off selection highlighting in the Behavior dialog box.

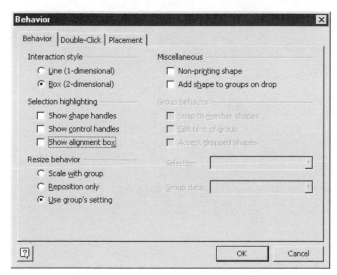

6. Click **OK**. Notice that the selection cues disappear from the shape.

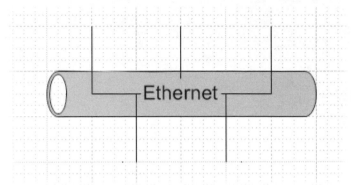

7. Press **Alt+F4** to exit Visio. Click **No** in response to the Save Changes dialog box.

This completes the hands-on activity for changing the behavior of shapes.

Module 34 | *Custom Properties*

Shape | Custom Properties
Tools | Report

Uses

In this chapter you'll learn about:

✓ **The Define Custom Properties dialog box**

✓ **Editing a shape's custom properties**

✓ **Adding a custom property**

✓ **Editing custom property fields**

✓ **Summarizing custom property data**

The **Custom Properties** selection of the **Shape** menu is used to edit the *custom* (defined by you) *properties* defined in the shape. These properties are not color or linetype; rather, they are data attached to a shape, such as its size, its model number, or its orientation. CAD software sometimes refers to properties as "attributes" or "tag data."

In Visio, custom properties sometimes already have values; other times, you need to fill in values or select values from a list. A custom property has three parts:

Label: The name of the property, such as "Cabinet Width."

Value: The value of the property, such as 33 inches.

Prompt: The message describing the property to the user, such as "Select a standard width from the list."

The three parts of a custom property.

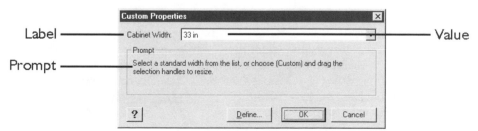

Custom properties are fully editable. The data itself is edited with the **Custom Properties** command; the data fields are edited with the **Custom Property Editor** command. New custom properties are created with **Define Custom Properties**.

Some custom properties, such as price or model number, do not affect the shape; other custom properties do. For example, the custom property of a door determines its swing. The Custom Properties dialog box can be made to limit the range of acceptable values. The custom property can also appear on the shape's shortcut menu.

The custom properties appear on the shortcut menu and in the dialog box.

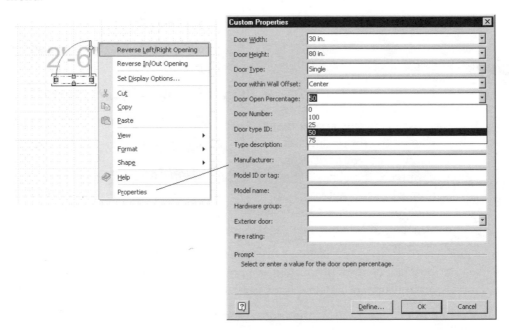

You summarize the information using the **Report** tool. (This replaces the Property Reporting Wizard, found in earlier releases of Visio.) These reports are excellent for counting shapes in a drawing, producing a bill of material, or creating an inventory report.

 Note: Most shapes do *not* have custom properties defined. When you use the Custom Properties command, older versions of Visio display a warning dialog box. Visio 2000 and 2002, on the other hand, ask if you would like to create custom properties for the shape.

This dialog box is displayed when the shape has no custom properties.

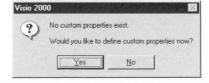

The Define Custom Properties Dialog Box

You use the Define Custom Properties dialog box to add custom properties to a shape. As mentioned previously, a custom property consists of just three parts: label, value, and prompt. The label and prompt are straightforward; the value is somewhat more involved.

When it comes to defining the value, Visio allows you to constrain acceptable responses. In a door shape, for example, you may want to limit the width to standard values, such as 24", 27", 30", 33", and 36". For this reason, there are three parameters to value: type, format, and initial value.

The upper half of the Define Custom Properties dialog box allows you to define five parameters (label, value type, value format, initial value, and prompt). The following illustration show how the areas of the dialog box relate to the Custom Property dialog box seen by the user.

The lower half summarizes the custom properties; recall that a shape can have more than one custom property.

The Define Custom Properties dialog box.

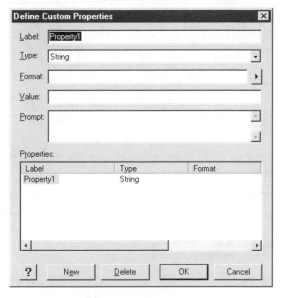

Label: Specifies the descriptive name for the custom property, such as "Cabinet Width" or "Model Number." The label appears next to where you enter the data.

Type: Specifies the type of data permitted for the custom property value; it can be up to 65,536 characters long.

The Type list box allows you to specify the data type.

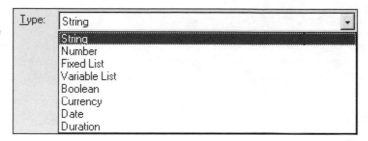

Type: String

- String
- Number
- Fixed List
- Variable List
- Boolean
- Currency
- Date
- Duration

▷ **String:** Accepts all input as text; text input by the user will be formatted according to the Format options (Normal, UPPERCASE, lowercase).

▷ **Number:** Expects a number, date, time, duration, currency, scalar, dimension, or angle; data input by the user will be formatted according to the Format options (General, General units, Whole number, Whole number with units, Floating point, Floating point with units, Fraction, Fraction with units).

▷ **Fixed List:** Displays a drop list from which the user can select a value specified by the **Format** field. The list of values are simply separated by semicolons. For example, the width of a door is limited to 24", 30", and 36". The Format section would be: **24 in.;30 in.;36 in.**

▷ **Variable List:** Displays a drop list from which the user can select a value (as specified by the Format field) or the user can type a value.

▷ **Boolean:** restricts the user to selecting either True or False.

▷ **Currency:** Accepts input as currency; data input by the user will be formatted according to the Format options (System settings, $x, $x.xx, x.xx dollar, x.xx USD).

▷ **Date:** Seconds, minutes, hours, days, months, and/or years; data input by the user will be formatted according to the Format options.

▷ **Duration:** Displays elapsed time; data input by the user will be formatted according to the Format options (Weeks, Days, Hours, Minutes, Seconds, HH:MM, MM:SS).

Format: Specifies the format of the value, as well as specific values.

▷ **String:** Formats the text as normal (upper- and lowercase as typed by the user), converted to all uppercase, or converted to all lowercase.

▷ **Number:** Formats the number as follows:

▷ **General:** Any number can be entered without units.

▷ **General Units:** Any number can be entered with units; if units are left out, the page's units are used.

▷ **Whole Number:** Numbers are rounded up to the nearest whole numbers; units are omitted.

▶ **Whole Number with Units:** (1 cm) The user can enter whole numbers followed by a unit (such as cm), but not fractions or decimals.

▶ **Floating Point Number:** (1.23) The user can enter whole numbers and decimal numbers, but not fractions.

▶ **Floating Point with Units:** (2.75 cm) The user can enter whole numbers and decimal numbers with units.

▶ **Fraction:** (15/16) The user can enter whole numbers and fractions, but not decimal numbers.

▶ **Fraction with Units:** (15/16 in.) The user can enter whole numbers and fractions followed by a unit (such as cm), but not decimal numbers.

▶ **Currency:** Formats the number entered by the user to one of the following: system settings, $x, $x.xx, x.xx dollar, or x.xx USD; the currency is specified by the Regional Settings set with Windows (to change, select **Start | Settings | Control Panel | Regional Settings | Currency** from the taskbar).

Date: Formats the number entered by the user to one of the following:

The formats available for dates.

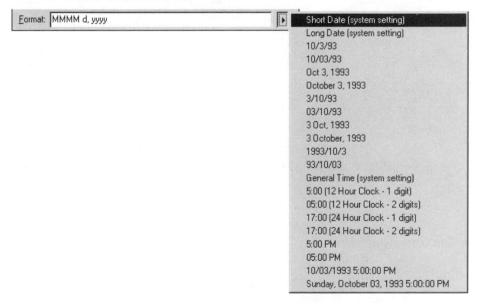

▶ **Duration:** Formats the number entered by the user to one of the following: Weeks, Days, Hours, Minutes, Seconds, HH:MM, or MM:SS.

Value: Specifies the initial (default) value; when the user enters a value in the Custom Properties dialog box, that value overwrites the default value.

Prompt: Specifies an instruction to the user for this custom property.

Properties: Displays a summary of custom property data for the shape.

> **Tip:** Developers can specify additional parameters for the custom property via its ShapeSheet. These include **SortKey** (specifies the order in which multiple custom properties appear), **Invisible** (hides the custom property from the user), and **Ask** (displays the Custom Properties dialog box when the shape is dragged onto the page).

Editing a Shape's Custom Properties

Use the following procedure to edit a shape's custom properties:

1. Select a shape. (Note that not all shapes contain custom properties.)

2. Select **Shape | Custom Properties**. Notice the Custom Properties dialog box.

Examples of Custom Properties dialog boxes.

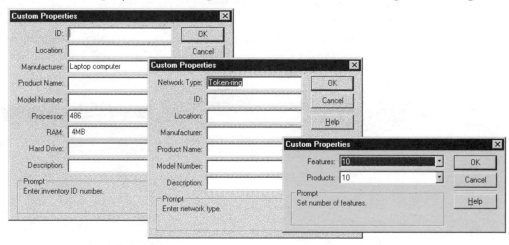

3. Add or change data in the text fields displayed by the Custom Properties dialog box.

4. Click **OK**.

Adding a Custom Property

Whether or not a shape already has custom properties, you can always add one more. Use the following procedure to add a custom property to a shape:

1. Select a shape.

2. Select **Shape | Custom Properties**.

   ▶ When the shape already has at least one custom property, notice that Visio displays the Custom Properties dialog box. Click **Define**.

   ▶ When the shape doesn't have any custom properties, notice that Visio displays a warning dialog box. Click **Yes**.

3. In either case, notice that Visio displays the Define Custom Properties dialog box.

    ▶ When the shape already has at least one custom property, notice that Visio displays data in the Define Custom Properties dialog box. Click **New**.

    ▶ When the shape doesn't have any custom properties, notice that Visio displays no data in the dialog box. Don't click anything, yet!

The Define Custom Properties dialog box: shape has at least one custom property (left); shape has no custom properties (right).

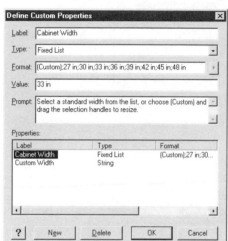
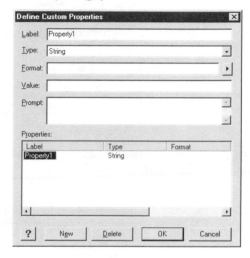

4. In the **Label** field, type a one- or two-word label for the property. For a door shape, you could enter "Door Width."

5. In the **Type** field, select the type of data you want represented. In most cases, this will likely be **String** (which accepts all input as text) or **Number**. For Door Width, you could select **Number**.

6. In the **Format** field, specify the format for the data; this is optional. In most cases, you will likely want to format dates, currencies, and numbers. For Door Width, you could select **Whole Number with Units**.

7. In the **Value** field, specify the default value; this is optional, and you may leave it blank. For Door Width, you could specify **30 in**.

8. In the **Prompt** field, type a one- or two-sentence description of the custom property; this is optional, and you may leave it blank. For Door Width, you could enter "Specify the width of the door in inches."

9. Click **OK**, and test your new custom property by entering a value.

Summarizing Custom Property Data

Use the following procedure to create a report from property fields:

1. Select **Tools | Report.** Notice the Report dialog box, which contains a variety of reports. Essentially, you select a report name, and then click Run to generate the report.

The Report dialog box.

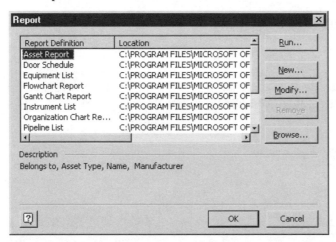

When you run a report, it extracts the custom property data from all relevant shapes, then creates the report in one of several formats. The reports can be divided into the following categories:

Buildings	Custom Properties
Asset Report	Belongs to, Asset Type, Name, Manufacturer
Space Report	Department, Room Number, Use, Area
Door Schedule	Door Number, Size, Type, Thickness
Window Schedule	Window Number, Size, Type
Process and Instrumentation	
Equipment List	Tag, Description, Material, Manufacturer, Model
Instrument List	Tag, Description, Connection Size, Service, Manufacturer, Model
Pipeline List	Tag, Description, Line Size, Schedule, Design Pressure, Design Temperature
Valve List	Tag, Description, Line Size, Valve Class, Manufacturer, Model
Flowcharts	
Flowchart Report	Displayed Text, Resources, Cost, Duration grouped by Master Name

Gantt Chart Report	Name, Start Date, End Date, Duration, User-defined Number, Percent Complete grouped by Resource
Organization Chart Report	Name, Title, Telephone grouped by Department
Visio Diagrams	
Shape Inventory	Displayed Text, Height, Width, X Location, Y Location grouped by Master Name
Report Definition	*None; for creating new report*

2. After selecting a report name, click **Run.** Notice the Run Report dialog box. Select the output format:

The Run Report dialog box.

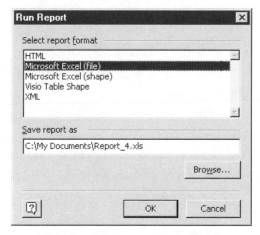

HTML creates a Web page.

Microsoft Excel (file) creates an XLS file.

Microsoft Excel (shape) creates a worksheet object inserted in the Visio diagram.

A Worksheet object inserted in a Visio diagram.

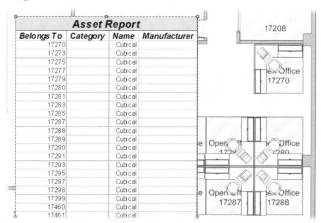

Visio Table Shape creates the report as a shape, which can be placed in the diagram.

XML exports the report in XML format.

3. Click **OK**. Notice that Visio collects the data. This process can take several minutes with large drawings on a slower computer.

4. When the report generation is complete, the report might appear in the Visio diagram, or Visio might ask if you wish to view it — depending on the output selected.

Hands-On Activity

In this activity, you create a report from a diagram. Start Visio.

1. Using **File | New | Browse Sample Drawings**, open the **Office Floor Plan** diagram found in the **Building Plan** folder.

2. From the menu bar, select **Tools | Report**. Notice the Report dialog box.

3. In the Report dialog box, select **Space Report**, which will create a report listing the department, room number, use, and area of each room in the diagram.

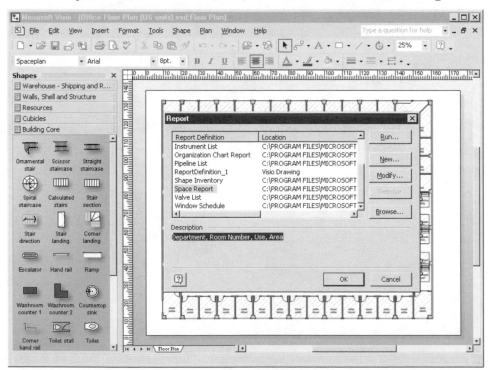

4. Click **Run**. Notice the Run Report dialog box.

5. Select **HTML** and click **OK**. Wait while Visio generates the report.

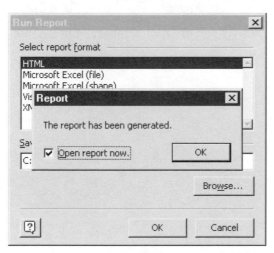

6. When complete, Visio asks if you wish to view the report. Click the check box next to **Open report now** and then click **OK**. Notice that the default Web browser opens with the report.

-	Department	Name	Use	Area
-	-	-	-	138.00 ft.^2
-	-	-	-	372.00 ft.^2
-	-	17490	Open Office	100.00 ft.^2
-	-	17491	Open Office	100.00 ft.^2
-	-	17493	Open Office	100.00 ft.^2
-	-	17495	Open Office	100.00 ft.^2
-	-	17497	Open Office	100.00 ft.^2
-	-	17498	Open Office	100.00 ft.^2
Total	-	-	-	8851.00 ft.^2

7. Back in Visio, select another report name from the Report dialog box, or click **OK** to close it.

8. Press Alt+F4 to exit Visio. Click No in response to the Save Changes dialog box.

This completes the hands-on activity for creating a report from custom properties.

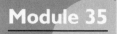

Module 35 **Internet Tools**

Insert | Hyperlink

Uses

Visio allows you to create hyperlinked versions of drawings in two different environments:

In this chapter you'll learn about:

✓ *Adding a hyperlink to a shape or page*

✓ *Editing a hyperlink*

✓ *Jumping to a hyperlink*

▸ Hyperlinks can be added to the Visio drawing, allowing you to jump from document to document on your own computer system.

▸ Visio drawings can be saved in HTML and VML format for viewing by Web browsers. (See Module 36 "Creating a Web Document.)

The **Hyperlinks** selection of the **Insert** menu places hyperlinks in the Visio drawing. A *hyperlink* is a filename with reaction: Click the hyperlink and Visio loads the file specified by the hyperlink. Visio calls the hyperlink the *address*. (A hyperlink is also known as a *URL*, short for "uniform resource locator," the universal file naming system used by the Internet.)

Some typical hyperlinks (or URLs) look like this:

Hyperlink	File Type
c:\visio\samples\block diagram.vsd	Visio drawing file
c:\visio\solutions\basic blocks.vss	Visio stencil file
c:\folder\index.htm	HTML document located on your computer
c:\graphics\filename.gif	Graphic file in GIF format
http://www.microsoft.com	Microsoft Web site
http://www.wordware.com	Wordware Publishing's Web site
http://www.upfrontezine.com	Author Ralph Grabowski's Web site

As you can see from the list, you can add a hyperlink to *any* kind of file in a Visio drawing — whether on your computer or on the Internet. When Visio is unable to display the file, it launches the appropriate application to display the file external to Visio. For example, to display an HTML document, Visio launches your Web browser; to display a graphic file, Visio launches your image editing program. Visio searches the Windows registry to determine which program to launch, based on the filename's extension.

When you pause the cursor over a hyperlinked shape in a Visio drawing, the cursor changes to show a tiny earth and a three-link chain.

In addition to linking to a filename, you can also select the page to display. Visio calls this the *sub-address*. In a multi-page Visio drawing, you can specify the page name.

You can also create internal hyperlinks, where the Visio drawing links to other parts of itself. More than one hyperlink can be attached to a shape.

Procedures

Before presenting the general procedures for adding and using hyperlinks, it is helpful to know about the shortcut key. It is:

Function	Keystroke	Menu	Toolbar Icon
Insert Hyperlinks	Ctrl+K	Insert | Hyperlink	

Adding a Hyperlink to a Shape or Page

Use the following procedure to insert a hyperlink in a Visio shape or page:

1. Select a shape.

2. Select **Insert | Hyperlinks** from the menu bar. Notice the Hyperlinks dialog box.

The Hyperlinks dialog box.

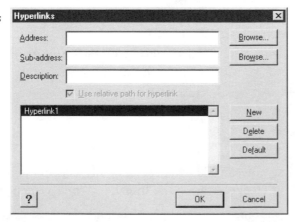

3. There are four areas to fill out in this dialog box, but only the first is required. Type a filename (or URL) in the **Address** text box.

4. If you don't remember the filename, click the **Browse** button. Notice the menu listing two choices: **Internet Address** and **Local File**.

    ▶ Selecting **Internet Address** launches your computer's Web browser.

    ▶ Selecting **Local File** displays the Link to File dialog box, which lets you select a file from your computer and networked drives.

Selecting an Internet address or a local file.

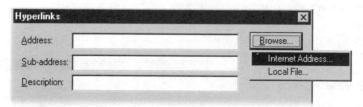

5. When the URL points to a Visio drawing, you have the option of specifying a particular page within the drawing in the Sub-address box. Although the Visio documentation states that you can also link to a location (also called an *anchor*) within an HTML file, attempting to do this results in a warning dialog box:

The sub-address can be a page or a shape in a Visio drawing.

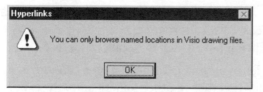

Tip: To link to another drawing page, leave the **Address** field blank. Click the **Browse** button located next to the **Sub-address** field. Visio displays another Hyperlink dialog box:

The Hyperlink dialog box for selecting a sub-address.

▶ Select a page name from the **Page** list box.

▶ (*Optional*) Specify the name of a shape in the **Shape** field; this is optional.

▶ (*Optional*) Select a **Zoom** level; this will cause Visio to zoom in on the shape.

Click **OK**.

 Note: The Hyperlink dialog box does not list the names of shapes in the Shape field, so you have to determine the name yourself. Visio assigns the name when you drag a shape from the stencil onto the page. The name is *name.n*. The *name* is a name, such as Sheet or Square, while *n* is a number that is incremented each time a shape is dragged onto the page, such as **Sheet.4**.

There are several ways to determine the name of a shape. One way is to select **Format | Special** from the menu bar. The Special dialog box displays the shape's name in the **Master** field. For example:

    Master: **Proess:Sheet.4**

"Process" is the name of the master, while "Sheet.4" is the name of the shape. (Recall that when you drag a shape from the stencil to the page, Visio makes a copy of the master.)

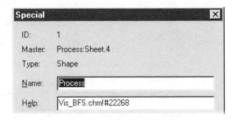

Determining the name of a shape in the Special dialog box. Use the name in the Name field.

---

6. When you pause the cursor over a hyperlinked shape, the cursor changes and a tooltip displays the address. As an alternative, you can type in a descriptive name of the link in the **Description** box, which is displayed instead.

7. When Use relative path for hyperlink is turned on, you can move the Visio drawing and its linked files together to other folders and drives, and the links will still work.

8. Click the **New** button to add another hyperlink to the shape. The **Delete** button removes the selected hyperlink. The **Default** button changes the list name from "Hyperlink 1" to the text in the Description field; this button also selects the default hyperlink, which is used by applications that recognize a single hyperlink only.

9. Click **OK**. Right-click the shape, and then choose the hyperlink to test the link.

Editing a Hyperlink

Use the following procedure to edit the URL and wording of a hyperlink:

1. Move the cursor over shapes to find one with a hyperlink. Notice how the cursor changes.

2. From the menu bar, select **Insert | Hyperlinks**. Notice the Hyperlinks dialog box.

3. Select a hyperlink from the list in the lower half of the dialog box.

4. Edit the entries in the **Address, Sub-address,** and **Description** fields.

5. Click **OK.**

6. Right-click the shape, and then choose the hyperlink to test the changes you made to the link.

Jumping to a Hyperlink

Use the following procedure to jump to a location specified by a hyperlink:

1. Move the cursor over shapes to find one with a hyperlink. Notice how the cursor changes.

2. Right-click the shape. Notice that the menu includes the name(s) of the hyperlink(s).

The shortcut menu shows the hyperlinks.

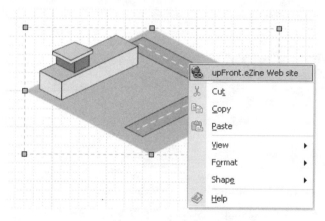

3. Select a hyperlink. Notice that Visio opens the file, or opens the related application to display the file or Web site.

Hands-On Activity

In this activity, you insert a hyperlink in a drawing. (This activity assumes that Excel or another spreadsheet program is installed on your computer.) Start Visio.

1. From the Choose Drawing Type window, open the **Basic Flowchart** template found in the **Flowchart** folder.

2. Drag the **Stored Data** shape onto the page.

3. Press **Ctrl+K** or select **Insert | Hyperlinks** from the menu bar. Notice the Hyperlinks dialog box.

4. Click **Browse** (next to the Address field). Select **Local File**. Notice that Visio displays the Link to File dialog box:

    Look in: **Visio 2002\Samples\Project Schedule**

    Files of type: **Office files**

    File name: **Sample Project Data.xls**

    Click **Open**.

5. For the **Description** field, type **Sample Project Data**. (This may be inserted by default.)

Hyperlink data filled in.

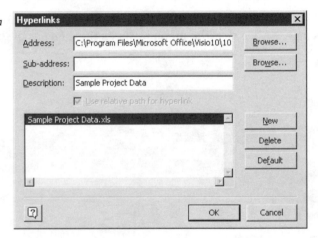

6. Click **OK**. Notice that the shape looks no different.

7. Pause the cursor over the shape. Notice the cursor changes and a tooltip displays the description, "Sample Project Data.xls." The change in cursor alerts you that the shape contains a hyperlink. When the shape contains more than one hyperlink, the tooltip reads "Multiple Hyperlinks…"

Internet cursor and descriptive tooltip.

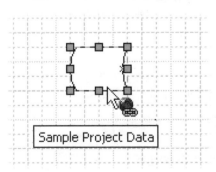

8. Right-click the shape. Notice that the shortcut menu lists the hyperlink.

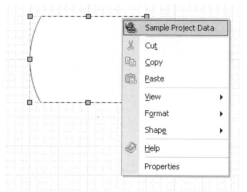

9. Select **Sample Project Data.xls** from the shortcut menu. Notice that Visio opens Excel with the spreadsheet.

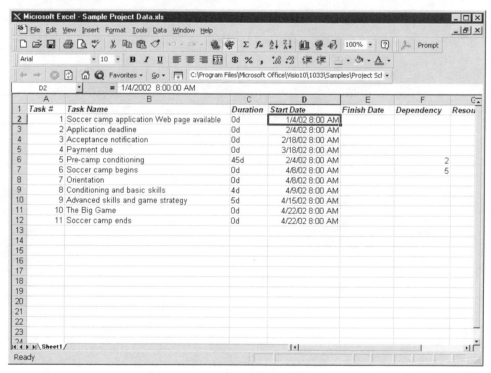

10. Exit Visio and Excel with **Alt+F4**. Click **No** in response to the Save Changes dialog box.

This completes the hands-on activity for creating and using hyperlinks.

Module 36 **Creating a Web Document**

File | Save as Web Page

Uses

> *In this chapter you'll learn about:*
> ✓ *Saving a drawing as an HTML file*

Visio drawings can be saved
in HTML format for viewing by Web browsers. The Visio drawing itself is converted
to a GIF, JPG, PNG, or VML file, with additional HTML code providing the "wrapper" for displaying multi-page drawings and custom properties.

Each page in the Visio drawing becomes a Web page. When you insert hyperlinks in
the Visio drawing, they are preserved in the Web documents. Your Visio drawing
cannot be edited when displayed by the Web browser, which can be considered a
form of security.

While you are probably familiar with GIF and JPG files, their drawback is that they
are raster formats, which means they lose their quality when zoomed. As an alternative, Visio can export its drawing in VML format (short for "vector markup
language"). The drawback to VML is that only Microsoft's Internet Explorer v5.x
(and higher) is able to display the files. The DWF (drawing Web format) introduced
by Visio 5.0 is no longer supported.

When Visio exports the drawing page as an HTML document, it generates the base HTML, plus a group of support files in a folder. In the following table, *filename* refers to the Visio drawing filename:

File	Purpose
filename.htm	The primary HTML page; this file uses the following files:
*filename*_frame.htm	Defines the frames (see illustration)
*filename*1_raster.htm	The HTML code that displays the raster image
*filename*1_raster.gif	The raster image generated from the Visio page (GIF, in this case)
*filename*1_vml.VML	The VML image generated from the Visio page
*filename*_nav.htm	The navigation frame; this file uses the following files:
*filename*_utils.js	The JavaScript code that activates the page turning
lt_off.gif	Left arrow
lt_over.gif	Left arrow displayed when selected
rt_off.gif	Right arrow
rt_over.gif	Right arrow displayed when selected

The HTML page generated by Visio.

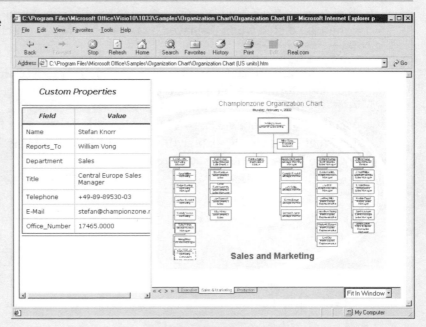

The filenames generated by Visio, such as Organization Chart1_raster.gif, can be decoded as follows:

▸ **Organization Chart**: Specifies the name of the source Visio drawing.

▶ **1_:** Specifies the Visio drawing page number.

▶ **raster:** Specifies the file is in raster format.

▶ **.gif:** Specifies the type of raster format, GIF in this case.

Tip: To view the source code of the HTML files generated by Visio, select **View | Page Source** in Netscape Navigator or **View | Source** in Internet Explorer.

```
Organization Chart (US units)_vml_2.htm - Notepad

File   Edit   Search   Help

<html xmlns:v="urn:schemas-microsoft-com:vml"
 xmlns="http://www.w3.org/TR/REC-html40">
<head>
<LINK REL="stylesheet" TYPE="text/css" HREF="Organization Chart (US
units).css">
<title>
Organization Chart (US units)
</title>
<style>
        v\:* { behavior: url(#default#VML); }

</style>
<script src="Organization Chart (US units)_utils.js"></script>
<script src="Organization Chart (US units)_vml_1.js"></script>
<script>
<!--
var m_viewMgr = new CViewMgr();
g_theApp.ActiveViewMgr = m_viewMgr;
m_viewMgr.ZoomIsPresent = true;
m_viewMgr.onResize = ViewMgrOnResize;
m_viewMgr.put_Zoom = ViewMgrSetZoom;
m_viewMgr.get_Zoom = ViewMgrGetZoom;
m_viewMgr.ApplyZoom = ViewMgrApplyZoom;
m_viewMgr.put_Location = null;
var cxmgn = 10;
```

The HTML source code.

Procedures

Before presenting the general procedures for creating a Web document, it is helpful to know about the shortcut key. It is:

Function	Keystroke	Menu	Toolbar Icon
Save as Web Page	Alt+FG	File	Save as Web Page	...

Saving as a Web Page

Use the following procedure to save the Visio drawing as a Web page:

1. Select **File | Save as Web Page** from the menu bar. Notice that the Save As dialog box has a couple of extra buttons specific to exporting the drawing as a Web page. Also, notice that the Save as type list box is set to "Web Page (*.htm,*.html)" automatically.

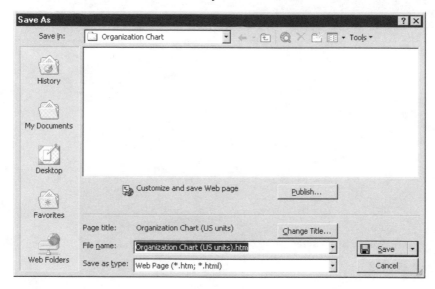

2. If necessary, specify a different filename, and select another folder and drive.

3. If you wish to change the text that appears on the title bar of the Web browser, click **Change Title**. Notice the Set Page Title dialog box.

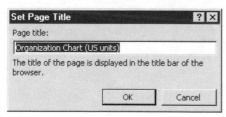

4. Enter new text for the page title. Click **OK**.

5. At this point, you have two options:

   ▶ Click **Save** to publish the drawing directly, without changing options.

   ▶ Click **Publish** to set options, then publish as a Web page.

6. Click **Publish**. Notice the Save As Web Page dialog box, which is separated into three tabs.

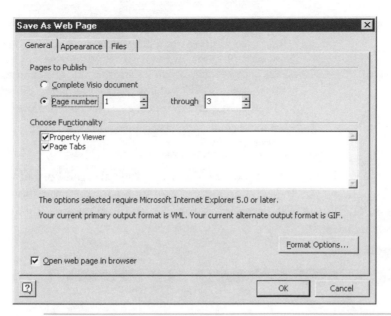

 Warning: When you click the Save As Web Page dialog box's OK button, Visio immediately begins to generate the Web page; it does not return to the previous dialog box, as you might expect.

General tab:

▶ **Pages to Publish** specifies whether all drawing pages are published, or a specific range of pages; this option is meaningless when the drawing consists of a single page. Background pages are not published separately, but appear as the background image in the Web page.

▶ **Choose Functionality** selects whether you want the Web page to display custom properties in a Web page sidebar called the Property Viewer. The Page Tabs option should be turned on for multi-page drawings.

▶ **Open web page in browser** automatically launches the default Web browser to display the Web pages after Visio completes exporting the drawing.

▶ **Format Options** displays a dialog box that allows you to choose the format into which the Visio drawing will be converted.

Format Option	Explanation
GIF	Raster format understood by all Web browsers; good for all types of images but may result in a larger file size than JPG.

Format Option	Explanation
JPG	Raster format understood by all Web browsers; best for photographic images but poor for Visio diagrams. JPG performs *lossy compression*, which means that fine lines and text found in Visio drawings become blurry.
PNG	Raster format understood by newer Web browsers;
VML	Vector format understood by newer Microsoft browsers; best format for Visio diagrams

Since VML is not understood by older Web browsers, the Format Options dialog box allows you to select an alternate graphics format. You should always choose GIF. If the Web browser cannot display the VML file, it will display the raster image instead.

Appearance tab:

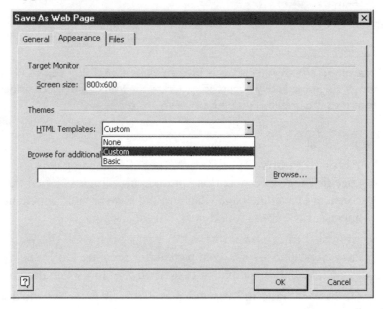

▸ **Screen size** specifies the size of the raster image (GIF, JPG, PNG). In most cases, accept the default 800x600 size. This option does not affect VML.

▸ **HTML Templates** allows you to select a predefined format for the Web page.

▸ **Browse for additional themes** becomes available when **HTML Templates** is set to **Custom**.

Files tab:

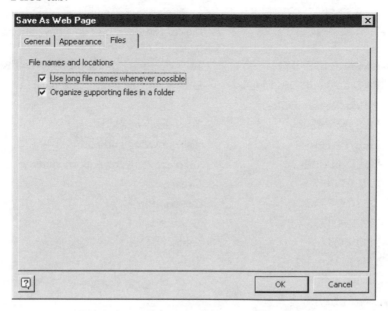

▶ **Use long file names whenever possible** should be left on, unless you know that the files will be viewed by an intranet that does not support long filenames.

▶ **Organize supporting files in a folder** places all of the support files needed by the Web page in a single folder. This is a useful option that should be left turned on.

Visio exports the drawing to one of three predefined HTML-formatted pages. You can, however, instruct Visio where to place elements in the HTML page via a *template*. Use an HTML template that contains *substitution codes*. Create the HTML file with a text editor, giving it an HTM extension. Visio recognizes the following substitution codes:

Codes	Meaning
<!--IMAGE-->	The Visio drawing
<!--CS_IMAGE_MAP-->	Map data containing hyperlinks
Navigation Buttons	
<!--NEXT_ANCHOR-->	Makes the Next button a navigational link to the next page
<!--NEXT_PAGE_BTN-->	Tags for the Next button graphic <IMG SRC="Next.GIF">

Codes	Meaning
<!--NEXT_ANCHOR_END-->	Ending anchor tag for the Next button
<! --BACK_ANCHOR-->	Makes the Back button a navigational link to the previous page
<!--BACK_PAGE_BTN-->	Back button graphic <IMG SRC="Back.GIF">
<!--BACK_ANCHOR_END-->	Ending anchor tag for the Back button
File | Properties Data	
<!--FILE_NAME-->	Visio drawing filename
<!--FILE_PATH-->	Visio drawing pathname
<!--FULL_NAME-->	Visio drawing drive, path, and file name
<!--CREATOR-->	Creator
<!--DESCRIPTION-->	Description
<!--KEYWORDS-->	Keywords
<!--SUBJECT-->	Subject
<!--TITLE-->	Title
<!--x-->	x = Category, Company, Manager, or Hyperlink_Base
Page Numbering	
<!--PAGE_COUNT-->	Total number of pages in the Visio drawing
<!--PAGE_INDEX-->	Page number relative to other pages in the Visio drawing
<!--PAGE_NAME-->	Name of Visio page saved in HTML format
<!--HTML_PAGE_COUNT-->	Total number of HTML pages
<!--HTML_PAGE_INDEX-->	HTML page number relative to other HTML pages

 Notes: The <! ... > is the HTML tag for a comment; this allows substitution codes to be ignored by the Web browser.

Visio retrieves some of the information from the File | Properties dialog box.

7. Click **OK**. Visio converts the drawing pages to raster and/or VML files. Notice that Visio launches your Web browser and loads the HTML file.

Hands-On Activity

In this activity, you export a drawing as a Web page format. Start Visio.

1. Open the **Organization Chart.Vsd** file found in the \Samples\Organization Chart folder.

2. From the menu bar, select **File | Save as Web Page**. Notice the Save As dialog box.

3. Click **Save.** Notice that Visio exports the drawing as a Web page. When finished, Visio launches your computer's default Web browser and loads the files.

4. The Web browser displays the Visio drawing, with page controls at the bottom. Click the tabs to move forward and backward through the pages.

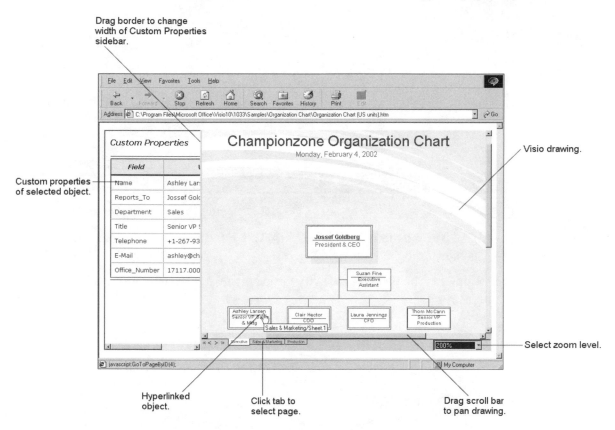

The Visio drawing displayed by Internet Explorer with page controls noted.

5. When you pass the cursor over an object in the drawing, the Web browser displays its custom properties (if it has any). This feature is available only in Microsoft's Web browser; other Web browsers, such as those from Netscape and Opera Software, display the pages and page tabs only.

The Visio drawing displayed by Netscape.

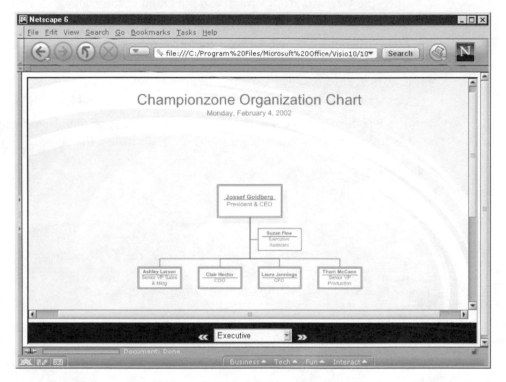

6. Exit Visio and the Web browser with **Alt+F4**. Click **No** in response to the Save Changes dialog box.

This completes the hands-on activity for exporting a Visio drawing as a Web document.

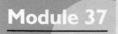 *Importing CAD Drawings*

Uses

Visio is sometimes used together with CAD (computer-aided design) software. Visio can display certain types of CAD drawings. Additionally, you can place Visio shapes on the CAD drawing, which "snap" to the CAD geometry.

Visio reads CAD drawings in these formats:

DWG: The file format for drawings created by versions of AutoCAD from v2.5 to 2002 (DWG is short for "drawing").

DGN: The file format for drawings created by Bentley Systems' MicroStation (DGN is short for "design") up to MicroStation/J (version 7).

DXF: A file format used to exchange drawings between CAD programs, as well as non-CAD programs (DXF is short for "drawing interchange format").

IGS: Another file format used to exchange drawings between CAD systems (IGS is short for "initial graphics exchange specification").

 Tip: If your CAD program is not supported directly by Visio, it might be able to save drawings in one of the four formats listed above.

After the drawing is placed on the page:

▶ Shapes snap automatically to the underlying geometry. For example, electrical outlets, HVAC ducts, and furniture shapes automatically rotate and snap into place.

▶ You can select layers to convert into Visio objects.

▶ The CAD drawing can be edited from within Visio using the OLE capabilities of the originating CAD package.

Caution: CAD drawings contain a great deal of information in addition to the lines and arcs that make up a typical Visio drawing. Even the color, line style, and layer name of a CAD drawing can contain legal information. For example, a property line might be shown in a specific color and linetype. The translation of a CAD drawing to a foreign program, unfortunately, often results in the loss of some data and the modification of other data.

CAD objects are erased when Visio is unable to convert them. Specifically, when importing an AutoCAD drawing, Visio does not display the following:

▶ Paper space (called "layouts" in AutoCAD 2002)

▶ Multiple model space viewports (only one is displayed)

▶ Proxy objects (or "zombie" objects)

▶ OLE object images

▶ 3D ACIS solids

▶ 2D ACIS regions

For example, if the AutoCAD drawing consists solely of ACIS solid models, the drawing will appear blank when opened in Visio 2002.

Other AutoCAD objects are partially displayed. Visio is able to display some of the object, but not all of it. The following are partially displayed:

▶ Raster image: Only the border is displayed.

▶ Complex linetypes: Only the straight line portions are displayed.

▶ TrueType fonts: AutoCAD's SHX fonts are substituted.

Also, there are some text justification problems; variable-width, splined polylines show some imperfection; lineweights are not shown (the lines are displayed one pixel wide); and 3D models are flattened to 2D, but 3D viewpoint is preserved.

The following figure shows the original text displayed by AutoCAD 2002 (at left) and the same text displayed by Visio 2002 (at right).

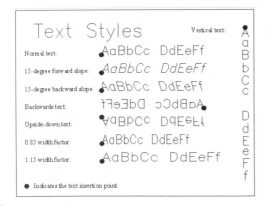

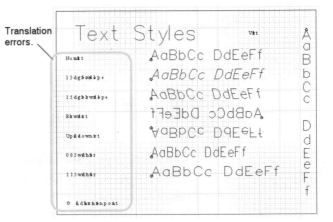

Procedures

As you can see from the above table, translation is *never* 100% accurate. With this caveat in mind, here are the procedures for importing AutoCAD DWG files. The shortcut keys are:

Function	Keystroke	Menu	Toolbar Icon
Open CAD File	...	File | Open | AutoCAD Drawing	...
Insert CAD File	Alt+IA	Insert | CAD Drawing	...

Importing a CAD Drawing

Use the following procedure to import an AutoCAD drawing into Visio for viewing only:

1. Select **File | Open** from the menu bar. Notice the **Open** dialog box.

2. From the **Files of type** list box, select a CAD drawing format:

   ▶ AutoCAD Drawing (*.dwg, *.dxf)

   ▶ MicroStation Drawing (*.dgn)

   ▶ IGES Drawing File Format (*.igs)

Tips: The procedure for importing DXF files is identical to DWG.
   To add a CAD drawing to an existing Visio page, select **Insert | CAD Drawing**; with this tool, however, the IGES format is not available.

---

3. Select the CAD drawing file.

4. Click **Open**. Notice the CAD Drawing Properties dialog box. The options of the **General** tab are:

   CAD Drawing Scale: Specifies the size of the CAD drawing relative to the Visio page. If you plan to place Visio shapes in the drawing, then you must scale the CAD drawing to fit the scale of the shapes. You can set the scale three ways:

   ▶ **Pre-defined Scale** causes Visio to scale the CAD drawing automatically; the *extents* of the drawing is scaled to fit the page ("extents" refers to a rectangle that encompasses all entities in the drawing). Click the **Page Scale** drop-down list to select a discipline: Architectural, Civil engineering, Mechanical engineering, or Metric.

   ▶ **Custom Scale** lets you specify any scale factor. The first number refers to the Visio page, while the second number refers to the CAD drawing. For example, **1 in = 40 in** means that one inch in the Visio page represents 40 inches in the CAD drawing.

▷ The **Page Setup** button lets you change the size and scale of the Visio page. See Module 4 "Setting Up Pages and Layers."

The CAD Drawing Properties dialog box's General tab.

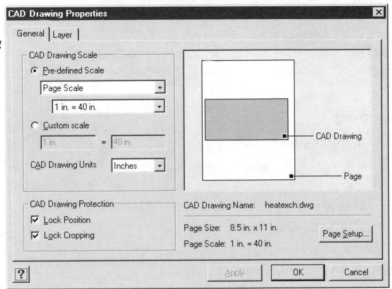

CAD Drawing Units: Specifies how to interpret CAD drawing units. (CAD software uses unitless units that are interpreted as real-world units.) Select a measurement unit, if you know what it should be.

Lock Position: Locks the CAD drawing so that is cannot be moved.

Lock Cropping: Locks the CAD drawing so that it cannot be cropped.

Tip: After the drawing is inserted on the page, you can change these properties. Right-click the drawing, and select **CAD Drawing Object | Properties**.

5. Click the **Layer** tab. It lets you specify some options related to layers in the CAD drawing:

*The CAD
Drawing
Properties dialog
box's Layer tab.*

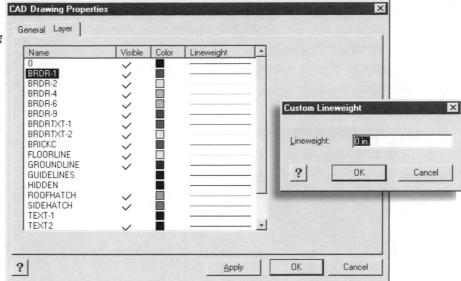

Name: Specifies the names of all layers found in the drawing, including externally referenced layers.

▶ Click the **Name** header to sort layer names in alphabetical order; click a second time to sort in reverse (Z to A) order.

▶ You cannot edit the name of layers.

Visible: Specifies whether entities on the layer are displayed; the default visibility is based on each layer's setting in the CAD drawing.

▶ A check mark means the layer is visible; click the check mark to turn off visibility.

▶ Click the **Visible** header to sort layers by visibility.

Color: Specifies the color of entities on the layer; the default color is based on the setting in the CAD drawing.

▶ Click a color square to display the Color dialog box, which lets you change the color of entities on the layer.

▶ Click the **Color** header to sort layer names by color, starting with red; click the header a second time to sort in reverse order, starting with white.

Lineweight: Specifies the weight (width) of lines making up entities; the default weight is 0, which means lines are drawn as thin as possible. Visio ignores lineweights specified in the CAD drawing.

▶ Click a line to display the Custom Lineweight dialog box, and specify a new weight.

▶ Click the **Lineweight** header to sort layer names by lineweight, starting with the lightest weight; click the header a second time to sort in reverse order, starting with the heaviest weight.

6. Click **OK**. Notice that Visio displays the CAD Drawing dialog box. This gives you another chance to match the CAD drawing scale to the Visio page scale. Select an option, and click **OK**. Notice the CAD drawing on the page.

The CAD Drawing dialog box.

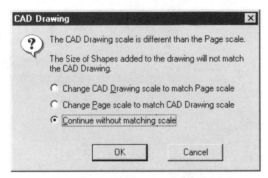

> **Tip:** If you do not see the CAD drawing, Visio may have located it off the page. To find the drawing, change the zoom to 1%, and look for the drawing on the pasteboard.

This concludes the procedures for inserting a CAD drawing in Visio 2002.

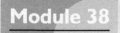 **Toolbar Customization**

View | Toolbars | Customize

Uses

In this chapter you'll learn about:

✓ *Changing toolbar options*

✓ *Creating a new toolbar*

All Windows programs, including Visio, have toolbars. The toolbar holds buttons and drop-down lists that allow you to directly select commands. Generally, it is quicker to select a command from a toolbar than from the menus because fewer mouse clicks are required.

The drawback to toolbars is that the button icons, such as on the Snap & Glue toolbar, can be sometimes confusing to figure out.

The following illustration shows the parts of a toolbar.

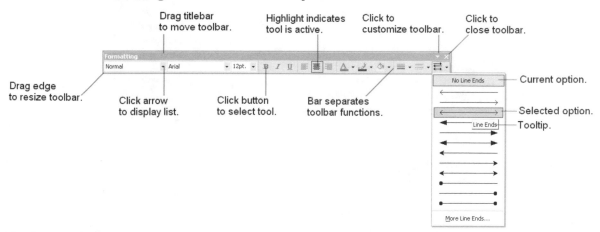

The elements of a floating toolbar.

Tip: When you drag a toolbar near the edge of the Visio window, the toolbar automatically docks. To prevent the toolbar from docking, hold down the **Ctrl** key while dragging the toolbar.

You can fully customize the toolbars. That means you can create and delete toolbars, and edit them to hold any Visio command.

Procedures

Before presenting the general procedures for customizing toolbars, it is helpful to know about the shortcut key:

Function	Keystroke	Menu	Toolbar Icon
Customize Toolbars	Alt+VTC	View | Toolbars | Customize	...

 Note: You can right-click any toolbar, and select **Customize** from the shortcut menu.

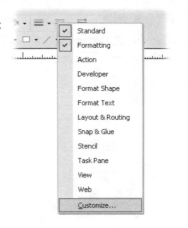

Right-click any toolbar to access the Customize command.

Changing Toolbar Options

Use the following procedure to change the "look and feel" of Visio toolbars:

1. Select **View | Toolbars | Customize** from the menu bar. Notice the Customize dialog box.

2. Select the **Options** tab.

3. Change any of the options:

The Options tab of the Customize dialog box.

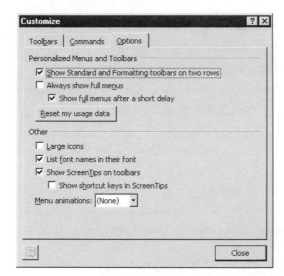

Show Standard and Formatting toolbars on two rows is a handy way to make Visio look like it should. Toolbars have a habit of being too slippery, and sometimes it's hard to get them back into their place easily.

Always show full menus is another option that could be turned on all the time. (I don't care much for the abbreviated menus that hide many options.)

Show full menus after a short delay means what it says; not a useful option, since it slows you down in your work.

Reset my usage data clears the settings made to menus and toolbars. This is useful for returning Visio's menus and toolbars to their original positions.

Large icons: When on, displays toolbar icons at twice their normal size.

List font names in their font: When font names are listed, Visio displays them in their font style. This can be useful for previewing the font.

Show ScreenTips on toolbars: When on, Visio displays a tooltip when the cursor lingers over a toolbar button. The tooltip describes the name of the toolbar button.

Show shortcut keys in ScreenTips: When on, the tooltip includes the short-cut keystroke, if one is available for the tool.

The look of large icons and ScreenTips.

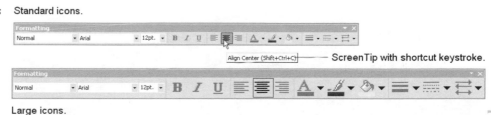

Standard icons.

ScreenTip with shortcut keystroke.

Large icons.

Menu animations: Determines how the menus open:

▶ **None:** The menu opens normally.

▶ **Random:** The menu opens by unfolding or sliding.

▶ **Unfold:** The menu opens by sliding open sideways and downwards.

▶ **Slide:** The menu opens by sliding down.

None is the best option because, once again, animated menus slow your work by forcing you to wait. On a fast computer, however, menu animations are not noticeable.

4. Click **Close** to see the effect of the options you changed.

Tips: Large icons are easier to see on a high-resolution screen, but take up more screen "real estate."

ScreenTips with shortcut keys are useful enough to always keep turned on.

Creating a New Toolbar

Use the following procedure to create a new toolbar:

1. Select **View | Toolbars | Customize** from the menu bar. Notice the Customize dialog box. If necessary, select the **Toolbars** tab.

2. Click **New.** Notice the New Toolbar dialog box.

The New Toolbar dialog box.

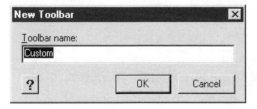

3. Enter a descriptive name for the toolbar. This name will appear on the toolbar's title bar, as well as on the list of available toolbars.

4. Click **OK.** Notice the new, empty toolbar.

The new, empty custom toolbar.

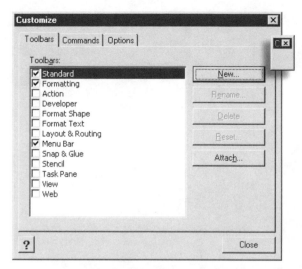

5.   Drag the toolbar away from the Customize dialog box so it doesn't disappear when you click another tab in the Customize dialog box. To fill the toolbar with buttons, drag icons into it. Here's how: Select the **Commands** tab of the Customize dialog box. Notice that all of Visio's commands are sorted by menu.

6.   Drag a command from the Customize dialog box into the new toolbar. For example, under **Categories**, select **Edit**. Under **Commands**, drag **Select All** to the new toolbar.

Drag a command into the new toolbar.

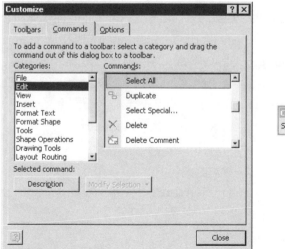

7.   To change the properties of the new button, right-click. Notice the shortcut menu.

     Reset: Resets the button's options.

Shortcut menu options for changing button properties.

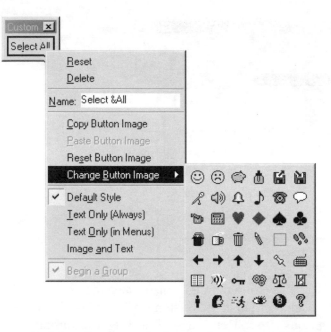

Delete: Removes the button from the toolbar.

Name: Specifies the name displayed by the ScreenTip and in the menu. The & (ampersand) prefixes the underlined character in menus, such as **Select All**. The underlnned character is used with the **Alt** key for shortcut keystrokes.

Copy Button Image: Copies the button's image to the Clipboard.

Paste Button Image: Pastes an image from the Clipboard onto the button.

Reset Button Image: Changes the image back to its original form.

Change Button Image: Allows you to select an alternative image for the icon.

Default Style: Displays text and/or an icon image on the face of the button.

Text Only (Always): Displays text only in menus and in toolbars.

Text Only (in Menus): Displays text only in menus.

Image and Text: Displays icon image and text.

Begin a Group: Defines a group of buttons (a.k.a. flyout).

8. Select the **Toolbars** tab, and click **Attach** to attach the toolbar to the drawing file. Notice that Visio displays the Attach Toolbars dialog box.

The Attach Toolbars dialog box.

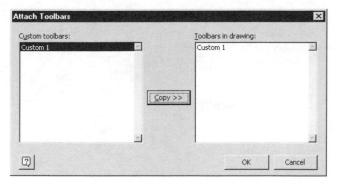

9. Select the toolbar name, then click **Copy**. This step is necessary because customized toolbars are available only on your computer. To make customized toolbars available anywhere the current drawing is opened, the toolbar must be attached to the drawing file.

10. Click **OK**.

11. Select the customized toolbar name in the Toolbars list. Notice that you can now rename and delete the toolbar.

12. Click **Close** to exit toolbar customization.

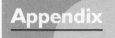

Mouse and Keyboard Shortcuts

> **In this chapter you'll learn about:**
> ✓ **Shortcuts by task**
> ✓ **Shortcuts by keystroke**

You may find that you work more quickly when you use Visio's shortcut keystrokes and mouse clicks. In this appendix, you find all shortcuts listed two ways: first in alphabetical order by tool name, and then in alphabetical order by keystroke.

Shortcuts by Task

General Tasks

Use the following mouse buttons and keystrokes to perform general tasks:

Select shape	Click
Highlight next shape	Tab; press Enter to select shape
Shortcut menu	Right-click
Customized operation	Double-click
Add to or remove from selection set	Shift and click
Nudge	Select an object, and then press cursor keys
Pixel nudge	Select object, Shift, and press cursor keys
Repeat last command	F4
Pointer	Ctrl+1

Pan & Zoom

Use the following shortcut keys to quickly zoom and pan your drawing:

Actual Size (100%)	Ctrl+Shift+I
Pan	Ctrl+Shift and drag while holding down the right-mouse button, or press cursor keys when no objects are selected.
Whole Page	Ctrl+W
Full screen	F5
Open the Zoom dialog box	F6
Zoom in	Ctrl+Shift and click
Zoom out	Shift+F6, or Ctrl+Shift and right-click
Zoom in on an area	Ctrl+Shift and drag a rectangle

Drawing Tools

Use the following shortcut keys to quickly switch between drawing tools:

Arc	Ctrl+7
Connection point	Ctrl+Shift+1
Connector	Ctrl+3
Crop image	Ctrl+Shift+2
Ellipse	Ctrl+9
Freeform	Ctrl+5
Line	Ctrl+6
Pencil	Ctrl+4
Rectangle	Ctrl+8
Rotation	Ctrl+0 (zero)
Stamp	Ctrl+Shift+3
Text	Ctrl+2
Text Block	Ctrl+Shift+4
Toggle between text edit and selection mode	Select a shape, then press F2

Menu Commands

For many of these shortcuts, you must select a shape first:

Align Shapes dialog box	F8
Bring selected shapes to front	Ctrl+Shift+F
Cascade windows	Alt+F7
Copy to Clipboard	Ctrl+C
Cut to Clipboard	Ctrl+X
Duplicate selected shapes	Ctrl+D
Field dialog box	Ctrl+F9
Fill dialog box	F3
Find dialog box	Ctrl+F
Flip horizontal	Ctrl+H
Flip vertical	Ctrl+J
Font tab, Text dialog box	F11
Glue toggle (on or off)	F9
Group selected shapes	Ctrl+G
Help	F1
Hyperlinks dialog box	Ctrl+K
Line dialog box	Shift+F3
Macros dialog box	Alt+F8
Microsoft Visio Help dialog box	F1
New drawing (based on current drawing)	Ctrl+N
Open dialog box	Ctrl+O
Paragraph tab, Text dialog box	Shift+F11
Paste from Clipboard	Ctrl+V
Print dialog box	Ctrl+P
Print preview	Ctlr+F2
Print Setup tab, Page Setup dialog box	Shift+F5
Redo	Ctrl+Y
Reorder Pages dialog box	Ctrl+Alt+P
Repeat last command	F4
Rotate left	Ctrl+L

347

Rotate right	Ctrl+R
Save drawing	Ctrl+S
Save As dialog box	F12
Select all	Ctrl+A
Send selected shapes to back	Ctrl+Shift+B
Size & Position window	Click the status bar
Snap toggle (on or off)	Shift+F9
Snap & Glue dialog box	Alt+F9
Spelling dialog box	F7
Tabs tab, Text dialog box	Ctrl+F11
Tile windows horizontally	Shift+F7
Tile windows vertically	Ctrl+Shift+F7
Undo	Ctrl+Z or Alt+Backspace
Ungroup selected groups	Ctrl+Shift+U
Visual Basic Editor	Alt+F11

Text Formatting

Use the following key combinations to apply and remove formatting to selected text:

Bold	Ctrl+B
Italic	Ctrl+I
SMALL CAPS	Ctrl+Shift+K
ALL CAPS	Ctrl+Shift+A
Sub$_{script}$	Ctrl+=
Super^{script}	Ctrl+Shift+=
Underline	Ctrl+U
Double underline	Ctrl+Shift+D
Increase font size	Ctrl+Shift++ (plus sign)
Decrease font size	Ctrl+Shift+− (minus sign)
Justification:	
Left	Ctrl+Shift+L
Center	Ctrl+Shift+C
Right	Ctrl+Shift+R
Full	Ctrl+Shift+J

Vertical Alignment:

Top	Ctrl+Shift+T
Middle	Ctrl+Shift+M
Bottom	Ctrl+Shift+V

Special Text Characters

Use the following key combinations to add special characters in text:

Beginning single-quote '	Ctrl+[
Ending single-quote '	Ctrl+]
Beginning double-quote "	Ctrl+Shift+[
Ending double-quote "	Ctrl+Shift+]
Bullet ●	Ctrl+Shift+8
En dash –	Ctrl+Alt+=
Em dash —	Ctrl+Shift+Alt+=
Discretionary hyphen -	Ctrl+hyphen
Nonbreaking hyphen -	Ctrl+Shift+- (hyphen)
Nonbreaking slash /	Ctrl+Shift+/
Nonbreaking backslash \	Ctrl+Shift+\
Section marker §	Ctrl+Shift+6
Paragraph marker ¶	Ctrl+Shift+7
Copyright symbol ©	Ctrl+Shift+Alt+C
Registered trademark ®	Ctrl+Shift+Alt+R

Text Fields

Use the following key combinations to add fields to text (without accessing the Field dialog box):

Height field	Ctrl+Shift+H or Ctrl+E
Rotation angle field	Ctrl+Shift+A
Width field	Ctrl+Shift+W

Full-screen Navigation

Use these keyboard shortcuts to navigate between Visio and another page when in full-screen view:

Forward	Ctrl+right arrow

Back	Ctrl+left arrow
Next Page	Ctrl+Page Down (not on the numeric keypad)
Previous Page	Ctrl+Page Up (not on the numeric keypad)

Windows Navigation

These keyboard shortcuts apply to almost all Windows applications:

Access menu bar	Alt or F10
Cycle through windows	Ctrl+Tab
Close window	Ctrl+F4
Exit Visio	Alt+F4

Shortcuts by Keystroke

Mouse Buttons

Click	Select shape
Double-click	Customized operation
Right-click	Shortcut menu
Shift and click	Add to or remove from selection set
Ctrl+Shift and click	Zoom in
Ctrl+Shift and right-click	Zoom out
Ctrl+Shift and drag a rectangle	Zoom in on an area
Ctrl+Shift and drag while holding down the right mouse button	Pan

Function Keys

F1	Microsoft Visio Help dialog box
F3	Fill dialog box
F4	Repeat last command
F5	Full screen
F6	Zoom dialog box
F7	Spelling dialog box
F8	Align Shapes dialog box
F9	Glue toggle (on or off)

F10	Access menu bar
F11	Text dialog box, Font tab
F12	Save As dialog box
Alt+F4	Exit Visio
Alt+F7	Cascade windows
Alt+F8	Macros dialog box
Alt+F9	Snap & Glue dialog box
Alt+F11	Visual Basic Editor
Ctrl+F2	Print preview
Ctrl+F4	Close window
Ctrl+F9	Field dialog box
Ctrl+F11	Text dialog box, Tabs tab
Ctrl+Shift+F7	Tile windows vertically
Shift+F3	Line dialog box
Shift+F5	Page Setup dialog box, Print Setup tab
Shift+F6	Zoom out
Shift+F7	Tile windows horizontally
Shift+F9	Snap toggle (on or off)
Shift+F11	Text dialog box, Paragraph tab
Select a shape, then press F2	Toggle between text edit and selection mode
Ctrl+0 (zero)	Rotation tool
Ctrl+1	Pointer tool
Ctrl+2	Text tool
Ctrl+3	Connector tool
Ctrl+4	Pencil tool
Ctrl+5	Freeform tool
Ctrl+6	Line tool
Ctrl+7	Arc tool
Ctrl+8	Rectangle tool
Ctrl+9	Ellipse tool
Ctrl+Shift+1	Connection point
Ctrl+Shift+2	Crop image
Ctrl+Shift+3	Stamp
Ctrl+Shift+4	Text Block

Ctrl+Shift+6	Section marker §
Ctrl+Shift+7	Paragraph marker ¶
Ctrl+Shift+8	Bullet ●
Ctrl+A	Select all
Ctrl+B	**Bold**
Ctrl+C	Copy to Clipboard
Ctrl+D	Duplicate selected shapes
Ctrl+E	Height field
Ctrl+F	Find dialog box
Ctrl+G	Group selected shapes
Ctrl+H	Flip horizontal
Ctrl+I	*Italic*
Ctrl+J	Flip vertical
Ctrl+K	Hyperlinks dialog box
Ctrl+L	Rotate left
Ctrl+N	New drawing (based on current drawing)
Ctrl+O	Open dialog box
Ctrl+P	Print dialog box
Ctrl+R	Rotate right
Ctrl+S	Save drawing
Ctrl+T	Select shape to place text
Ctrl+U	Underline
Ctrl+V	Paste from Clipboard
Ctrl+W	Whole Page
Ctrl+X	Cut to Clipboard
Ctrl+Y	Redo
Ctrl+Z	Undo
Ctrl+Alt+P	Reorder Pages dialog box
Ctrl+Shift+A	ALL CAPS
Ctrl+Shift+A	Rotation angle field (inside Field dialog box)
Ctrl+Shift+B	Send selected shapes to back
Ctrl+Shift+C	Justification: Center
Ctrl+Shift+D	Double underline
Ctrl+Shift+F	Bring selected shapes to front

Ctrl+Shift+H	Height field (in Field dialog box)
Ctrl+Shift+I	Actual Size (100%)
Ctrl+Shift+J	Full justification
Ctrl+Shift+K	SMALL CAPS
Ctrl+Shift+L	Full justification
Ctrl+Shift+M	Vertical Alignment: Middle
Ctrl+Shift+R	Right justification
Ctrl+Shift+T	Vertical Alignment: Top
Ctrl+Shift+U	Ungroup selected groups
Ctrl+Shift+V	Vertical Alignment: Bottom
Ctrl+Shift+W	Width field (inside Field dialog box)
Ctrl+Shift+Alt+C	Copyright symbol ©
Ctrl+Shift+Alt+R	Registered trademark ®

Punctuation and Other Keys

Alt	Access menu bar
Alt+Backspace	Undo
Ctrl+[	Beginning single-quote '
Ctrl+]	Ending single-quote '
Ctrl+=	Sub$_{script}$
Ctrl+- (hyphen)	Discretionary hyphen -
Ctrl+Alt+=	En dash –
Ctrl+Shift++ (plus sign)	Increase font size
Ctrl+Shift+– (minus sign)	Decrease font size
Ctrl+Shift+/	Nonbreaking slash /
Ctrl+Shift+[	Beginning double-quote "
Ctrl+Shift+\	Nonbreaking backslash \
Ctrl+Shift+]	Ending double-quote "
Ctrl+Shift+=	Super^{script}
Ctrl+Shift+- (hyphen)	Nonbreaking hyphen -
Ctrl+Shift+Alt+=	Em dash —
Tab; press Enter to select shape	Highlight next shape
Ctrl+Tab	Cycle through windows
Ctrl+left arrow	Back

Ctrl+right arrow	Forward
Ctrl+Page Down (not on the numeric keypad)	Next Page
Ctrl+Page Up (not on the numeric keypad)	Previous Page
Select an object, then press cursor keys	Nudge
Select object, Shift, and press cursor keys	Pixel nudge
Press cursor keys when no objects are selected	Pan

Index

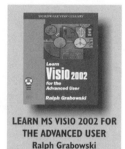

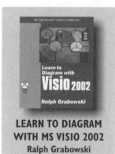